International Political Economy Series

Series Editor: **Timothy M. Shaw**, Visiting Professor, University of Massachusetts Boston, USA and Emeritus Professor, University of London, UK

The global political economy is in flux as a series of cumulative crises impacts its organization and governance. The IPE series has tracked its development in both analysis and structure over the last three decades. It has always had a concentration on the global South. Now the South increasingly challenges the North as the centre of development, also reflected in a growing number of submissions and publications on indebted Eurozone economies in Southern Europe.

An indispensable resource for scholars and researchers, the series examines a variety of capitalisms and connections by focusing on emerging economies, companies and sectors, debates and policies. It informs diverse policy communities as the established trans-Atlantic North declines and "the rest", especially the BRICS, rise.

Titles include:

Geoffrey Allen Pigman
TRADE DIPLOMACY TRANSFORMED
Why Trade Matters for Global Prosperity

Kristian Coates Ulrichsen
THE GULF STATES IN INTERNATIONAL POLITICAL ECONOMY

Eleonora Poli
ANTITRUST INSTITUTIONS AND POLICIES IN THE GLOBALISING ECONOMY

Andrea C. Simonelli
GOVERNING CLIMATE INDUCED MIGRATION AND DISPLACEMENT
IGO Expansions and Global Policy Implications

Victoria Higgins
ALLIANCE CAPITALISM, INNOVATION AND THE CHINESE STATE
The Global Wireless Sector

Andrei V. Belyi
TRANSNATIONAL GAS MARKETS AND EURO-RUSSIAN ENERGY RELATIONS

Silvia Pepino
SOVEREIGN RISK AND FINANCIAL CRISIS
The International Political Economy of the Eurozone

Ryan David Kiggins (*editor*)
THE POLITICAL ECONOMY OF RARE EARTH ELEMENTS. RISING POWERS AND TECHNOLOGICAL CHANGE

Seán Ó Riain, Felix Behling, Rossella Ciccia and Eoin Flaherty (*editors*)
THE CHANGING WORLDS AND WORKPLACES OF CAPITALISM

Alexander Korolev and Jing Huang
INTERNATIONAL COOPERATION IN THE DEVELOPMENT OF RUSSIA'S FAR EAST AND SIBERIA

Roman Goldbach
GLOBAL GOVERNANCE AND REGULATORY FAILURE
The Political Economy of Banking

Kate Ervine and Gavin Fridell (*editors*)
BEYOND FREE TRADE
Alternative Approaches to Trade, Politics and Power

Ray Kiely
THE BRICS, US 'DECLINE' AND GLOBAL TRANSFORMATIONS

Philip Fountain, Robin Bush and R. Michael Feener (*editors*)
RELIGION AND THE POLITICS OF DEVELOPMENT
Critical Perspectives on Asia

Markus Fraundorfer
BRAZIL'S EMERGING ROLE IN GLOBAL SECTORAL GOVERNANCE
Health, Food Security and Bioenergy

Katherine Hirschfeld
GANGSTER STATES
Organized Crime, Kleptocracy and Political Collapse

Matthew Webb and Albert Wijeweera (*editors*)
THE POLITICAL ECONOMY OF CONFLICT IN SOUTH ASIA

Matthias Ebenau, Ian Bruff and Christian May (*editors*)
NEW DIRECTIONS IN COMPARATIVE CAPITALISMS RESEARCH
Critical and Global Perspectives

Jeffrey Dayton-Johnson
LATIN AMERICA'S EMERGING MIDDLE CLASSES
Economic Perspectives

Andrei Belyi and Kim Talus
STATES AND MARKETS IN HYDROCARBON SECTORS

Dries Lesage and Thijs Van de Graaf
RISING POWERS AND MULTILATERAL INSTITUTIONS

Leslie Elliott Armijo and Saori N. Katada (*editors)*
THE FINANCIAL STATECRAFT OF EMERGING POWERS
Shield and Sword in Asia and Latin America

Md Mizanur Rahman, Tan Tai Yong, Ahsan Ullah (*editors)*
MIGRANT REMITTANCES IN SOUTH ASIA
Social, Economic and Political Implications

Bartholomew Paudyn
CREDIT RATINGS AND SOVEREIGN DEBT
The Political Economy of Creditworthiness through Risk and Uncertainty

Lourdes Casanova and Julian Kassum
THE POLITICAL ECONOMY OF AN EMERGING GLOBAL POWER
In Search of the Brazil Dream

International Political Economy Series
Series Standing Order ISBN 978–0–333–71708–0 hardcover
Series Standing Order ISBN 978–0–333–71110–1 paperback

You can receive future titles in this series as they are published by placing a standing order. Please contact your bookseller or, in case of difficulty, write to us at the address below with your name and address, the title of the series and one of the ISBNs quoted above.

Customer Services Department, Macmillan Distribution Ltd, Houndmills, Basingstoke, Hampshire RG21 6XS, England

---

Social Justice in the Globalization of Production

Labor, Gender, and the Environment Nexus

Md Saidul Islam
Assistant Professor, Nanyang Technological University, Singapore

and

Md Ismail Hossain
Professor, Shahjalal University of Science and Technology, Bangladesh

palgrave
macmillan

First published 2016 by
PALGRAVE MACMILLAN

Palgrave Macmillan in the UK is an imprint of Macmillan Publishers Limited, registered in England, company number 785998, of Houndmills, Basingstoke, Hampshire RG21 6XS.

Palgrave Macmillan in the US is a division of St Martin's Press LLC, 175 Fifth Avenue, New York, NY 10010.

Palgrave Macmillan is the global academic imprint of the above companies and has companies and representatives throughout the world.

Palgrave® and Macmillan® are registered trademarks in the United States, the United Kingdom, Europe and other countries.

ISBN: 978–1–137–43400–5

This book is printed on paper suitable for recycling and made from fully managed and sustained forest sources. Logging, pulping and manufacturing processes are expected to conform to the environmental regulations of the country of origin.

A catalogue record for this book is available from the British Library.

A catalog record for this book is available from the Library of Congress.

To the women, men and children killed and affected by the Rana Plaza, Tazreen Fashions and all other industrial disasters

Contents

List of Illustrations

Box

Figure

Tables

Preface

On April 24, 2013, the world witnessed the collapse of Rana Plaza, the deadliest garment-factory disaster in history, killing over a thousand people. Exactly five months before, on November 24, 2012, Tazreen Fashions, another factory in Bangladesh's capital city, Dhaka, caught fire and killed over a hundred workers. These two accidents clearly show that garment workers, the biggest contributors to the local economy, are constantly in death traps. Along with horrible working conditions, as emerged later partly because of local and international uproar, the exploitation of the workers, the gendered dimension of this exploitation and environmental contamination are linked with global commodity networks stretching into the powerful supermarkets in the global North. These industrial tragedies are essentially a product of class exploitation in the global production system and are reflective of the notion that profit accumulation has overshadowed the lives of many in Third World countries. These immediately call for a robust investigation and a formulation of social justice for the downtrodden masses in the globalization of production.

The issues of labor, gender and the environment have formed a "critical nexus" in the wake of "flexible accumulation" and intense market competition under the neoliberal globalization of production. As the entire society serves the market economy, economic growth continues, albeit concentrating in increasingly fewer hands, at the expense of labor justice, gender equity and long-term environmental sustainability. Only a minority of working people today hold jobs that are well-paid and well-secured, while the majority of them are confronting inhuman working conditions. Female laborers are particularly vulnerable, as they dominate the lower end of the global commodity chains, which are characterized by low pay, long hours and informal working arrangements. Despite these dire conditions, women need their jobs at global factories to survive. The precarious conditions and vulnerabilities of women ironically appear as an "advantage" for the continued accumulation of capital, generating a paradox often known as "comparative advantages of women's disadvantages".

Along with precarious labor conditions and exploitative gender relations, this global "treadmill of production" is also generating a global treadmill of environmental destruction. The cost calculus driving the relocation of manufacturing to the Third World includes avoidance of stringent environmental regulations. The use of different toxic chemicals in factories generally results in chronic illness, such as headaches, sore throat and drowsiness among the workers. Chemical discharges from *maquiladoras* into open ditches adjacent to shantytowns, for example, have been linked to cancer, birth defects, and brain damage, and factories in export processing zones (EPZs) have been associated with the dumping of pollutants into local waters, affecting drinking water and fisheries. While environmental issues are often treated as an "externality" to be addressed at a later time, in fact, they are an indispensable ingredient in the globalization of production.

Much ink has been spilt on the question of labor, gender and the environment – albeit separately; however, we still lack a complete and coherent account of the complex nexus in the globalization of production. What patterns of labor and environmental conditions as well as gender relations does globalization of production with its flexible accumulation generate? Why and how are outsourcing, displacement, informalization and global relocation becoming common features of global economy today? What future trajectories are we heading toward? How can we empower labor, ensure gender justice and maintain environmental protection while maintaining flexibility? With an analytic framework comprising political economy, global commodity chains, feminist approaches, treadmill of productions and social justice, and drawing on empirical evidence from Bangladesh's ready-made garment industries and shrimp factories, labor migrants in Malaysia and Singapore, and "world factories" and other EPZs in China and elsewhere, *Social Justice in the Globalization of Production* provides a comprehensive look at the political economy of labor, gender and the environment in the context of neoliberal flexible accumulation. We will not only delineate the trajectories and conditions of labor, gender and the environment, but also postulate solutions using a social justice frameworks.

Acknowledgments

Social Justice in the Globalization of Production was made possible by research funding from the Italian Ministry of Education, University, and Research (MIUR) in Italy as well as the Ministry of Education, Singapore (through its Tier-1 grant). We would like to acknowledge our debt to these funding agencies. We are grateful to the series editor, commissioning editor and editorial assistant of Palgrave Macmillan for their diligent and crucial support and timely response in every phase of this publication. Special thanks to Vidhya Jayaprakash and her production team of Newgen Knowledge Works Pvt Ltd.

Our enormous debt, of course, is to all our informants for their warmth and hospitality and for providing us with necessary information patiently, the reviewers of the book and our mentors including Renata Semenza (University of Milan, Italy) and Golam M. Mathbor (Monmouth University, USA). For assistance and support during our fieldwork and writing phases, we would like to thank Md Tauhidur Rahman, Md Saiful Islam, Sonia, Opu, Lopa, and Md Saiful Islam, and a number of our students. We remember our colleagues at Nanyang Technological University (NTU) in Singapore and Shahjalal University of Science and Technology (SUST) in Bangladesh for their support and encouragements. Furqan Akram Khan and Md Nazrul Islam (Professor of Statistics, SUST) provided some crucial help with editing and thoughtful comments on our earlier drafts. The continuous support from Zhou Min (NTU), Syed Serajul Islam (Lakehead University), Samuel Cohn (Texas A&M University), Mustafa Koc (Ryerson University), Peter Vandergeest and Hira Singh (York University), Abu Yusuf and Md Rejaul Islam (SUST), and Md Shariful Islam (University of Dhaka) is also notable.

Finally, our family members have been loving and supportive throughout the long years of this project. Salma Sultana (wife of Saidul Islam) and Sohely Tamanna (wife of Ismail Hossain) have been a great source of encouragement and support. We also remember our parents, siblings and children (Ulfat Tahseen, Rawsab Said and Musab Said) for their priceless emotional support. During our fieldwork, we lost two of our most valuable pillars of life – Sakina Khatun (mother of Ismail Hossain) and Md Abul Hossain (father of Saidul Islam), who always pushed us towards academic excellence. We cannot simply repay our debt to them. May their souls rest in peace.

About the Authors

Md Saidul Islam, Assistant Professor, Division of Sociology, Nanyang Technological University, Singapore

Md Ismail Hossain, Professor, Department of Social Work, Shahjalal University of Science and Technology, Bangladesh

Tommy Kevin is a researcher in the Division of Sociology, Nanyang Technological University, Singapore.

Iris Carla De Jesus is a graduate student at Humboldt University, Berlin, Germany.

Md Saiful Islam is a graduate student in the Department of Social Work, Shahjalal University of Science and Technology, Bangladesh.

List of Abbreviations and Glossary

ADB	Asian Development Bank
AFL	American Federation of Labor
AFMA	Agriculture and Fisheries Modernization Act
AIDS	acquired immune deficiency syndrome
ANZCERTA	Australia and New Zealand Closer Economic Relations Trade Agreement
ASA	Association for Social Advancement
ASEAN	Association of South East Asian Nations
BBS	Bangladesh Bureau of Statistics
BECC	Border Environmental Cooperation Commission
BEF	Bangladesh Employment Federation
BEPB	Bangladesh Export Promotion Bureau
BEPZA	Bangladesh Export Processing Zones Authority
BGMEA	Bangladesh Garments Manufacturers and Exporters Association
BIGUF	Bangladesh Independent Garments Workers Union Federation
BILS	Bangladesh Institute of Labour Studies
BIRDEM	Bangladesh Institute of Research & Rehabilitation in Diabetes, Endocrine and Metabolic Disorders
BKMEA	Bangladesh Knitwear Manufacturers and Exporters Association
BLAST	Bangladesh Legal Aid and Services Trust
BNP	Bangladesh Nationalist Party
BRAC	Bangladesh Rural Advancement Committee
BSCI	Business Sourcing Compliance Initiative
BSTI	Bangladesh Standards and Testing Institution
CCC	Clean Clothes Campaign
CEN	Coalition of Environmental NGOs
CEO	Chief Executive Officer
CIO	Congress of Industrial Organizations
CRP	Centre for Rehabilitation of the Paralysed
DEPC	Department of Environment and Pollution Control
DIFE	Department of Inspection of Factories and Establishments
EDI	electronic document interchange

EFP	Employment Provident Fund
EOI	Export-Oriented Industry
EPZ	Export Processing Zone
ETI	Ethical Trading Initiative
FAO	Food and Agriculture Organization of the United Nations
FDI	Foreign Direct Investment
FDW	Foreign Domestic Workers
FLA	Fair Labor Association
FPE	Feminist Political Economy
FSCD	Fire Service and Civil Defense
GATS	General Agreement on Trade in Services
GCC	Global Commodity Chain
GDP	Gross Domestic Product
GIFT	Genetic Improvement of Farmed Tilapia
GIZ	German Institute for Cooperation Development
GPN	Global Production Network
GSC	Global Steering Committee
GSI	global sex industries
GSP	Generalized System of Preferences
GVC	Global Value Chain
HACCP	Hazard Analysis and Critical Control Point
HIV	human immunodeficiency virus
HOME	Humanitarian Organization for Migration Economics
HRM	Human Resource Management
HVFs	high-value foods
HYVs	high-yielding varieties
IBC	Industrial Bangladesh Council
ICCPR	International Covenant on Civil and Political Rights
ICESCR	International Covenant on Economic Social and Cultural Rights
ICT	information and communication technologies
IFPRI	International Food Policy Research Institute
ILO	International Labour Organization
IMF	International Monetary Fund
KN	*Karmajibi Nari* (Working Women)
LWO	Labour Welfare Officers
MEP	Ministry of Environment Protection
MFA	Multi Fibre Arrangement
MIC	Military Industrial Complex
MM2H	Malaysia My Second Home

MNCs	Multinational Corporations
MoEF	Ministry of Environment and Forests
MOU	Memorandum of Understanding
NACA	Network of Aquaculture Centres in Asia-Pacific
NAFTA	North America Free Trade Agreement
NCCWE	National Coordination Committee for Workers' Education
NEMAP	National Environment Management Action Plan
NGO	Non-Governmental Organization
NICs	Newly Industrializing Countries
NIDL	new international division of labor
NOC	No Objection Certificate
NTPA	National Tripartite Plan of Action
OECD	Organisation for Economic Co-operation and Development
PEA	Political Economy Approach
RAJUK	Rajdhani Unnayan Korttripokkho (Capital City Development Authority)
RMG	readymade garments
SAI	Social Accountability International
SAPTA	SAARC Preferential Trading Arrangement
SCP	Sustainable Consumption Pattern
SEMP	Sustainable Environment Management Project
SEZs	special economic zones
ShAD	Shrimp Aquaculture Dialogue
SSOQ	Shrimp Seal of Quality
TFN	transnational feminist network
ToP	treadmill of production
TSD	treatment, storage, and disposal
TWC2	Transient Workers Count Too
UDHR	Universal Declaration of Human Rights
UN	United Nations
UNDP	United Nations Development Programme
UNEP	United Nations Environment Programme
USA	United States of America
USAID	US Agency for International Development
WASA	Water Supply Authority
WB	World Bank
WRC	Worker Rights Consortium
WTO	World Trade Organization
WWF	World Wildlife Fund
Ain O Salish Kendra	Centre for Law and Justice

Baire	Outside
Nari Uddog Kendra	Centre for Women's Initiative
Purdah	Seclusion/veil
Odhikar	Right

1 The Globalization of Production

With Tommy Kevin

The relation between human labor and the environment

From the beginning, it has been part of the human condition to labor collectively and utilize our surroundings and local resources for survival and reproduction. Since the beginning, the dynamics of labor, gender and the environment have affected the production and perpetuation of human social lives.

Prior to modern humans, there were documented cases of environmental degradation in pre-*Homo sapiens* societies. *Homo erectus* (1.8 million years ago) experienced an unexpected population boom simply by throwing rocks to hunt and using fire to cook. They were known to set fires to open vegetation for travel, to attract game animals and to drive animals for hunt (Richerson et al., 1991: 392). While the specifics of cooperation and competition varied among *Homo sapiens* populations, early hunter-gatherers lived in kinship bands and were known to cause ecological disaster through over-hunting and over-gathering. The first farmers over-farmed, leading to deforestation, soil erosion and species extinction. Flooding occurred frequently in the Yellow River region, which resulted in destroyed villages. In the Fertile Crescent (8500 BC), the Middle East region's highly productive vegetation areas became deserts, and entire civilizations were wiped out (Diamond, 1997, 2005; Chew, 2001).

The history of mankind contains certain recurring features in the cycle of expansion and social and environmental crisis regardless of the mode of production; that is, they live in social groupings and labor collectively to make use of the environment. Perhaps because it is often too effective in exploitation – be it of fellow human beings or of nature – excesses appear to be a trend in production, based on the social collective. Solutions to the problems are typically either physical – by expanding into new frontiers when they have exhausted the natural resources of the previous area, conquering other groups of humans – and/or technological, with innovations in new tools leading to new methods of production. With environmental changes, hunter-gatherers gradually settled for horticulture. Sedentary collectives generated surpluses to produce innovations in culture and technology, and through sociocultural evolutionary processes, gender dynamics shifted from rather egalitarian practices of hunting-gathering societies to the patriarchal arrangements of agrarian, and subsequently industrial, societies. Bands, tribes, chiefdoms, empires and nation-states either expanded at the expense of others or experienced downfall, amid differing forms. Such is the intersection of labor, gender and the environment. This nexus continues today – in the age of globalization – with more complex dynamics and varying outcomes.

From reflexive modernity to flexible accumulation

Production – how to make a living – drives both individuals and the social collective. A cornucopia of literature in the anthropological fields traces the sociocultural, economic, political and technological evolution of production from the earliest days to the present. For the sake of brevity, we shall focus on the most recent shift to the current dominant mode of production: the trajectory that shifted the characteristics of production from (industrial) development to (contemporary postindustrial) globalization (Islam, 2009).

Before the industrial order, the economy was a function of the society in question. Since the industrial revolution (1760–1840), which is based on the engines of production and consumption of goods and services, we see a peculiarity where society is made to serve the economy (Polanyi, 1944). Whereas in other types of society "economy, as a rule, submerged in... social relationships" (Polanyi, 1968: 46), in the case of the industrial capitalist market economy "[i]nstead of economy being embedded in social relations, social relations are embedded in the economic systems" (ibid., 57). The turmoil of current developments and social changes across much of the Third World stems from "Southern" societies being embedded in a global capitalist system in which their societies are made to serve the needs and interests of "Northern" economies, via an international division of labor. While the specific form has shifted somewhat with a change in political context, the essence of its unequal exchange mechanism has remained. In the colonial era, mother states accumulated capital through extracting raw materials from the colonies on the cheap and returned the trade with higher-valued manufactured products, thereby accumulating capital in the mother states at the expense of the colonies' natural environment. Under the current global age, the newly industrializing countries (NICs) provide the site and labor for cheap production while the postindustrial nations control the design, services and investments inputs, thereby accumulating financial and knowledge capital in the First World at the risk of environmental and workplace hazards in the Third.

While first modernity is used as the term for the breakdown of agricultural society in favor of an industrial mode of production – and its implications to the changes in political, economic, social and cultural characteristics – in the aftermath of the industrial revolution, Ulrich Beck and Anthony Giddens (1991) separately describe a second modernity, or "reflexive modernization", as reassessing sociology as a science of the present by moving beyond the early 20th century conceptual framework to provide a counterbalance to the postmodernist paradigm offering a reconstructive view alongside deconstruction (Beck et al., 2003) so as to reflect the transition from an industrial to a networked information society (Castells, 1996). Using this framework to analyze the global production system, Fordism, of the late 1900s, where capital accumulates through breaking down production into simple steps along an assembly line so that large quantities of standardized, mass-produced items may be sold in the market, has been replaced by post-Fordist forms of production in the late 20th century. In this consumerist-geared mechanism, products are no longer homogenous, straightforward, or mass-produced, but contain a varying set of characteristics that are increasingly customized in the minute details so as to target differentiated sets of consumers through flexible specialization (Piore and Sabel, 1984) of producing, if necessary, small volumes of a wide and rapidly changing range of products.

In order to produce goods and services in ever-evolving and specialized conditions, neoliberal globalization is practiced through outsourcing, displacement, informalization and recolonization, where inputs beyond raw material (e.g., land, labor) are increasingly commoditized (Michael, 2008), the value of which is determined through the process of exchange rather than their use (Harvey, 1991), so that capital (i.e., financial, social, knowledge) is accumulated "flexibility".

In the wake of this flexible accumulation under the conditions of neoliberal globalization (Munck, 2002; Smart, 2003; Harvey, 2005; Islam, 2013), the issue of labor has become both significant and challenging. While only a minority of working people today hold jobs that are well-paid, where their fundamental rights are respected, and where they can enjoy to some extent social security in case of job loss, personal or family illness or other difficulties, the majority of them are faced with inhuman working conditions and are living in poverty (Dahan et al., 2011). "Good jobs are getting harder and harder to find and *keep*; while bad jobs seem to be getting worse even as they are more plentiful than ever" (Islam, 2008: 212). According to the International Labor Organization (ILO), 39 percent of the world's workforce is living in poverty (earning less than $2 a day) and 21 percent live in extreme poverty (less than $1.25 a day) in 2008 (ILO, 2010a). A majority of the workers are in the informal economy, which is mostly associated with low wages, unsteady job security and extreme conditions of labor exploitation. The gender wage gap is at the center, as women are engaged in segregated sectors that are generally characterized by low pay, long hours and often informal working arrangements (Bulut and Lane, 2011; ILO, 2010b; McMichael, 2008; Islam, 2008; O'Brien, 2004). Despite these dire conditions, women need their jobs at global factories to survive. The precarious conditions and vulnerabilities of women ironically appear as an "advantage" for the capitalists' continued accumulation, generating a paradox known as "comparative advantages of women's disadvantages" (Arizpe and Aranda, 1981: 453). This juxtaposing situation of workers is not unique to a specific country, but rather a common feature of most developing countries that are connected to the global production system.

Globalization of production and the nexus

Supporters argue that globalization brings positive changes in the lives of women workers in various forms, such as expansion of employment opportunities leading to higher incomes (Barrientos et al., 2004; Razavi, 2001), subversion of century-old exploitative patriarchal relationships (Lim, 1997), an increase of self-awareness about rights and duties (Kabeer, 2004) and a shift in affirmative gender roles and value structures, as well as a reconfiguration of the public–private and production–reproduction dichotomies (Unni, 2002). Critics of neoliberal globalization, however, reject the claim of economic benefit to women resulting from economic globalization, stating instead that it is pushing women into even more vulnerable situations than they were in before (Elson and Pearson, 1981, 1997; Nash and Fernandez-Kelly, 1983; Acker, 2004; Standing, 2009). They argue that the entry of women into the paid workforce does not make any significant change in hierarchal gender relations, since a new sexual division of labor is created in factories. Working conditions in the factories are characterized by, for instance, extremely long hours, little training, absence of seniority payments, unhygienic work conditions, and little occupational and employment security. All of these in turn reduce the labor costs, leading to a profit haven for many multinational corporations (Jaggar, 2001; Acker, 2004; O'Brien, 2004). These critics therefore maintain that women workers are a vital resource for economic globalization and are subject to capitalist exploitation.

In Harvey (2005), developing nations are unable to transform into First World economies through internalized neoliberal mechanisms because exploitation is rampant. It examines how a neoliberalized, global, political economy benefits few at the expense of many, which has resulted in the recreation of class distinction through "accumulation by dispossession". That is, some groups of people (namely, the upper and middle classes of the First World and the elites of the Third) accumulate wealth, power and material possessions at the expense of disempowering and povertizing others (namely, the global masses) through the global economic order. Klein (2000) argues that manufacturing and industrial jobs have been offshored from developed countries (i.e., United States and Western Europe) to developing countries, particularly to export processing zones (EPZs). She highlighted that because normal labor laws and environmental regulations do not apply to sweatshops located within these EPZs, semi- and unskilled workers face exploitation through long working hours, dangerous work conditions, inhumane treatment and low wages, sometimes barely above subsistence levels. Under the new system, the companies no longer own the means of production nor manage the manufacturing process. The actual manufacturing of the physical goods is contracted out to factory and plant owners who are able to keep costs down by employing methods as described previously. Portions of the work can be further subcontracted with even greater cost savings albeit to higher degrees of worker exploitation at each level. With the manufacturing of the goods no longer under the purview of the corporations, they now focus heavily on branding and marketing, using the surplus monies generated by the cost savings of offshoring and contracting. Klein rationalized that the corporations are able to get away with these misdeeds due to two main reasons. First, the developing countries are trapped in a negative feedback loop where, in order to compete with other developing economies for foreign investment dollars, the countries had to offer cutthroat deals such as relaxing regulations and control. In addition, the corporation deals with only the contractor, and only prices are on the agenda. Micromanagement and law abatement are the concerns and legal liability of the contractor.

These polarizing trajectories in the existing literature, however, often obscure the extent to which labor practices at global manufacturing are just and fair, leaving little or no room for considering and enhancing labor justice. This book attempts to explore the relationship between labor and the environment in the context of globalization. Compounded by the feminization of marginalized Third World labor and the associated social problems that arose with said globalization, these three topics (labor, gender and the environment) and their dynamics in relation to production form the "nexus" through which we examine the global economic and social order of our times. Drawing on the social justice framework propounded by, among others, Amartya Sen (2009), we will unpack this critical nexus. In other words, we will investigate how neoliberal flexible accumulation generates unique conditions, contradictions and confrontations in labor, gender and environmental relations; and whether and how a broader global social justice can mitigate the tensions and improve the conditions.

Methodology

This book is based on a robust analysis of secondary sources found in various social science disciplines and a content analysis of "grey" literature (see Cadman, 2011: 21). This analysis has been substantiated by a number of primary researches conducted on the garment industry in Bangladesh, labor migrants in Malaysia and foreign domestic workers in Singapore. In addition, the authors, over the past decade, engaged and participated in discussions with various stakeholders related to the issue of labor from the global South to the North. Grounded largely in the discipline of sociology, social work, philosophy, history and economics, the book offers an interdisciplinary perspective on the critical nexus of labor, gender and the environment in the globalization of production.

Study on ready-made garments in Bangladesh

A great deal of primary data, qualitative in nature, were collected through a robust study on the ready-made garments (RMG) industry in Dhaka, the capital of Bangladesh, during the period of October 2011 to June 2012. The Bangladesh RMG industry has been taken as an empirical site for this study for several pressing reasons. First, it's a pressing example of global manufacturing that illuminates the global chain of production, feminization of labor and low standards of labor rights and benefits (Paul-Majumder and Begum, 2006; Rahman et al., 2008; Standing, 1999). Two recent RMG industrial disasters in Dhaka (a fire breakout killing over a hundred and a factory collapse killing over a thousand) highlight the precarious working conditions and significance of this study. Second, the RMG industry is the largest export-oriented industry (EOI) in Bangladesh, generating about US$2 billion (about 80 percent) foreign exchange annually and the second largest in the world, in terms of RMG exports, after China. The growth of this industry over the years has therefore been exponential. While there were only 0.12 million workers employed in 384 factories during the year 1983–84 in Bangladesh, it has reached to 4 million in 5400 factories in the year of 2011–12 (BGMEA, 2013). Finally, the Bangladesh RMG industry is increasingly becoming a promising place – albeit with various challenges – for many multinational corporations after the rising labor costs in China and elsewhere (Wassener, 2011). In terms of operational flexibility and reduction of labor costs – two major considerations for neoliberal flexible accumulation – Dhaka remains an ideal place for multinational corporations (MNCs). Leading MNCs such as Walmart, Nike, Reebok, Levi Strauss, Disney, Li & Fung, Sears, Hallmark, GAP, Hasbro and TakaraTomy, Haines & Martinez, and Tesco import garment items from Bangladesh, linking the nation with the global commodity networks.

While Dhaka is the main hub of RMG manufacturing, its plants are congregated in different places around the city, and the labor rights situation varies from factory to factory (Hossain, 2011). Therefore, for empirical investigation, we purposively selected eight manufacturing enterprises, considering the size and location of the firms. For a credible representation, both large and small, export processing zones (EPZs) and non-EPZ areas were covered while drawing our sample. A methodological triangulation – an in-depth qualitative interview substantiated by ethnography, focus group discussions and a document search – was employed in this study to represent diverse stakeholders and to capture broad pictures. We conducted in-depth interviews with 71 respondents that include 32 factory workers, 16 employer/management staffs, 6 representatives from 6 workers' unions (one from each union), 3 representatives from the government agencies (Ministry of Labor, Directorate of the Inspection of Factory and Establishment, and Bangladesh Export Promotion Zone Authority (BEPZA)), 2 representatives from Bangladesh Garments Manufacturers and Exporters Association (BGMEA), 2 NGO staff members working on the labor issues, 6 representatives from brand companies and 3 labor experts. The women workers, selected through snowball sampling for interviews, were between 18 and 45 years old and had experience working in the RMG industry for at least two years, demonstrating that they are "key informants" for interview.

For acquiring appropriate information, we used different interview schedules for each type of participant (e.g., workers, employers, union leaders). The interviews contained many semi-structured, open-ended questions dealing with various critical issues; for instance, whether and why the employers prefer to have women workers instead of men, what the current situation of worker rights and labor benefits is, to what extent they follow the international standards, types of problems and challenges women workers face at the workplace, in case of injustice whether and how workers voice out, and what roles different actors (i.e., state, employers' association and unions) are playing and with what outcomes.

Respondents in each stratum were identified as "key individuals" for this study and therefore spoke with relative authority on the subject matters. Second, although a significant amount of primary data was generated through in-depth qualitative interviews providing a substantial basis for this book, some ethnographic techniques in the forms of direct observation and conversation with local people added significant value to this study. The researchers stayed six months in the research areas and spent a large amount of time engaging in informal talks with local people residing in workers' residential areas, including workers' family members, and tried to get their opinions about women's employment in RMG industry. Third, for a final consistency check, the researchers also arranged four focus group discussions involving workers from different factories and local people. Each group, comprising 10–12 participants, shared their views about, among other things, their daily experiences and collective resistance against harassment faced inside and outside factories. Finally, a robust document search was conducted to make a comparative gauge between our primary data and locally available secondary sources. Along with online sources, the researchers spent more than a month in Dhaka solely to collect different documentary information such as annual reports, brochures, periodicals, bulletins and study reports from concerned offices, such as BGMEA and BEPZA.

Follow-up research on the Rana Plaza disaster

On April 24, 2013, Bangladesh experienced the deadliest garment-factory accident in history. Eight-storied Rana Plaza in Dhaka EPZ collapsed, burying five garment factories and 3000 people. A total of 1129 people died, most of whom were poorly paid female garment workers (CNN, 2013). It was later revealed that the plaza's foundation was exceedingly unstable, having only been built on a pond filled with sand to keep construction costs low (Ali, 2013). Plaza owner Sohel Rana had ignored warnings by both police and industrial trade group BGMEA just the previous day about huge cracks that had appeared at the side of the building, boasting that the building would stand "for a hundred years" (Al-Mahmood and Harding, 2013). It was revealed that many safety regulations were circumvented in the process of building the Rana Plaza due to corruption. Rana himself was a politician of the ruling Awami League, although he was more commonly known as a *mastan* – a gangster – who gets his power and money from providing thug services to other politicians (Islam and Mustafa, 2013). It was his political allies who gave him the permits necessary to increase the number of floors from five to eight, even though the building could only withstand five (Yardley, 2013).

During the period from November to December 2014, we conducted a follow-up study on the Rana Plaza disaster and collected data using four kinds of methods – documents reviews, observation, in-depth interviews and focus group discussions. To get access to the respondents, we stayed a few days in the Savar areas to identify the Rana Plaza survivors, engaging in informal talks with gatekeepers, including NGO staffs, union leaders and local people residing around the collapsed building. We first found a Rana Plaza rescuer and then located a medical center operated by Bangladesh Institute of Labor Studies (BILS), a labor research institute, and collected the list of survivors who were connected with the BILS for physiotherapy and other medical services. From that list, we randomly picked ten cases for in-depth interviews. Following prior appointments with phone calls, we visited the living places of the survivors and held informal talks with them. During interviews, the interviewees were asked about their experiences during the disaster; support provided by the government, NGOs, and brand companies; the current state of physical conditions; and medical and other needs and required services. We also conducted informal talks with some labor activists concerning these issues. In addition, we arranged two focus group discussions involving the family members and survivors.

Study in Malaysia and Singapore

Both Singapore and Malaysia are hubs for labor migrants coming largely from other Southeast/South Asian countries. We conducted two separate studies: labor migrants in Malaysia and foreign domestic workers in Singapore. In both countries, we interviewed over 100 workers (90 labor migrants in Malaysia and 10 foreign domestic workers in Singapore), about a dozen local residents, and five human rights and social justice activists. We also made several purposeful visits in labor-crowded areas in Singapore (Mustafa Centre and Lucky Plaza) and Malaysia (Kuala

Lumpur, Klang Valley, Gombak, Perak and Perlis) and held informal conversations to gain a broader picture of, for example, their national and gender compositions, social and environmental conditions, and common complaints.

In case of inconsistency in the above studies, the researchers relied more on the primary data and the repeated cited secondary sources. Taken as a whole, these data sources provided a robust and in-depth understanding of the complex issues and questions regarding the employment conditions and labor rights in the globalization of production.

Prospectus

With this opening context and background, we have outlined the key questions relating to the critical nexus among labor, gender and the environment. The next chapter (Chapter 2) presents a comparative discussion of existing approaches for understanding labor, gender and the environment, reviewing available approaches such as political economy, feminism, global value chain, and human rights. We show that despite various strengths and strands, these approaches have narrow focus as they provide only a partial view of understanding the critical nexus between labor, gender and the environment. The chapter then complements these conceptual threads with a social justice approach, particularly the "capability approach", drawing largely from Amartya Sen (2009). We show that the social justice approach has much wider focus covering many of the key themes of other approaches. The "capability approach" is used to understand and to propose notions of labor justice, gender justice and environmental sustainability.

Chapter 3 elucidates the complex intersection between gender, labor and global manufacturing by drawing on the existing literatures and central debates concerning employment of women in global manufacturing enterprises. The literature reviewed under this study is organized into three central themes. First, this group of literature explicates the relationship between feminization of the workforce and global manufacturing. The second group of literature explores how feminization and labor vulnerability intersects in global factories. The third group of literature explores the policy debates of labor regulations. Drawing on the views from the literature, this chapter concludes that the impact of globalization on women is a paradox. While it provides many women, mainly in the global South, a way of survival through expansion of employment opportunities, women workers face multiple oppressions where gender identity is used as a resource for globalizing the capital.

The fourth chapter discusses the trajectories of women's employment and development from tradition to "modernity". Based on empirical evidence from Bangladesh and elsewhere, this chapter illustrates how gendered beliefs and cultural practices shape the gender division of labor and then sketches out how women's labor-market participation and vulnerability are influenced by these beliefs – portraying the shifting trends of women's employment from traditional agriculture to modernized production – and discusses the antecedents of transforming and accelerating this shift. We also trace the development path of the industrial relations system and labor regulation policies.

Based on theoretical framework outlined in Chapter 2 and drawing on the empirical evidence from the Bangladesh Readymade Garments (RMG) industry, Chapter 5 examines whether the current labor practices are just and fair. Upon discussing the rise of Third World industrialization, we first examine the practices, policies and strategies of labor regulation in the RMG industry and elsewhere and how they contribute to maintain labor rights, and examine to what extent existing labor practices are just and fair. Second, we explore the role of the actors (both traditional and new actors) in ensuring labor justice and injustice. Finally, we conclude that a coordinated role of different actors is needed for ensuring true labor justice.

Chapter 6 explores how, in the global agro-food system, consumer concern has cantered not only around long-established issues like food safety and environmental degradation but also included questions of, among other things, labor exploitation in food-producing countries. To address these issues, we explicate two great food revolutions – the green and the blue – that dramatically altered both agrarian and environmental landscapes. Taking evidence from shrimp-processing factories in Bangladesh, we show labor patterns, gender relations and environmental conditions. We investigate whether there is a gap between labor standards in private regulatory regimes and actual labor practices. As the local labor practices are largely influenced by local ecological (e.g., monthly cycles, when processing factories get an abundant supply of shrimp) and social (e.g., abundance of cheap labor) conditions, fundamental questions arise as to whether and how the private certification schemes/regimes can address the labor issues. Who is setting standards for whom, and with what effects? Do they consult with the local stakeholders regarding labor standards that would be consistent with local ecological and social conditions? How will the emerging certification regimes pinpoint these problems and broadly address the labor issues for complete certification?

Chapter 7 explores the conditions, contradictions and confrontations encountered by migrant labor through linking it with some conditions of neoliberal globalization such as outsourcing, displacements, informalization and global relocation. We examine migrant labor, labor in global sex industries and human trafficking. Taking examples of the "Orang Bangla" (Bangladeshi migrant labor in Malaysia and Singapore), foreign domestic workers in Singapore, global sex labor and global human trafficking, we look at not only the trials and tribulations of the migrant labor but also scopes for mitigations and social justice.

Chapter 8 focuses on workplace environment and safety issues at global manufacturing industries with particular focus on the RMG industry in Bangladesh. This chapter reviews the major industrial accidents/disasters that have taken place in the RMG industry over the years, and the regulatory measures for improving the work environment, and assesses the long-term consequences on the lives of workers. We also highlight some tragic stories of survivors who lost parts of their bodies in the factory building collapse and long-term consequences on the well-being of family members after the death of their sole breadwinners. The chapter finally evaluates the corporate responsibility for compensation and rehabilitation of the disaster victims.

Chapter 9 contemplates the treadmill of production in relation to the environment. The treadmill of production refers to the endless cycle of production processes inherent in our current capitalistic mode of production in the modern industrial society. This cycle of endless production processes generates large quantities of often toxic waste, which is usually dumped back into the environment. The resultant degradation impacts upon natural ecosystems and human well-being. Taking evidences from the "world factory", export processing zones and the military industrial complex, as well as drawing on the literature focusing on environmental conditions and consequences elsewhere, this chapter argues that the global treadmill of production is in fact generating a global treadmill of destruction. We also highlight environmental regulations and certifications issues as well as a way to mitigate the problem.

Referring to and taking insights from earlier chapters, the concluding chapter (Chapter 10) brings forth the discourse of social justice, focusing on different paradigms. Particular attention is paid to the notion of "capability approach" propounded by Nobel Laureate Amartya Sen and is applied to the globalization of production after locating it in the broader analysis of labor justice, gender justice and environmental sustainability/protection. The chapter also highlights the issues of environmental justice and other forthcoming issues in the study of the globalization of production.

2
Labor, Gender and the Environment: Analytic Framework

This chapter will look into a range of theories that have been propounded to explain the issue of labor and gender justice. The understandings and policy initiatives demonstrated concerning social justice are not limited to a singular approach but rather a myriad of distinct and unique conceptual underpinnings. This chapter will go on to discuss five dominant approaches currently in practice (political economy, feminist political economy, global value chain, human rights, and social justice) and will justify the choice of "capability approach" as the main theoretical framework to explore the issues of labor, gender and the environment presented in the subsequent chapters in this book.

Political economy approach

The political economy approach (PEA) is one of the dominant contributions in political economy literature. The PEA, a study of society as an integrated system, departs from the traditional economic approach, which mainly deals with the demand and supply of goods and services in a free market economy. It identifies and analyzes social relations as they relate to the economic system of production and treats economics as an extension of politics and relations of power as they influence the production, distribution and consumption of goods and services as well as management of these economic variables, relationships and functions (Inter Pares, 2004). The main focus of this approach is to shift the traditional institutional mechanism to newly structured economic power and institutions to serve people. The change of the global economy destabilizes the traditional methods that have been constructed to confront patriarchal economic power (e.g., the power of the state, the pervasive and unregulated power of capital and male privilege). Many of the strategies that have been developed to improve the living and working conditions of the employees are no longer productive. The failure of traditional institutions in regulating the labor market has led to various economic institutions sprouting at the international level to govern the global economy. This severely questions whether state power is subsumed at the level of the international economic power or if it is reconfigured in the new globalized economy (Cohen, 2004). This issue has been thoroughly discussed in the political economy discourse and has led to two distinct forms of arguments: the global imperative approach and the national management approach (Bergeron, 2001).

The global imperative approach contends that the economic logic of capitalism has created a truly global economic, social and cultural system that can only be countered by a global resistance movement (Banuri and Schor, 1992; Dirlik, 1994). It conceives that once upon a time, nation-states were capable of managing national economy and meeting citizens' demands for economic stability, environmental regulations, labor regulations and social safety nets, and accordingly kept up with the economic interests and well-being of their citizens. However, the recent transformation of the global economy, characterized by interdependence and competitiveness, external forces such as structural adjustment policies imposed by the World Bank (WB) and the International Monetary Fund (IMF), and the increasing number of free trade agreements, whether global (General Agreement on Trade in Services, GATS), regional (North American Free Trade Agreement, NAFTA) or bilateral (Australia New Zealand Closer Economic Agreement, ANZCERTA), are shaping state policy. National states are forced to cut tariffs and taxes to attract foreign direct investment (FDI) from TNCs that are subject to shrinking budgetary allocation to social services that hinders the nation-state from crafting economic policies that promote national interests or that undertake extensive security programs (Yeats, 2001; Rudra, 2002). Many governments around the world have followed a privatization policy for state institutions in order to shift resources from the public sector (Cohen, 2004). Thus, scholars contend that the global order of transnational production and finance calls for a new institutional system of economic regulation that inadvertently destabilizes the nation-state (Banuri and Schor, 1992).

In contrast, *the national management approach* conceives that a state is not an idle, passive or powerless actor but rather a key creator and mediator of globalization (Weiss, 2003). National states reserve some power to manage the economy and bargain with global capital to secure the rights of citizens and to protect the vulnerable groups (e.g., Kayatekin and

Ruccio, 1998; Reich, 1991). Proponents hold the view that the institutions that are being established are not democratic and hence are unable to replace the market-controlling function of nations, which leads to a shift in power decidedly in the favor of multinational corporations (Cohen, 2001). They contend that a national government can best contribute to the welfare of its citizens by pursuing a competitiveness-enhancing strategy, such as enhancing education and training of the workforce, protecting national firms and workers by taking safety nets, restricting the movement of capital across national borders, and opposing World Trade Organization (WTO) agreements in case of the failure to provide for the desired working conditions as stated by the national law. The changing economic and political spectrums do not jeopardize the role of the state, which retains the power to manage its affairs in a more progressive way (Taylor, 1995). It is a denationalization process that supposedly revitalizes the national capabilities toward the implementation of global projects (Esping-Anderson, 1990; Sassen, 2006).

The apparent controversy on the role of the state in political economy literature continues to create interest among scholars to further research the issue and seek new insights in managing the global capital. Bergeron (2001) notes that both the global imperative and the national management approaches invoke different ideas about the power of global capital, economic subjectivity and strategies for resistance, but they do not maintain any specific boundary regarding the use of one or the other of these frameworks. Overcoming the drawbacks of these approaches, Hirst and Thompson (1996) suggest a hybrid approach combining both the national and international public policies to cope with global market forces.

Feminist political economy approach

The feminist political economy (FPE) approach focuses simply on the market economy and hence seeks to challenge the reigning, orthodox, neoliberal economic model whose primary goal is growth and accumulation. The FPE approach departs from conventional economics on the grounds that gendered assumptions and effects are generally invisible in mainstream theories. It employs gender[1] as a defining category and focuses on the actual lived experience of women, men and their families and the elements of life, community and social relations and considers them not only as economic definers and qualifiers but also as human beings. A feminist political economy approach "reveals and clarifies how gender determines or influences the social and political relationships and structures of power and the differential economic effects that flow from these relationships and structures" (Inter Pares, 2004: 4). Explaining the feature of FPE, Lordes Beneria (2003: 47) notes:

> On the one hand, it addresses the social construction and economic bases of women's subordination with important implications for our understanding of the factors generating the various forms of gender inequality and hierarchical power relations and for policy action. It also addresses the questions of women's interests and needs. On the other hand, it challenges some fundamental tenets and basic assumptions in the discipline of economics, either joining other critiques from different perspectives or representing unique feminist contributions. In this sense, feminist economics transcends the more explicit project by questioning the very nature for the profession as a whole.

Since FPE seeks to explore gender relations embedded in sociopolitical institutions and gender inequality in outcomes, it does not merely consider production but both production and reproduction, and focuses on the provisioning of human needs and well-being (Riley, 2008). The underlying assumption of FPE is that under the current reign of neoliberalism, the accumulation of wealth within and among countries (for neoliberal economists the sign of a healthy economy) is diminishing the possibility of social provisioning for a growing number of people in poverty and in the middle class. The gap between poverty and wealth is increasing (Riley, 2008). Feminist political economists point to this poverty wealth gap and call into question the contribution of unfettered market economy in increasing productivity and the resultant consequence on the benefit of society at large, irrespective of gender and the role of the state. The FPE approach does not consider the state as a universal safeguard; rather it sees the state as either the main enemy or savior (Armstrong and Connelly, 1999). Feminist political economists argue that there is no gender-neutral perspective. The masculine value system, based on dynamics of power and domination, promotes historical, social, political and economic marginalization of women and gendered division of labor. Without challenging discriminatory power relations and gendered division of labor, it is difficult for women to take their fair share in the material and societal resources as Riley (2008: 3) notes:

> The unequal power dynamics between women and men intersects with, mirrors and reinforces other power dynamics embedded

> in institutions and relationships.... These power dynamics limit autonomy and agency – on the personal level for women and so-called minority groups, for people in poverty and for countries in the global south – creating systemic inequality across the social sectors, including the household. Because of the intersection of gender power dynamics with all other forms of power over, the struggle for women's autonomy and agency cannot be separated from the larger context of class, race/ethnicity, sexual preference and geographic location.

Riley (2008) implies that women must have the opportunity to engage in processes that allow them to challenge the diverse forms of subordination and develop the capacity to take power and control over their lives, their organizations, and their specific cultural, economic, political and social context. To ensure effective participation of women in social, cultural, political and economic life, FPE focuses on women's empowerment and capability enhancement. Women's engagement in the struggles and resistance movement, dialogue and coalition building are effective ways of challenging women's oppression and promoting women's human rights (Brenner, 2003; Antrobus, 2004).

While many scholars have acknowledged the state as a primary site of women's resistance, emphasizing the role that national policy can play by instituting national restrictions on international capital, social safety nets, fair pay laws and health and safety regulations (Cagatay, Elson and Grown, 1995; Collier, 1994), others hold the view that equality issues that take transnational form cannot be tackled at the level of national resistance. It requires a global collective decision of regulating labor markets. Feminist discourse of globalization contends that nation-states and national subjectivities are no longer meaningful in the changing contours of the global economic and political space. The best resistance strategies for women are based on the new realities of global identity, which lays the foundation for a global women's movement (Moghadam, 1999). This global feminist politics calls for a globalized women's movement and transformation of institutional structure at the global level. However, many feminists argue that global resistance based on international solidarity cannot meaningfully interpret the needs at the local context. They call for the establishment of a "strategic sisterhood" that recognizes the different articulations of economic processes in the areas of common concern and intervention in the transnational arena (Grewal and Kaplan, 1994; Spivak, 1996; Agarwal, 1996).

Global value chain approach

The global value chain (GVC) approach is mostly used in global trade and labor rights issues. This approach originated in the work of Hopkins and Wallerstein, who defined it as "a network of labor and production process whose end result is a finished commodity" (1986: 159), and it was popularized by Gereffi and Korzeniewicz (1994), who explored how the linkage between production distribution and consumption of products are globally interconnected along commodity or value chains. Gereffi (1994) pointed out two types of governance chain structures: producer-driven and buyer-driven. Producer-driven chains are typical of capital- and technology-intensive industries where transnational manufacturing firms drive the chain by controlling the core technologies and production facilities, often through vertical integration. Buyer-driven chains, however, possess large retailers or brand-name companies that make key decisions about the structure and activities of actors in the chain though they do not own any production facilities. A key factor in buyer-driven chains is the social and economic context in which the chain operates. Powerful lead firms not only decide what is to be produced but also how and under what conditions it is to be produced, often due to pressure from consumers. In the globalized world, consumers are well aware of quality and safety, as well as the social and environmental conditions under which products are produced. This has led to firms developing their own codes of conduct and inspection mechanisms to avoid the risk in competitive markets that have been part of the GVC approach. However, the GVC approach lacks a crucial consideration – that of gender.

Many scholars (e.g., Grown, Elson and Cagatay, 2000; Whitehead, 2001: Elson, 2005) note that labor market institutions are embedded within and constructed by a gendered economy. They reflect a social division of gender roles that are situated at the intersection between productive (paid) and reproductive (unpaid) work. Labor market regulations and norms have traditionally reinforced this gendered division of labor. This gendered speculation is also reflected in trade union practices as well as labor laws. The codes of conduct that are drawn up and implemented within the value chains also reflect the gendered forms as these codes only cover the rights of formal employees, excluding temporary and flexible workers who often make up the majority and are mostly women. Thus, scholars (e.g., Barrientos, Dolan and Tallontire, 2003; Rai, 2002) argue that if codes are to address the employment issues faced by the majority of informal workers, gender sensitivity needs to be enhanced to incorporate broader employment-related issues that are of concern to women workers in particular. This new approach is known as the "gendered value chain approach." However, gender analysis in GVCs is still at an early stage and as such it is still a matter of research on how best to incorporate gender sensitivity in the global chain of production as multinationals tend to move toward a flexible workforce to cut off labor benefits (Barrientoes, Dolan and Tallontire, 2003).

In the case of the garment industry, a central focus in our book, we can discern a value chain focusing on capital flow, supply and price pressure (Figure 2.1). Since the lower end of the chain is dominated by a women's labor force, known as the "feminization of labor", the vulnerable work conditions have more negative impacts on women than men.

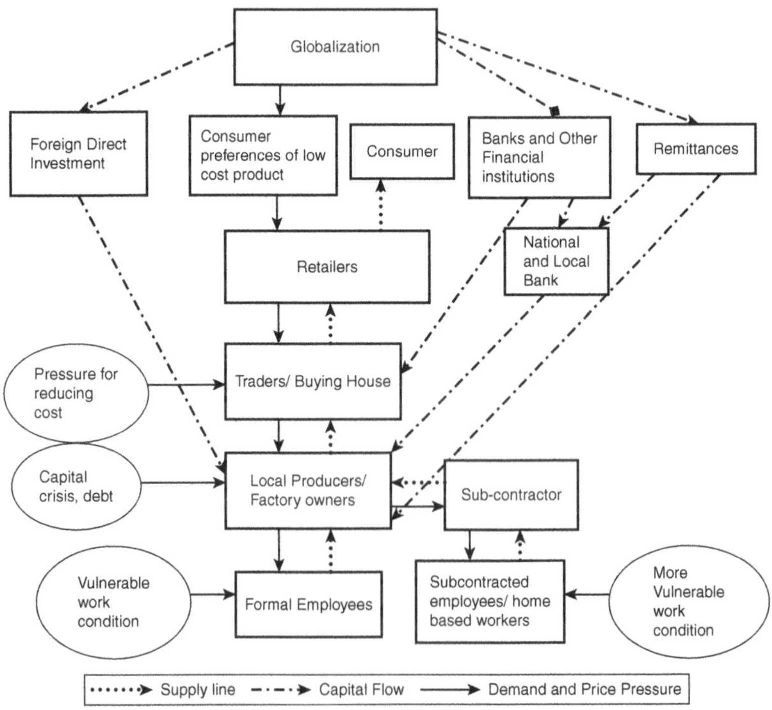

Figure 2.1 Global chain of capital flow, garment supply and price pressure
Sources: Frynas (2000), Ahmed (2006) and authors' investigation.

Human rights approach

An idea often invoked in contemporary political discussions is that every person anywhere in the world irrespective of citizenship, residence, race, class, caste or community has some basic rights that others should respect – in other words, human rights. The entitlement of these rights is predicated solely on the basis of being human. The idea of human rights has a strong ethical pronouncement, which underscores a need for action to be taken. These claims are not only those that are already realized by legal provisions but also those that initiate fresh legislation (Sen, 2005). The issue of human rights is not a contemporary one; rather, there is a history of its use over a long period, which includes particularly the invoking of "inalienable rights" in the American Declaration of Independence and the French declaration of "the rights of man" in the 18th century, and the later adoption of the "Universal Declaration of Human Rights" in 1948 by the United Nations (MacNaughton and Frey, 2011). The recurrent questions are: what kind of rights should be regarded as human rights and what are the grounds for having these rights? T.H. Marshall's classic account in his 1949 Cambridge lectures on "Citizenship and Social Class" is very instructive in this regard. He identifies three distinctive elements of citizenship entitlements – civil, political and social – which corresponded to distinctive sets of rights (Marshall, 2009). *Civil and political rights* are regarded as fundamental, universal, individual, absolute and also negative, where the state is not obliged to provide for resources. These are seen as "first generation rights" that derive from the 18th-century enlightenment theories of natural rights, equally applicable to all and justifiable or enforceable in the courts. In contrast, *social rights* are seen as imposing different types of obligations, either positive obligations on the state to provide services or negative and positive obligations on private actors. Social rights are seen as "second generation rights" that may require differential treatment and lack juridical status (Marshall, 2009). Most of the labor rights belong to the second category. Marshall conceives collective labor rights as a category of secondary rights based on industrial citizenship outside the core triad of civil, political and social rights (Fudge, 2007). Colin Crouch's definition of "industrial citizenship" provides a broad range of labor rights:

> [Industrial citizenship is] the acquisition by employees of rights within the employment relationship, rights which go beyond, and are secured by forces external to, the position which employees are

> able to win purely through market forces…these rights cover such matters as: individual rights to a safe and healthy working environment; to protection from arbitrary management action; to certain entitlements to free time; guarantees of some protection of standard living in the case of inability to work as a result of loss of employment, poor health or old age; [and] collective rights to representation by autonomous organizations in relations between employees and employers. (Fudge, 2007: 207)

Industrial citizenship entails the collective use of civil rights in order to assert claims for social justice; and it cannot be reduced to an individual civil right, although individual civil rights are crucial for the emergence of trade unions. Due to the interconnectedness and interdependency of various rights, a number of international agreements and declarations are used to bring all of these issues into one unified system that gives equal importance to all of these rights as human rights. The Universal Declaration of Human Rights (UDHR) is the onset toward this effort, which states that "everyone is entitled to a social and international order in which the rights and freedoms set forth in this declaration can be fully realized" (UN, 1948). It implies a holistic framework that recognizes the social, economic and political structures, both at the national and international level, that are required to support the realization of all categories of human rights. This holistic approach is also reinforced by subsequent declarations and covenants, including the Declaration on the Right to Development of 1986, the Vienna Declaration and Programme of Action of 1993, the International Covenant on Civil and Political Rights (ICCPR) and the International Covenant of Economic, Social and Cultural Rights (ICESCR), all of which acknowledges the indivisibility and interdependency of all human rights and calls for equal attention to the implementation of civil, political, economic, social and cultural rights (Marks, 2005). The holistic human rights approach rejects the traditional hierarchical distinction between civil and political rights on the one hand and economic social and cultural rights on the other (Nickel, 2008). This holistic framework is notably reaffirmed in the Vienna Declaration (UN, 1993):

> All human rights are universal, indivisible and interdependent and interrelated. The international community must treat human rights globally in a fair and equal manner, on the same footing, and with the same emphasis. While the significance of national and regional particularities and various historical, cultural and religious

> backgrounds must be borne in mind, it is the duty of the states, regardless of their political, economic and cultural systems, to promote and protect all human rights and fundamental freedoms.

The above declaration clearly presents three key features of the holistic human rights approach that are briefly discussed below.

Universality and inalienability

The most important feature of the holistic human rights approach is the universality and inalienability of human rights. Universality means that all people are entitled to human rights at all times. Inalienability means that people cannot surrender their own human rights or the human rights of others voluntarily or involuntarily. The UDHR (UN, 1948) acknowledges the universality and inalienability of human rights, which states that "All human beings are born free and equal in dignity and rights ... in a spirit of brotherhood" (article 1) and "Everyone is entitled to all the rights and freedoms set forth in this Declaration, without distinction of any kind ... of sovereignty" (article 2). This feature ensures that all persons are entitled to have certain rights of being a human. These rights are inevitable for survival and can never be surrendered, whatever the demands of the social situation (Donnelly, 2003).

Interrelatedness, interdependency and indivisibility

Human rights are also interrelated, interdependent and indivisible. They are interrelated in the sense that they are all intricately connected to one another. The UDHR recognizes the interrelatedness of different human rights. For example, the "right to work" (article 23) and the "right to rest and leisure" (article 24) is related to the "right to a standard of living" and the "right to security in the event of unemployment, sickness, disability" (article 25). Similarly, the "right to freedom of peaceful assembly and association" (article 20) is linked to the "right to form and to join trade unions" for the protection of his interests (article 23) while "equal pay for equal work" (article 23) is connected to the prohibition against discrimination (article 2) and the equality between men and women (article 3). Human rights are interdependent in two senses. The first sense captures the interdependency of rights, which is that the realization of one human right requires the implementation of other. For example, the right to health is dependent upon the rights to food, education, employment and so on, as these are the determinants of health (ECOSOC, 2000). In the second sense, as Scott (1999) explains, interdependency may be understood in terms of the relationships between people. For example, in the court's decision to grant injunctive relief in the context of a dismissal of a group of workers, a judge might consider the rights of the workers' children and other dependents. Along with interrelatedness and interdependency, human rights are also indivisible. Confirming this feature, Donnelly (2003: 31) states that "the universal declaration model treats internationally recognized human rights holistically as an indivisible structure in which the value of each right is significantly augmented by the presence of many others".

Equality of rights

All human rights are intrinsically associated with human dignity. The starting line of UDHR states that the "recognition of the inherent dignity and of the equal and inalienable rights of all members of the human family is the foundation of freedom, justice and peace in the world" (UN, 1948). The same words are reiterated in the preambles to ICESCR and the ICCPR. The equal status was also reaffirmed in the Vienna Declaration of 1993, which states that the international community and national governments should treat all human rights "in a fair and equal manner." This feature respects the inherent dignity of the individual and recognizes the right of the individual without making any distinction in terms of race, sex, location, beliefs and so on.

Though the human rights approach has made worthwhile contributions in reducing inequality, this approach has some limitations in analyzing and understanding labor rights. First, the conception of human rights is much contested. There are many different conceptions of rights, which provoke questions, such as what rights are human rights? What are the bases of these rights? Do they belong to the individual or a group? Are they correlated with duties? Are rights pre-political or artifacts of laws and institutions? Therefore, the use of right language may invite further questions. Second, the language of rights is historically associated with civil and political liberties while its association to social and economic entitlement is a very recent phenomenon. Many of the social and economic rights, particularly labor rights, are still under scrutiny and questioned as to whether they should be included as fundamental entitlements. Third, the human rights approach is mostly criticized by feminist scholars for being male-centered and for not including fundamental entitlements, abilities and opportunities that are essential in women's struggle against sex inequality (Nussbaum, 2003). Fourth, the human rights approach establishes universal norms of rights for men and women by virtue of being a human, which is defended by both feminist and cultural relativists. Feminists argue that universal norms ensure rights for men, not for women, because gender inequality and freedom from discrimination of women is given low priority. Cultural relativists argue that there is no such thing as universal human rights – the source of human rights is culture and since cultures are diverse, universal norms cannot protect human rights.

Social justice approach

Though the human rights approach, which seeks to establish a universal norm, is a more comprehensive approach for understanding rights, it remains ineffective due to the contestation of the right language as to whether labor rights are human rights. Perhaps the most influential approach that surpasses this debate and has been discussed widely in the wake of global inequality is social justice. The term social justice denotes various meanings throughout the literature in the social sciences. Flynn (1995) defines social justice as the embodiment of fairness, equity and equality in the distribution of resources. Barker (2003: 404–05) defines social justice as "an ideal condition in which all members of a society has the same basic rights, protection, opportunities, obligation and social benefits". Beverly and McSweeney's (1987) definition of social justice emphasizes distributive equality as well. To them, social justice means "fairness in the relationships" between people; "acquisition of resources" based on some kind of valid claim to share those resources. The justice or injustice of a particular policy or situation is determined by looking at the fairness of the distribution of resources in relation to the claims or demands made for those resources (1987: 5).

This definition of social justice emphasizes the fair distribution of resources and access to opportunities. Some crucial questions then arise: What is the way of bringing justice into the society? What should be the basis of entitlements of certain rights? And what should be the principles in distributing scarce resources? There are, however, different perspectives in distributive justice, such as the utilitarian (e.g., Mill, 1963), egalitarian (Rawls, 1971) and libertarian (Nozick, 1974; Sen, 2009) perspectives. Among these various forms of distributive justice, two major theories – "justice as fairness" and "capability approach" – have been much deliberated in the social sciences literature.

Justice as fairness

"Justice as fairness" was developed by John Rawls in his book *A Theory of Justice* (Rawls, 1971, 1999, 2001). Rawls (1999) notes that justice of a social scheme is essentially dependent on how fundamental rights and duties are assigned and how economic opportunities and social conditions in the various sectors of society are distributed. The intuitive idea of "justice as fairness" is that since the well-being of people is largely dependent on the social system of cooperation, without which worthy living is impossible, the distribution of advantages and opportunities should be made in such a way that everyone taking part in it can benefit, and that which offers greater prosperity for someone at the expense of others is not just. Rawls notes: "Institutions are just when no arbitrary distinctions are made between persons in the assigning of basic rights and duties and when the rules determine a proper balance between competing claims to the advantages of social life" (1999: 5). Rawls places a greater importance on social institutions because the distribution of fundamental rights and duties are determined by these institutions. He adds: "The primary subject of social justice is the basic structure of the society, the way in which the major social institutions distribute fundamental rights and duties and determine the division of advantages from social cooperation" (1995: 6).

Rawls' distributive justice has two essential requirements. First, Rawls considers society as a fair system of social cooperation between free and equal citizens. Thus, citizens and institutions must cooperate to fulfill basic needs. This social cooperation entails three basic features: First, publicly recognized rules and procedures that regulate individual conduct, beliefs in reciprocity or mutual benefits and rational advantages of each participant. Second, the government must regulate social, economic and political institutions, and determine the rights and obligations of citizens and institutions based on the two principles of justice (equal basic liberties and fair equality opportunity and difference; more below). Finally, when these conditions are met, the benefits and burdens of social cooperation are fairly distributed among all citizens and relegate distributive justice.

In the context of labor, social cooperation means investment would be made by those who have the capital to produce goods and services while wage labor would be supplied by those who do not have the capital to invest. In such a system, pay and other benefits would be predetermined through a contract between two parties considering the individual's ability, merit, effort and contribution as well as the market's willingness to pay for such labor based on demand and supply. People judged to have talent will be of higher demand in the market, and as such their return would be higher than others who show less potential and are deemed less talented. Individuals unhappy with their wages will then be encouraged to enhance their educational and occupational skills to increase their earning capability. Thus, there is a mutual negotiation between two groups that takes place in a more or less free market economy where the state should regulate only to prevent the formation of monopolies (Rawls, 1971, 1999, 2001).

Since social negotiation takes place in a free market economy, individuals are not indifferent about their own rights; they are intended to pursue greater benefits produced by their cooperation that may lead to unfair distribution of the resources. Therefore, a set of principles are needed which Rawls calls the principles of justice. Rawls (1971, 1999, 2001) formulated two principles of justice to ensure a fair distribution of resources so that no one is devoid of access. In a revised statement[2] of the two principles of justice, Rawls (2001: 42–43) notes:

> Each person has the same indefeasible claim to a fully adequate scheme of equal basic liberties, which is compatible with the same scheme of liberties for all; and social and economic inequalities are to satisfy two conditions: first they are to be attached to offices and positions open to all under conditions of fair quality of opportunity; and second, they are to be the greatest benefit of the least-advantaged members of society.

The two principles of justice stated above (e.g., equal basic liberties and fair equality opportunity and difference) follow a lexical order, which means that the first principle is prior to the second and the first part (fair equality opportunity) is prior to the last part of the second principle (difference). For a greater understanding of social justice, we have further elaborated these principles here.

(1) *Principle of equal basic liberty:* The first principle of justice is known as the equal liberty principle based on the idea of free and equal persons. Liberty is a pattern of social forms that applies to everyone equally and is imposed by institutions. It allows for the most extensive liberty compatible with a like liberty for all. Equal liberty means that a person should have the equal right of basic liberties compatible with a similar scheme that holds to another person residing in the same society. The rights and basic liberties refer to those which are defined by the public rules of the basic structure and guarantee equal basic political and civil rights such as freedom of speech, assembly, religion, property ownership and political participation to all (Rawls, 2001). It is important to note here that justice as fairness is a political conception of justice for a democratic society

where social cooperation is a basic requirement. Since citizens are regarded as equal and active participants in social cooperation, they should require two moral powers: firstly, the capacity for a sense of justice, which is the capacity to understand, to apply and to act from the principles of political justice; and secondly, the capacity for a conception of good, which is the capacity to have, to revise and to rationally pursue a conception of the good. Rawls (2001) assumes that citizens have these requisite capacities to engage in mutually beneficial social cooperation and they are free to take part in the process for their own sake.

The meaning of a free person, in justice as fairness, is drawn from the political culture, but it has very little or no connection with the freedom of wills as discussed in philosophy of mind. In justice as fairness, Rawls (2001) explains that citizens are regarded as free persons in two respects: First, citizens are free in the sense that they conceive of themselves and of others as having moral power to have a conception of good. They are capable of revising and changing the conception of good on reasonable and rational grounds, and they do so of their own volition. Due to their moral power in revising and forming the conception of good, the public or legal identity as free persons is not affected by changes over time in their life if it is not reasonable and rational from their view. Second, citizens are free in the sense that they consider themselves as self-authenticated sources of valid claims. It means that citizens hold the conception that they are entitled to make claims on their institutions. The moral doctrine as well as the duties and obligations they are owed by society lay the basis for this self-authenticated claim.

(2) *Principle of fair equality of opportunity and difference:* The second principle of justice consists of two parts. The first part is known as the fair equality of opportunity that guarantees fair access for all citizens with equal ability and talent irrespective of their socioeconomic background. To accomplish this aim, certain requirements must be imposed on the basic structure beyond the system of natural liberty. According to Rawls, "a free market system is to be incorporated within a framework of political and legal institutions to prevent excessive concentration of wealth and opportunity to a particular group especially those likely to lead to political domination" (2001: 44). The fair equality of opportunity is primarily concerned about education, which might allow for higher income and wealth. It does

> not guarantee equal access for all but ensures fair access to education and work, which means that all people with equal talents, irrespective of their class background, would have equal access to education. However, Rawls does not dismiss the influence of class background and socioeconomic condition on individuals' ability and talents. Recognizing this influence, he recommended that the government should budget a fair amount for the education of children who are economically disadvantaged, but not make it obligatory. The ground for valid claims of this need is dependent on three circumstances – people who cooperate with the economy and work but fail to make a living wage; people who are unable to work because of ill health; people who remain unemployed due to the seasonal or temporary nature of jobs – and they will receive an amount pegged to the "social minimum". However, this approach does not address what the social minimum amount should be but hints that the social minimum should always be lower than the market value in order to retain the incentive for work (Banerjee, 2011).

The second part of the second principle is known as the difference principle that accepts economic and social inequality to some extent if it fulfills the greatest interest of the least advantaged. One of the key features of the difference principle is the principle of reciprocity that respects mutual benefit. Rawls says, "Reciprocity is a moral idea situated between impartiality...and mutual advantage" (2001: 77). According to this principle, the person who holds more capital should invest so that the underprivileged are able to secure a job and earn a market wage. At the same time, the people who have less income and assets should not be an annoyance to those who have more. The least advantaged people would be identified based on the access of five primary goods, such as basic rights and liberties; freedom of movement and free choice of occupation from diverse opportunities; powers and prerogatives of offices, and positions of authority and responsibility; income and wealth; and social bases of respect. Rawls notes that "all these primary goods are to be distributed equally unless an unequal distribution of any, or all, of these values is to everyone's advantage" (1999: 54). However, he later changed his position and clarified that the "least advantaged" are those who have the lowest index of the five primary goods (2001). Which means that a fair share of citizens would be determined based on the appropriate contributions made by the citizen. Thus, a citizen's index of primary goods would be low, medium or high based on the market value of contribution.

Rawls' contribution to social justice is regarded as a vanguard of social justice theory; however, it is not without its shortcomings. First, one of the major limitations of this approach is that it ignores the moral worth in distributive justice. He states, "moral worth would be utterly impracticable as a criterion when applied to questions of distributive justice...only God could make those judgments" (2001: 73). This position contradicts with the concept of rights since a right is viewed as a moral principle defining and sanctioning a human's freedom of action in a social context (Rand, 1961). Second, this approach is unable to deal with the rights issue of global workers or migrant labor as it emphasizes the social contract. The contractual approach cannot ensure a balance between two unequal parties due to the differential power status. Rawls seems to imagine the bargain taking place between the United States and the nations of Europe or Australia, which can be claimed to be at least of equal standing. However, in the case of a bargain between a developed and Third World country, the negotiation cannot be claimed as balanced and equal (Rasmussen, 1974). Third, Rawls' second principle is contradictory in nature. While he acknowledges that primary goods should be distributed among the citizens so that they can enhance their moral power, he also says that distribution should be made based on their contribution. The distribution of primary goods based on contribution may lead to a widening gap between rich and poor. Fourth, Rawls' theory of justice ignores the needs of disabled people. In the theory of justice, Rawls classified nonworking people into two groups: able-bodied poor who are unwilling to work (surfers) and people with health issues (hard cases). He did not support social assistance for people who are unwilled to work, noting that surfers must somehow support themselves (2001: 179), but he did not discuss people who are unable to work as he viewed all people within a normal range. In a footnote, however, he mentioned that it is a duty to help people with disability issues but stresses that it cannot be covered under the purview of a political conception of justice (Banerjee, 2011).

Capability approach

Rawls' approach emphasizes fair distribution of primary goods based on a person's contribution that ignores the differences of individual potentials and power, which further leads to inequality. This issue is well illustrated by Nobel laureate economist and philosopher Amartya Sen, who has been preoccupied with questions of social justice throughout his career. The most extensive and thoughtful explanation was made toward social justice in his book, *The Idea of Justice* (2009). However, to get an actual idea of what Sen conceives as justice, we must focus on his other writings, such as Social Choice (Sen, 1998), Rationality (Sen, 2002), Human Rights (Sen, 2004), Justice (Sen, 1990, 1992, 1995), and Women's Agency (Sen, 1990).

Sen's idea of justice derives a good part of its motivations and structure from the approach of "justice as fairness", but his idea then departs significantly from Rawls'. Sen conceives that a theory of justice based on fairness should focus on the extent to which people are capable of taking control over resources rather than what goods and resources he or she holds (Sen, 1985, 1990). The concept of capabilities is now widely known as the "capability approach"; it accommodates social, economic and political analysis and holds that the well-being of the person ought to be assessed in the space of capabilities, not on the distribution of the resources (Deneulin and McGregor, 2010).

The term capability originates from the concept of "entitlement" from Sen's famous study, "Poverty and Famines", where he argues that the growing trend of poverty and famines is not merely caused by the decline of food production and supply but because of people's "entitlements failure" and "loss of purchasing power" to acquire and access food (Sen, 1981). He later refines the concept of entitlements[3] into capabilities and put emphasis on capabilities in evaluating social justice. Sen proposes that people's well-being and standing in society should be assessed based on their "capabilities to function", the effective opportunities to undertake the actions and activities that they have reason to value. Simultaneously, he acknowledges that people's functioning or achievement can vary even if they reside in a similar set of opportunities due to the influence of various conversion factors, such as personal heterogeneities (physical condition, intelligence, skills, sex); diversities in the physical environment (climate, geographical location and structural development); variation in social climate (social conditions and public policies) and differences in relation perspectives (social norms, discriminating practices, gender norms and roles, power relation and societal hierarchies). Thus, the focus of the capability approach is not just on what a person has done, but also on what he or she is in fact able to do. It does not matter whether he or she has chosen or not to take that opportunity (Sen, 2009). The capability approach gives prime focus to a person's freedom to promote or achieve valuable functioning. Sen defines freedom as "the real opportunity that we have to accomplish what we value" (Sen, 1992: 31). It does not include the opportunities that a person might hold theoretically or legally but only those that are within their reach. Sen (1990: 111–21) remarks:

> In the capability-based assessment of justice, individual claims are not to be assessed in terms of the resources or primary goods the persons respectively hold, but in terms of the freedoms they actually enjoy to choose between different ways of living that they can have reason to value. It is this actual freedom that is represented by the person's "capability" to achieve various alternative combinations of functioning that is doings and beings.

The term freedom involves two distinct elements: opportunity and process. The opportunity aspect is concerned with the person's ability to achieve what they reason to value irrespective of the outcome of the process involved. The process aspect exemplifies that the chosen action or activities shall not be forced because of the constraints imposed by others. This relates to the concept of agency that relegates the moral obligations and responsibilities to others. For example, Sen (2009) refers to two different cases of hunger and undernourishment: one is voluntarily fasting for political or religious reasons, and another is a famine victim. Though the outcome of these two different cases (long-term fasting and consequent undernourishment) is the same, there is inherently a significant difference between them in terms of the opportunity and the process aspects of freedom. In the first case, the person has the opportunity to choose to starve themselves or not; but in the second case the person starves and suffers for lack of alternative possibilities. The latter involves the immediate violation of the process aspect of freedom since the constraint of the unavailability of food is forcing him or her to starve. The opportunity aspect of freedom is also affected as no alternative possibility exists that he or she can choose. It is very relevant to ask how capability links with the well-being of a person. Sen puts much effort into explain this issue, and for this purpose he presents two important distinctions that are the key features of the capability approach: freedom and achievement, and well-being and agency.

(1) *Freedom and achievement:* One of the most important features of the capability approach is the broad informational perspective of freedom, which distinguishes capabilities from achieved functioning. Sen uses "capability" as a freedom to choose from possible alternatives but not as the capability set that he or she has chosen.

He says, "capability, as a kind of freedom, refers to the extent to which the person is able to choose particular combinations of functioning (including inter alia, such things as being well-nourished), no matter what the person actually decides to choose" (Sen, 2004: 334). In his analysis of capabilities, the perspective of capability and freedom is more meaningful and useful than achieved functioning in an assessment of a person's well-being for the following reasons. First, the reliance on achieved functioning cannot tell us the exact feature of a person's advantages or disadvantages as even the same achieved functioning of two persons can differ in terms of their ability to choose. For example, in the previous case, the person who starves for religious or other political reasons has higher capability to function than the other. The freedom-based capability can identify the different substantial opportunities even though they reside exactly in the same set of means. Second, the capability to choose between different affiliations in cultural life can have both personal and political importance. For example, the freedom of an immigrant in practicing ancestral, cultural and religious traditions and lifestyles cannot be adequately assessed without distinguishing between doing something and being free to do something. Third, policy-related issues are better addressed in the capability perspective because freedom-based capability, the agency aspect of freedom, is more concerned about responsibilities and obligations of the societies.

(2) *Well-being and agency:* Sen's concept of functioning corresponds to two distinct but interrelated goals: well-being and agency. Well-being refers to the individual's own advantage from a particular functioning. Well-being freedom is ensured through social provisions in the form of providing material benefits. Agency, on the other hand, refers to all the goals that a person adopts, not for pursuing his own interest but for others. In the case of agency, the individual interest is supplemented with commitments and obligations. The person is characterized here as a "rational agent of constructivism" following Rawls' "Kantian constructivism". The agency aspect here makes a man socially responsible. In the absence of the agency aspect, a person's functioning is merely devoted to his own well-being. A person's agency objective may include, inter alia, his or her own well-being, and thus agency and well-being may have something in common. However, it is important to note here that there has been a substantial interconnection between the two, and it is most often the proven way to enhance a person's well-being.

In assessing a person's well-being advantage, Sen combines these two different distinctions of "between freedom and achievement" and "between well-being and agency" and proposes four different spaces of human advantages, such as, well-being achievement, agency achievement, well-being freedom and agency freedom. Well-being achievement should be measured based on the functioning of the person, whereas well-being freedom is assessed based on capability set. In both cases, persons are completely free from adhering to any moral obligation for people living in the society. The agency aspect shifts the focus from seeing the person as just a vehicle of well-being, ignoring the importance of the person's own judgment, and prioritizes the social commitment with which the capabilities are concerned. A person's agency freedom refers to the freedom of doing the things that are more valuable for society than one's own well-being. A person's agency aspect cannot be understood without taking note of his or her aims, objectives, allegiances, obligations and – in a broad sense – the person's conception of the good.

Sen contends that a person's capability ought to be seen in the space of agency freedom (the freedom to advance whatever goals and values a person reasons to advance) and well-being freedom (the freedom to advance one's own well-being). While the former may be of general interest to public policy, the latter can be seen as being of primary interest to the persons involved. Sen also acknowledges that although agency freedom does include well-being freedom, there is a real possibility of the latter going down while the former goes up (Sen, 1985). For example, a protest by a fellow coworker to protect the job of a worker who wishes to resume her duty after her maternity leave but is still dismissed. This sort of protest may result in a universal benefit of maternity leave for all workers but may also negatively affect his or her personal well-being either by being fired from the job or by being locked up by police for being accused of inciting unrest in the factory. At this point, it is common to struggle with what the matter of concern for a person would be in either pursuing his or her own well-being freedom or agency freedom. If the person gives up pursuing his or her own well-being, then why should it matter whether the person had well-being freedom or not? Responding to this issue, Sen says that both agency freedom and well-being freedom are equally important but for different reasons. The well-being aspect may be particularly important in some specific contexts; for example, making public provision for social security or planning for the fulfillment of basic needs. Sometimes agency freedom can be seen as more advantageous or as inevitable for the greater interest of the society over his or her own well-being, as in the case of Gandhi's decision on fasting to free Indian people (Sen, 2009). Simultaneously, even though the agency freedom is broader than the well-being freedom, the former cannot subsume the latter (Sen, 1984).

There are, however, some criticisms to Sen's capability approach, one of which is the absence of the listing of capabilities. Capability theorist Martha Nussbaum argues that Sen's capability approach does not have any significance as long as he does not endorse a particular list of capabilities (Nussbaum, 2003). Second, the capability approach is too individualistic and does not pay attention to groups and communities (Robeyns, 2005). Third, this approach, under specific conditions, leads to well-being conflict among different contested groups. There is a very real possibility of sacrificing the well-being strategies and aspirations of a powerless group to accommodate or fit with the goals of other more powerful actors (Deneulin and McGregor, 2010). Finally, it is argued that the capability approach cannot be seen as a comprehensive theory of social justice because it cannot possibly adequately deal with the process aspect of freedom. Seguino (2013) argues that a person's well-being is not only dependent on opportunity but also on equality of outcome. If it is not possible to ensure the equality of outcomes, inequality will persist between the people because some will reap greater benefits than others.

Conclusion

The chapter discusses a number of relevant approaches, namely political economy, feminist political economy, global value chain, human rights, and social justice for understanding the issue of labor, gender and the environment. The PEA approach focuses on the power of the state in governing the global economy so that it can protect the issues of labor rights. Although there is a debate about the effectiveness of state power in controlling the global economy and labor, the power of the state cannot be neglected. Criticizing the unwillingness or inability of the state, the feminist approach focuses on the agency of women since global industries are dominated by women workers, and the "feminization of the workforce" is used as a resource for globalizing the capital. It emphasizes the collective resistance of women workers to realize their demands and regards the making of solidarity of international women's organization as essential. The human rights approach focuses on citizenship in general and industrial citizenship in particular as the basis of claiming human rights. Universal norms of rights, both for men and women, are highly criticized by feminist scholars. In a society where sociocultural practices treat men and women differently, universal norms are far beyond the reach of women. Since human rights have a culture-specific context, and social inequality and discrimination are widespread, the rights-based approach encounters major challenges in defining the universal boundary of human rights. To address the needs of the underprivileged and disadvantaged people, "justice as fairness" focuses on the fair distribution of resources depending on two principles that are inherently in conflict.

From the comparative analysis of the approaches presented above, the capability theory of social justice seems to be more meaningful and appropriate in assessing the rights of workers, gender relations and environmental impacts. The transformation of entitlements into capabilities gives this approach a normative standard that can be used in wide areas of human well-being. As Ingrid Robeyns notes, "the capability approach is a broad normative framework for the evaluation and assessment of individual wellbeing and social arrangements, the design of policies and proposals about social change in society" (2005: 94). Despite certain shortcomings, capability approach is much more able to cope with globalization, and at the same time, it is also an incremental-adaptable approach for some essential features inherent within the approach, such as a consideration of individual ability and social context, integration of social and market features, beliefs in universality and human diversity, and provoking social action and change.

3
Globalization, Gender and Labor Rights: Trends and Trajectories

This chapter explores the complex intersection between gender and labor in the globalization of production. By reviewing the existing literature, this chapter draws on the central debates concerning the employment of women in global manufacturing enterprises, which will be organized into three central themes: the relationship between feminization of workforce and global manufacturing; how feminization and labor vulnerability intersect in global factories; and the policy debates of labor regulations. Drawing views from the existing literature, this chapter will conclude that the impact of globalization on women is a paradox. While it provides many women, mainly in the global South, a way of survival through expansion of employment opportunities, women workers face multiple oppressions where gender identity is used as a resource for globalizing the capital. The chapter raises a number of questions that correspond to how globalization of the economy shapes the dynamics of employment and rights of workers.

Capitalist transformations toward neoliberal globalization

The term capitalism refers to a system through which goods and services, ranging from life's basic necessities to luxury commodities, are produced for the purpose of generating profits. This is achieved through the purchase and use of human labor power as a form of commodity as well as a dependence on the market. The downfall of Communism during the 1980s and 1990s has reaffirmed the belief held by many that capitalism is a "natural human condition" that promotes the basic inclinations of human beings (Wood, 2002). However, an exploration of the trajectory of capitalism's development reveals that despite its triumph over Communism, capitalism has had its share of problems ever since its inception. This in turn has caused capitalism to shift from one form to another in order to pull out of these problems.

Colonization was one of the earlier waves of and a necessary condition for the rise and development of capitalism (Islam, 2013). During the era of colonization, development was understood as having colonies, organizing the European societies and their labor and market forces by disorganizing the non-European colonies (McMichael, 2008). The notion of development during the colonial era had debilitating effects on the colonized subjects. It created a huge resource gap between the colonized territories and the European colonial empires, dismantled the political and social structures of the colonized territories, launched a cultural genocide and marginalized indigenous populations. It led the colonial subjects to react in various forms, ranging from death through submission and internalization of inferiority to a variety of resistances from everyday forms through sporadic uprisings to mass political mobilization.

In the postcolonial world, newly independent states emerged, and political leaders had to operate in an international framework that was not of their making but through which they needed political legitimacy. In the first place, their newly independent states were materially disorganized and required economic stimulation. Second, the acceptable model of economic stimulation was a European model of development. Third, the source of stimulation was European economic aid. In short, the framework within which political independence was realized was that of European conception of development. The adoption of a European model across the formerly colonial world in the post–World War II era was the underpinnings of what we call the "development project" (McMichael, 2008; Islam, 2013). The United States was a powerful reality at that time. Asian and African decolonization started at the time when the United States was at the height of its power and prosperity, and eager to reconstruct the postwar world to expand markets and the flow of raw materials. Reconstructing a war-torn world was an international project, inspired by a vision of development as a national enterprise to be repeated across the world of newly independent states (McMichael, 2008). One of the important developments at that time was the creation of the Third World. Escobar's path-breaking writing delineates "how the 'third world' has been produced by the discourses and practices of development since their inception in the early post–World War II period" (1995: 4) and how the development discourses have "created an extremely efficient apparatus for producing knowledge about, and exercise of power over, the Third World.... In sum, it has successfully deployed a regime of government over the Third World, a 'space for "subject peoples"' that ensures certain control over it" (p. 9). From the part of the West, especially from the United States, this development was viewed as a concept based on "democratic fair dealing" (McMichael, 2008). For the Americans and their allies, this was a liberal vision projected globally – a vision of universal political opportunity to pursue national economic growth. Therefore, the discourse of development assumed additional meanings to be understood more as a "natural" process, with universal application, than the colonial initiative. That is, development could be administered by non-Europeans. This new development paradigm, however, ignored and obscured the contribution of colonies to European development.

The pursuit of economic growth by countries across the globe, however, required international support. These supports were an essential part of the development project. Foreign aid, technology transfer, stable currency exchange, robust international trade – all were deemed necessary to sustain national development policies. The dominant roles were played by the different international agencies/organizations. The United States spearheaded two initiatives to reconstruct the world economy: the Marshall Plan and the Bretton Woods program. The Marshall Plan was in fact a vast, bilateral transfer of billions of dollars to European states and Japan, serving US geopolitical goals in the Cold War. The Bretton Woods system, on the other hand, managed an international exchange between the First and Third Worlds that resembled the "colonial division of labor" at a more intensive remove.

If we examine the patterns of Western foreign aid in the postwar era, we see that the patterns of development assistance contradicted the universalism of the development project. The US aid programs to selected countries functioned as military outposts in securing the perimeters of the so-called free world and in preventing a "domino effect" of defections to the Soviet bloc. For the United States and its First World allies, then, the development project was more than a transmission belt for Western technology and economic institutions to the Third World. So long as the Third World, a vital source for strategic raw materials and minerals, was under threat from an alternative political-economic vision such as socialism, the survival of the First World was at stake (McMichael, 2008). Not only that, development and survival of the West was articulated as the underdevelopment of the non-West. This view was clearly articulated by an influential development economist named Walt Rostow: "our military security and our way of life as well as the fate of Western Europe and Japan are at stake in the evolution of the underdeveloped areas" (quoted in McMichael, 2008: 62).

Until the 1970s, development was understood as primarily a national process of economic and social transformation; however, by then, two trends were becoming clear. First, the First World was not waiting for the Third World to catch up. Indeed, the gap between these world regions was expanding. Second, a strategy emerging among some Third World states was to attempt to reduce the gap by aggressive exporting of manufactured goods. In the 1970s, "development" was redefined by the World Bank as "successful participation in the world market". The prescription was that Third World countries should now follow the example of the newly industrializing countries, pursuing a strategy of export-oriented industrialization. Specialization in the world economy, rather than specialization of economic activities within a national framework, was emerging as the criterion of "development" (McMichael, 2008; Islam, 2013).

The 1980s' debt crisis consolidated two distinct trends that had been emerging in the 1970s: (1) the unfolding of the Third World as a collective entity, as economic growth rates diverged among states; and (2) global managerialism, in which the world economy was managed through coordinated, rule-based procedures – the debt regime. The debt regime, which ultimately led to neoliberal globalization, provided a further pattern of meaning to "development". The rise of a global banking system, matched by international financial liberalization, laid the foundation of what is termed "globalization" today. The "global managerialism" is the reformulation of economic policy-making according to global rather than national considerations. In short, we can discern the following characteristics of the neoliberal globalization today, as summarized in McMichael (2008: 151):

- A Washington-based consensus among global managers/policy-makers favoring market-based rather than state-managed development strategies
- Centralized management of global market rules by the G-8 states (US, UK, France, Germany, Japan, Italy, Russia and Canada)
- Implementation of these rules through multilateral agencies (World Bank, International Monetary Fund, World Trade Organization)
- Concentration of market power in the hands of transnational corporations (TNCs) and financial power in the hands of transnational banks (TNBs)
- Subjection of all states to economic disciplines (trade, financial, labor), varying by position in the state system (North/South/East), global currency hierarchy, debt load, resource endowments and so forth;

- Realization of global development via new gender, race and ethnic inequalities
- A countermovement at all levels, from marginalized communities to state managers to factions even within multilateral institutions, contesting and second-guessing unbridled market rule

Under the conditions of neoliberal globalization, the multilateral institutions compelled states to adopt policies privileging global, over national, economic relationships. The states had no choice but to collaborate. The states surrendered their powers to manage their national economic growth. Sale of public enterprises and reduction of social subsidies effectively remade the Third World states and restructured societies, placing the burden on the lower classes, especially women in these lower classes. Considerable amounts of state autonomy and sovereignty were lost to the global managers (IMF, World Bank, WTO, and GATT) (McMichael, 2008; Islam, 2013). An apparent tension occurred between the governments and the public as the governments had to give priority to the global market over their people's welfare. This often led some governments to respond in repressive ways. Labor patterns, gender relations and the environmental conditions in developing nations are largely reconstituted under the conditions of neoliberal globalization. Feminization and labor flexibility are two dominant trends.

Feminization and labor flexibility

The presence of women workers in global manufacturing factories is one of the dominant images of globalization. Generally, feminization of the workforce entails mass entry of women into the formal labor force (Momen, 2006). This concept became the center of academic discussion after the publication of Ester Boserup's book *Women's Role in Economic Development* (1970). The term "feminization of labor" is mainly used to denote two different meanings. First, it is used to refer to the sharp increase of women in labor-force participation, particularly in a shift from the agricultural to the industrial sector. Second, the term "feminization of labor" is used to describe the increased flexibility of women's labor. Labor flexibility refers to temporary employment constituted by part-time and casual workers where employers are able to increase workforces when they have higher production volumes and reduce the workforce when they have small volumes of production (Ofreneo, 2010). In practice, flexibilization denotes a very pervasive meaning, the "gradual weakening of the conditions that characterize regular employment"

(Arnold and Bongiovi, 2013: 296). Limited job opportunities for women combined with urgent family needs often force women to work in these global industries even though employment is often temporary, without any formal contract and with limited or no labor benefits.

Neoliberalism opens fierce competition among the producers. Corporations adopt three main strategies to compete in the global market: cutting labor costs by employing temporary workers in the place of permanent workers, moving to subcontracting and transferring plants to other countries where labor is cheap, and bringing diversification to the production process by upgrading technology and improving labor capacity (Carr and Chen, 2004). In fact, multinational corporations relocate their firms, mostly labor-intensive assembly operations, to cheaper production sites overseas, mainly in Third World countries where the supply of cheap labor is abundant. This relocation of labor-intensive firms to Third World countries has provided an ample employment opportunity for women who were previously jobless (e.g., Nash and Fernandez-Kelly, 1983; Barrientos, Kabeer and Hossain, 2004). As a result, the presence of women workers in global manufacturing industries is overwhelming, which characterizes the feature of the feminization of workforce. For example, the share of women workers in the garment industry constituted 85 percent in Bangladesh, 90 percent in Cambodia, 70 percent in Morocco and 60 percent in Honduras; and in the cut-flower industry, 65 percent in Colombia, 75 percent in Kenya and 87 percent in Zimbabwe (Kidder and Raworth, 2005).

Producers or multinational corporations (MNCs) prefer women workers because they are "comparatively cheap", resulting from a combination of patriarchy and capitalism (Elson and Pearson, 1981; Lim, 1997; Harvey, 2010). Explaining the reason for female preference by MNCs, Elson and Pearson note, "female labor must either be cheaper to employ than comparable male labor, or have higher productivity, or some combination of both; the net result being that unit costs of production are lower with female labor" (1981: 92). The recent trend in most countries is to allow the employers to use temporary employment contracts, and the consequent outcome is greater flexibility and heightened insecurity in the labor market. Increasing competition in the global market leads MNCs to move toward a mixed workforce constituted by both full-time and part-time workers because it legally frees them from providing labor benefits, helping to keep production costs down. This flexible labor force is primarily comprised of women workers (Standing, 1989; Beneria, 2001; Walby, 2002; CCC, 2005; Chang, 2009). In fact, feminization and labor flexibility are conjoined and undifferentiated. The combination of "feminization" and "labor flexibility" forms a two-fold process that involves the increased labor-force participation of women and simultaneously an increase in nonstandard jobs. Women tend to work even though the employment contract is temporary, which means having no labor benefits except wage because they desperately need the job for survival. On the other side, employers can run the factory depending on flexible labor because surplus labor constituted by women is abundant (Smithson and Stokoe, 2005). Their employment is totally dependent on the needs of the firm, leading to nonexistent job security as the firms will hire and fire workers based solely on their production needs. This is particularly the case for labor-intensive industries like garment manufacturing, where workers do not need advanced skills. A worker can perform all tasks if he or she has basic skills in operating the sewing machine. Therefore, employers are not heavily dependent particularly on skilled workers, who are easily replaceable. Employers can substitute the labor force anytime without hampering production.

The existing literature has mentioned at least two main arguments in favor of feminization of labor in the global manufacturing industry. The first argument emphasizes economic forces of cheap labor. Scholars have argued that the increase in the feminized workforce occurs as a process of searching for cheap labor. The second argument places importance on feminist discourse that highlights gender discourses of work – ideas and practices about men and women that provide distinct forms of labor or gender divisions of labor. Scholars of this stream are also feminist economists, but they slightly differ from the previous argument by highlighting the diversity of gendered labor practices in the global economy. They claim that gender discourses of work influence employers to prefer women workers and provide justification to maintain gendered division of work. Among many of these, some notable and widely used discourses are: women are careful, diligent, disciplined, patient, easier to manage or control, better suited for light and monotonous work, less likely to go on strike and protest, have less of a desire for higher wages and promotion, have less occupational mobility and so on (Caraway, 2005, 2007; Hossain, Mathbor and Renata, 2013). Whether women workers may or may not possess these traits, the fact is that managers believe and shape practices around them. As Leslie Salzinger (2003) noted, these images are important not because they reflect reality but because they produce it. Caraway (2007) argues that gendered discourses not only illuminate the process of job allocation and reallocation at the firm level but also provide a means of connecting shop-floor gender divisions of labor with a broader gendered pattern of industrialization. These gendered discourses are important, and very often more important than wages for feminization of manufacturing industries, and are crucial for understanding the sexual politics of globalization.

The debate of comparative influence of "wage" and "gendered discourses of work" may ask for further research and may lead to different conclusions, but scholars largely agree on a point that a feminized and flexible workforce – two important features of global manufacturing industries – is used for exploiting labor. Many scholars (Stiglitz, 2002; Standing, 2008; Chang, 2009; Kalleberg, 2009) have argued that labor market flexibility increases and shifts the risk from employers to employees by reducing employment security and job benefits. It is women who suffer more than men, since global factories are dominated by women workers, violations mostly relate to women, and traditional gender norms restrict women from raising their collective voices. Thus, it is argued that women workers are the resource for economic globalization and are subject to capitalist exploitation (Elson, 1999; Acker, 2004; Caraway, 2007). Based on empirical evidence from some Asian countries (India, Bangladesh and Japan), Custers (2012) notes that traditional gender norms shape the sexual division of labor in such a way that preserves male power over female and greater economic exploitation of women in pursuit of capitalist interests. Women workers are the source of extraction of absolute and relative surplus value. She also notes that employers have chosen to increase their female labor force as a means of raising productivity because women are more willing to accept low wages, long working hours, unpleasant and often unhealthy or hazardous working conditions, and they typically do not engage in collective bargaining or any protest movement to increase labor conditions that are shaped by dominant gender discourse found within the social community.

The above literature throws up a number of questions, such as: How do gender-stereotyped beliefs and ideas persist in the workplace? Is there any relationship between gendered beliefs and global forces of capitalism? If yes, what is the form of this relationship? How do these beliefs influence the work pattern and employment relations, and how are these associated with labor rights? We will address some of these questions in the sections below.

Women workers and labor justice

The effect of economic globalization on ensuring labor rights is contradictory, and it has spurred endless debate among scholars. A number of studies have shown that economic globalization allows all countries to become wealthier and hence prosperous by stimulating economic growth because it helps them best utilize resources in the production of goods and services, which, in turn, increases income opportunities. It eventually enhances living standards and leads to a greater respect for human rights (e.g., Apodaca, 2001; Richards, Gelleny and Sacko, 2001; Elliot and Freeman, 2003; Richards and Gelleny, 2007). On the other hand, critics of globalization state that neoliberal globalization is widening the gap between rich and poor instead of bringing universal prosperity. The economic restructuring, trade and financial liberalization increases the global competition, which makes states less capable of enforcing or willing to enforce human rights obligations. Neoliberal economists consider labor as an input of production like any other commodities (Eichengreen, 1997; Rodrik, 1998; Stiglitz, 2002). Entrepreneurs are reluctant to improve employment conditions because it increases the production costs and thus makes them less competitive (Doumbia-Henry and Gravel, 2006).

In the same vein, counterarguments are found on the impacts of globalization on women workers. Some argue that globalization brings positive changes to the lives of women workers in various forms, such as the expansion of employment opportunities leading to increased income, breaking the patriarchal bond, growth of self-awareness about rights, duties, and participation in the collective bargaining association, shifts in gender roles and value structure, and reconfiguration of the public-private and production-reproduction dichotomies (Lim, 1997; Razavi, 2001; Gills, 2002; Unni, 2002; Kabeer, 2000). In a comparative study based on in-depth interviews with Bangladeshi workers in London and Dhaka, Kabeer (2000) shows that global restructuring widens the labor market opportunity for women, and cash earnings help women to renegotiate the *Purdha* (veil) norms; husbands and community, in general, allow and encourage women working outside of the family because they need their income. But the study highlights that the status of workers in developing countries is more inferior compared to the industrialized countries. A similar argument is suggested by Shally Feldman (2001, 2009), who notes that there has been an overwhelming change in the lives of women workers. The presence of women in public spaces is a dramatic shift within a strict cultural norm that restricts women's movement outside of the home, particularly for employment. In a review article, Khosla (2009) shows that women workers gain greater economic independence, respect, social standing and voice than they had before, but she mentions that gender-based harassment and exploitation still persist.

Other critics (e.g., Seguino, 2000; Collins, 2003; Raworth, 2004; Ngai, 2005) reject the claim of an overall economic benefit to women resulting from economic globalization; rather, they argue that employment in global factories pushes women into more vulnerable and precarious situations than they had been in prior to working in the factories. For them, the entry of women into the paid workforce does not result in any change in hierarchal gender relations, since a new sexual division of labor is created in the factories. Increasing competition in the global market pushes entrepreneurs to look for a flexible workforce constituted by women workers. Women, compared to their male counterparts, are predominantly employed in low-skilled and low-paying jobs. Working conditions in most factories are characterized by long hours, little training, absence of seniority payments, unhygienic and even dangerous work conditions, a low standard of occupational safety and an insecurity of employment. All of these in turn reduce the labor cost, and multinational corporations find it profitable to employ this low-cost female labor. Seguino (2000) observed that major export-oriented industries such as textile, clothing and electronics in South Korea, Taiwan, Hong Kong and Singapore – all are industrializing countries with EPZs experiencing rapid growth – employed a high concentration of women coupled with high wage differentials between men and women. In a comparative study of two prominent US apparel firms in Virginia and Mexico, Collins (2003) provides a history of the garment industry based on interviews with factory workers and management. In both companies, she concludes that globalization, characterized by a free market economy, is unlikely to improve the harsh and precarious working conditions. She shows how, although conditions in firms differed, workers are burdened with long working hours, a stressful environment (which is increased by the imposition of stricter standards of management and control) and complicated work assignments, and become disillusioned, failing to voice grievances due to weak unions. Collins (2003), however, is optimistic that the situation will change as women have begun to challenge these conditions by organizing themselves at the workplace and in their communities through the help of various nongovernmental organizations. An Oxfam report, prepared by Kate Raworth (2004) through a comprehensive research in 12 partner countries, presents a dismal picture of how workers' rights are violated in the global supply chain. This report explains that workers are contributing to rising global prosperity and to the profits of some of the world's most powerful companies, but they are systematically denied their share of the benefits. Moving away from the factory floor, the hidden costs of precarious work are much higher; for example, children are out of school and suffering from diseases due to unhygienic accommodations and malnutrition, and workers are struggling with long-term ill health caused by unhealthy working conditions and long working hours. In absence of global institutions that are widely trusted and empowered to protect the rights of workers in the global economy, workers' rights are traded away by corporations. Based on ethnography in an electronics factory in Shenzen special economic zones in Southern China, Ngai (2005) similarly shows a passionate indictment of the social violence brought about by global capitalism. She notes that the sufferings of rural migrant women to urban areas does not simply end with low wages, arduous working conditions and temporary employment; rather, a number of social prejudices undermine their social dignity though their labor has been crucial to the expansion of Chinese manufacturing. An edited volume based on evidences from global garment-producing countries, shows that global women workers bear the cost of the capitalist drive for profit maximization, and perception of gender plays an important role in propelling precarious labor practices that cost beyond the workplace. However, workers are not aware of their rights, and they often shy away from raising their collective voices for lack of workers' interest organizations (CCC, 2005).

The above discussion provides two polarizing trends concerning the labor conditions in the globalization of production. These trends and paradoxes raise a number of questions: What is the current state of labor rights in global manufacturing? Are they just and fair? Why do women workers tend to work at global factories despite the poor labor rights situation? What benefits, if any, are women workers harvesting from the globalization of production? Is there any space for women workers to resist unfair treatment and inhuman working conditions?

Actors and labor market regulation

One key challenge is how to improve the condition of workers at manufacturing industries in the global production network. Current literature on labor market regulation and policy practices offer diverse and sometimes contested connotations and policy frameworks. One focus of the literature is internal management and work organization. The literature in this domain shows that employers and workplace management can ensure labor justice through better management practices. Based on a comparative case study on two of Nike's suppliers in Mexico, Locke et al. (2007) shows that employing modern production work, work organization and an employee voice mechanism improves performance on both production and employee-centered outcomes.

A second focus of the literature concentrates on increasing workers' power for organizing themselves and raising their collective voice. O'Brien (2004) notes that the fate of workers depends on the ability of the labor movement, keeping pressure upon the state and corporate authorities. A labor force that organizes itself and is capable of producing a collective voice of the workers translates into labor power. Based on the evidence of Maria Elena Cuadra (MEC) in Nicaragua, Jennifer Bickman Mendez's book (2005) *From the Revolution to the Maquiladoras: Gender, Labor and Globalization in Nicaragua* affirms that organizing at the grassroots level can confront the challenges of global capitalism. In contrast, Valentine M. Moghadam's book (2005) *Globalizing Women: Transnational Feminist Networks* shows that structural adjustment and global trade policies have increased social inequality around the world, especially for women who are a source of cheap labor for economies in developing regions. She contends that feminist activism has extended into the global arena by the expanding networks that transcend national boundaries, which she refers to as "transnational feminist networks" (TFNs) and suggests a closer alignment of global feminism with the global labor movement to transform and reorient the globalization process from being market driven to becoming people driven.

A third trend in the literature concentrates on state regulation and protection. Scholars belonging to this trend (e.g., Chan and Wang, 2005; Yu, 2008; So, 2011) argue that, historically, the state has been the main safeguard for its people, responsible for protecting their rights through law enforcement and deploying social protection systems; and even in the wake of globalization under neoliberal trade regimes, the importance of the state has not diminished. Wang (2005) studied certain corporations' factories, comparing factories in Vietnam with those in China. The study found that labor conditions in Vietnam are better than those in China, suggesting that the host countries' rules and practices cause a differentiation in labor practices and thus the particular state in which a factory is located still matters. Yu's study (2008) similarly depicts that Reebok labor-related codes have resulted in a "race to ethical and legal minimum" workplace standards because codes are driven by commercial incentives for long-term profitability, not for the benefit of the workers. She concludes that a state's legislation and international laws have a particularly crucial role to play in regulating labor practices where only codes can supplement this initiative. Similarly, Alvin So (2010) shows that labor rights in China have been upgraded not by multinational corporations but by the state party. However, the capacity of the state to regulate economic behavior and to set restrictions on market exchange is in decline under neoliberal globalization (Scherer and Palazzo, 2011). Globalization adversely affects welfare spending of developing countries and thus the state's protection of citizens is gradually shrinking (Rudra, 2002; McMichael, 2008; Islam, 2013). In the absence of state power, a number of private institutions and actors at the global, national and local levels are taking part in a regulation process through which a new form of transnational regulation is emerging above and beyond the state.

A fourth trend literature focuses on the role of multinational corporations within the value chain. Scholars who subscribe to this trend (e.g., Islam, 2008; Gereffi, 1994; Dolan and Humphrey, 2000; Schrage, 2004; Mamic, 2004) hold the idea that under the conditions of neoliberal globalization, states hold little power and regulatory agencies of developing countries are too corrupt and weak in enforcing local laws to improve working conditions. In contrast, corporations hold enormous power and therefore can improve working conditions. It is in fact the interest of the corporations to improve the working conditions as consumers' movement against firms for violating labor rights jeopardizes the name and reputation of the company and thus significantly reduces their market competitiveness. Therefore, multinational corporations have developed their own "codes of conduct" combining core conventions of ILO and local labor laws to regulate labor practices of their overseas suppliers (Kaufman et al., 2004; Mamic, 2004). Rodriguez-Garavito (2005) explains that codes of conduct have the potential to facilitate worker organization and sustainable gains in working conditions, but she highlights creating institutional designs and mechanisms to bolster the effects. For example, workers' unions need to be empowered, the individual capacity of the worker is to be strengthened through popular education and training, and legal measures must be implemented to enhance the protection of rights and the involvement of umbrella organizations in transnational organizing campaigns. Since global industries are dominated by women workers, feminist scholars urged gender-sensitive codes of conduct to address the gender-related issues, including sexual harassment, maternity leave and child care (Barrientos, Dolan and Tallontire, 2003; Tallontire et al., 2005). Expanding on this view, Rossi's study (2011), based on the Moroccan garment industry, shows that producers adopt two categories of employees: regular workers who are senior and experienced, thereby guaranteeing high skills and good quality; and irregular workers who are employed in unskilled segments of the production chain, such as packaging, checking and quality control. These two types of workers face very different opportunities and challenges for social upgrading. Regular workers have enjoyed more security in employment protection and benefits that reduce their fear of reprisals and thus enhance their enabling rights. In contrast, irregular workers are less able to avail of employment protection and often face discrimination on account of both their social and employment status. Following this study, Barrientos, Gereffi and Rossi (2011) have suggested for both economic and social upgrading to protect workers in global production networks.

However, critics identify a number of conflicting interests in codes of conduct and actors involved in this process. Esbenshade's study (2004) notes that brand-name companies have avoided taking responsibility for ensuring labor rights in subcontracting factories. The code of conduct still remains at the second priority level while price, product quality and customer satisfaction are at the first. Esbenshade argues that the voluntary character of corporations' code of conduct does not put enough pressure on the producers, and egregious violators escape punishment. She concludes that independent monitoring cannot bring expected change until trade unions, democratic governments and labor laws come into real enforcement. As indicated earlier, Xiaomin Yu's (2008) study on Reebok's athletic footwear factory in China shows that the impact of Reebok's labor-related codes are a "race to the ethical and legal minimum" in the workplace. She mentions that inhuman labor practices (being required to work long hours for pay that is below the legal minimum wage, unsafe and unhealthy working conditions, corporal punishments to discipline workers, child labor, etc.) exist in all global factories, but workers' agency and voices are almost absent for lack of freedom to form associations and collective bargaining. Being forced by an authoritarian management, workers' unions functioned more like a "company union" rather than representing workers' interests. Corporations' codes of conduct rarely put emphasis on workers' union rights. A similar argument has been suggested by Mark Anner (2012), who notes that corporations' codes are designed to detect the violation of minimal standards in areas of wages, hours and occupational safety and health because violations of these rights may provoke activist campaigns and increase market risk. But, she points out, these voluntary codes rarely emphasize workers' democratic rights to form independent organizations, collective bargaining and the ability to strike because these rights are perceived as a threat of managerial control. Codes of conduct focus more on the quality of the commodity produced rather than the producers (labor) themselves.

A fifth trend in the literature concentrates on global actors. Beyond enterprise level initiatives, a number of strategic alliances are formed to pursue a system of accountability. A wide range of actors are involved in private sector initiatives across the globe including, for example, Transnational Trade and Financial Agreements (North Atlantic Free Trade Agreement, NAFTA), NGOs (Fair Labor Association, FLA; Social Accountability International, SAI; Ethical Trading Initiative, ETI) and hybrid coalitions between enterprises, workers, NGOs, investors and others (Workers Rights Consortium, WRC) (Diller, 1999; Hutter, 2006; Wegner and Zwart, 2011; CCC, 2009). Polaski (2006) affirms that trade agreements are positively associated with higher labor standards. Based on a comparative analysis between two garment exporting countries, Bangladesh and Cambodia, she shows that the widespread problems in Bangladesh include incorrect payment of wages and excessive hours or forced overtime work along with violations of health and safety, freedom of association and collective bargaining. The situation is far better in Cambodia, which is due to the trade agreement between Cambodia and the United States, the largest garment exporter from Cambodia. Santoro (2003) explains that MNCs do not care about ethical business unless some pressure comes from students groups, labor rights activists, consumer groups and NGOs. To create effective pressure on MNCs, NGOs organize global movements and campaigns for fair labor standards. Both the cooperational and confrontational roles of NGOs, despite tension being sometimes created between these two, have shaped the history of the labor movement. Some scholars (e.g., Bellemare, 2000; Elliot and Freeman, 2003) argue that consumers' demand for maintaining labor standards gives power to the anti-sweatshop movement. If consumers demand "guilt-free" commodities and improved working conditions, corporations cannot readily dismiss this demand. Different survey results (e.g., Marymount University, 1999; Prasad et al., 2004) also show that consumers are willing to buy the products and even willing to pay slightly more if goods are produced under improved working conditions.

The above diverse policy debates lead to an examination of some of the questions, such as: What are the roles played by different actors for securing labor justice in global factories? What are the effective mechanisms of ensuring fair labor practices? Is a single actor able to bring labor justice to the global chain of production or is there any necessity of a coordinated role by multiple actors? Do nonstate actors free the state of taking roles or extend the array of state responsibility? In the upcoming chapters, we will address some of these issues with more empirical evidences.

Conclusion

We found that along with local dynamics, neoliberal globalization of production generates unique labor conditions and gender relations. The reviews in this chapter clearly indicate that the existing literature offers diverse and contested perspectives in understanding the complex intersection between gender and labor rights under the global chain of production. The current global economy, comprising a complex interplay of gender, capitalist forces of globalization, and multiple actors in global production networks, is shaping a new regime of labor regulation and industrial relations, which in turn influences the rights of women workers in global manufacturing industries. Feminization of the labor force is the dominant feature of global manufacturing, and it is used as a resource for globalizing the capital. On the contrary, one undeniable fact is that global factories are perhaps the best places for the employment of women. Global consumers have therefore pushed the global brand companies to maintain labor standard at the factory levels where goods are produced. Various efforts have also been executed to improve labor conditions. Therefore, the gender effect of global manufacturing cannot be stated in a simple straight line; rather, it has many turns and twists that raise many questions which have been presented in this chapter. The understanding of all these largely depends on the answers to the following questions: What is the current state of rights of women workers in global factories? How do gender norms and capitalist forces of production shape the terrain of labor rights in the workplace? And what are the roles played by the traditional and nontraditional (newly emerging) actors for ensuring labor rights of women workers?

4
Women in Employment: Local Dynamics, Global Pressures

Women's involvement in wage-earning activities is viewed as a process of empowering them. This is particularly important in Third World countries where hierarchical gender relations exist between men and women. Women's earnings change the status of women in the family and increase their participation in decision making, transforming the patriarchal power relations into greater gender equity, as documented in a number of studies. This chapter explores the trajectories of women employment and development, focusing on the case of Bangladesh. It will show how gendered beliefs and cultural practices shape the gender division of labor and how women's labor market participation and vulnerability are influenced by these beliefs. It will then go on to discuss the shifting trends of women employment from traditional agriculture to modernized production, the antecedents of transforming and accelerating this shift and the development path of industrial relations system and labor regulation policies. It will also highlight the connection of labor rights with global capital and RMG trade.

Historical background of women employment

Historically, the level of participation of women in wage labor has been dwarfed by that of men. Modernity, however, has seen the unprecedented participation of women in the global labor force, in terms of the scale of participation (Psacharopoulos and Tzannatos, 1989). However, the participation of women in labor markets has not played out equally, resulting in the vulnerability of women as compared to their male counterparts. We find that women today are forced into unequal labor arrangements that are not of their own making, even across the socioeconomic range of women, thus risks are being passed down to them (Gills and Piper, 2002). Modern gender vulnerability in labor is a result that continues to be shaped by economic as well as cultural forces, which need to be addressed at the institutional roots in order to achieve substantive progress toward gender equality. Using Lorber's (1994) systematic account of techno-economic bases of society as well as Kendall's (2006) analysis of these bases, we can discern the historical conditions leading up to the gendered division of labor (Table 4.1).

Here, we will examine more in the case of Bangladesh, a South-Asian country, which became independent in 1971 from the ruling of Pakistan. It is an overpopulated country consisting of 149,772,364 people of which 74,980,368 are women in the area of 147,570 square kilometers, and the annual growth rate for 2011 is 1.37 percent (BBS, 2011). The country was ravaged by acute food shortages and famines during the early years of its independence (Mahmud, 2008). Moreover, due to the discriminating state policy of the Pakistan government, the initial period of Bangladesh displayed a dismal picture in terms of various social development indicators. However, this scenario has gradually been changed from the last quarter of the 1970s. Life expectancy has risen from 50 to 63 years, the child mortality rate of 240 per thousand births has been decreased by 70 percent, the literacy rate has improved to 66 percent and total fertility rate (TFR) declined from 6.3 births per woman in the mid-1970s to about

Table 4.1 Women in economic structures

	Hunting and gathering	Horticultural and pastoral	Agrarian	Industrial	Postindustrial
Change from prior society	-	Use of hand tools, such as digging stick and hoe	Use of animal-drawn ploughs and equipment	Invention of steam engine	Invention of computer and development of high-tech society
Economic characteristics	Hunting game, gathering roots and berries	Planting crops, domestication of animals for food	Labor-intensive farming	Mechanized production of goods	Information and service economy
Control of surplus	None	Men begin to control societies	Men who own land or herds	Men who own means of production	Corporate shareholders and high-tech entrepreneurs
Women's status	Relative equality	Decreasing in move to pastoralism	Low	Low	Varies by class, race and age

Source: Adapted from Lorber (1994) and Kendall (2006).

3.0 in recent years (NIPORT, 2011; BBS, 2010). Most of these gains have taken place with respect to accelerated growth in per capita GDP, which is currently 6 percent (WB, 2013). Among many factors that contributed to the growth of the annual GDP, most notable are the increase of foreign direct investment (FDI), remittances, foreign aid, and above all an increase of employment and income-earning opportunities for women. However, women participation in the labor force is still low in Bangladesh when compared to their male counterparts.

Women's labor force participation in a patriarchal society is constrained by a traditional normative family system, a system which restricts the women's mobility outside the home in the name of *Purdah*[1] (Feldman, 2009). Women are confined within the home compound unless any emergency occurs (Hossain, Al-Amin and Alam, 2012). This seclusion of women is linked with the ideological apparatus of the people, which conceives that women's appearance outside the domain of the home undermines the status of family (Feldman, 2001). Social and cultural practices have given shape to the "male breadwinner model" where maintenance of financial needs belongs solely to men. Women are free from carrying the financial responsibility and hence the economic role of women is considered as secondary and only to supplement the male income, whereas reproductive and caring roles are seen as their primary role (Rahman, 2005). Moreover, women cannot participate in paid employment outside the home without first obtaining the consent of male house heads. This patriarchal belief influences women's labor force participation and supports the male priority in getting jobs (Cain, 1977; Westergaard, 1983). A study conducted in Mozambique and Tanzania has shown that husbands and fathers prevent women from taking part in paid work outside the home particularly in places where they were likely to come into close contact with men (Oya, 2010). Another study in Mexico showed that husbands were openly against or at best dubious about the spouse's engagement outside the home (Appendini, 2010). Being a traditional patriarchal society, women in Bangladesh are to follow a similar course of action. Since the main source of employment of Bangladeshi people is agriculture and its related activities,[2] mainly done outside the home, economic participation of women is very low. Statistics shows that there are 30.9 million people in the labor force of which women constitute 14.1 percent compared to 79.8 percent of men (BBS, 2011). It is in upward trend in the following years (Table 4.2).

It should be noted that gendered differential beliefs do not relieve women from performing economic activities. Crops processing (post-harvesting) activities are mostly done in the home where maximum

Table 4.2 Labor force, employment and participation rate

	Labor force (Millions)			Employment (Millions)			Participation rate (%)		
Year	Female	Male	Both	Female	Male	Both	Female	Male	Both
1990–1991	4.0	26.9	30.9	4.0	26.7	30.7	14.1	79.6	–
1999–2000	8.5	32.2	40.7	7.9	31.1	39.0	22.8	84.0	–
2005–2006	12.1	37.4	49.5	11.3	36.1	47.4	29.2	86.8	58.5
2010–2011	17.2	39.5	56.7	16.2	37.9	54.1	36.0	82.5	59.3

Sources: Labor Force Survey (various years), Bangladesh Bureau of Statistics.

contribution comes from women but no cash benefit reaches them. To gain monetary benefit, women need control over the earnings that come from selling the products. Generally, being the head of the family, men are responsible in bringing the agricultural products to the market and as a result, the earnings from selling the products go into men's hands. Through this process, women's contribution remains unpaid, and women are excluded from active participation in the labor force. This scenario is under gradual change though, and women are no longer passive participants in the labor market. Due to the increase in women's education and women's movement for securing rights and mobility, their economic participation outside the home has increased substantially. Many women are now taking part in cultivation alongside men and even taking responsibility of maintaining the family, thus breaking the rule of "male bread winner and female care giver". This shift mostly happened through the intervention of some nongovernmental organizations (NGOs) that started their work just after the independence war in 1971, when many people fell into the trap of poverty resulting in them having no source of income. Considering the deep shock of war and devastation, many NGOs (e.g., Bangladesh Rural Advancement Committee, Grameen Bank, Association for Social Advancement, etc.) came forward to help the poor people through relief and rehabilitation activities and later redirected their activities to make the rural poor, particularly women, self-reliant (Feldman, 2009; Hossain, Al-Amin and Alam, 2012). During the 1990s, NGOs' activities had achieved greater success in creating self-employment through microfinance. Currently, the number of group-based microcredit borrowers has reached 25 million who are running credit-based, small enterprises (Khandker, Faruqee and Samad, 2013). In addition to micro-credit, other NGO-led activities such as social awareness about health, education, nutrition, social forestry and legal rights, have led to a transformation in women's lives by promoting social interaction and mobility for women. The most possible outcome from these changes is the sharp increase in women's labor-force participation (Mahmud, 2008). Female participation rates rose faster during the period of 1983 to 2000 than that of the male participation rate, which was 8.2 percent, 14.1 percent, 22.8 percent and 29.2 percent in 1983, 1991, 2000, and 2006 respectively (Rahman, 2005). In spite of the sharp increase of labor-force participation of both men and women, higher growth of the labor force and low employment potentials accelerated the size of total unemployment (an increase to 2.7 million in 2006 from 2.1 million in 2000). Although the unemployment rate of women had declined from 7 percent to 5.8 percent in the years 2005 and 2010, respectively, 30.5 million women are still not in the labor force

Table 4.3 Sector-wise employment by sex

	Total employment (millions)			Percentage (2010)		
Major sectors	**2002–03**	**2005–06**	**2009–10**	**Both**	**Male**	**Female**
Agriculture, forestry and fisheries	22.9	22.8	25.7	49.2	50.2	45.6
Mining and quarrying	0.1	0.1	0.1	0.5	0.3	1.3
Manufacturing	4.3	5.2	6.7	9.5	7.4	17.7
Electricity gas and water	0.1	0.1	0.1	0.3	0.3	0.0
Construction	1.5	1.5	2.6	2.8	4.2	1.3
Trade hotel and restaurant	6.7	7.8	8.4	15.7	18.3	6.3
Transport, storage and communication	3.0	4.0	4.0	6.4	7.7	1.3
Finance, business and real estate	0.3	0.8	1.0	1.0	1.2	0.0
Health education, public administration and defense	2.5	2.6	2.3	5.7	5.9	6.1
Community and personal services	2.7	2.6	4.4	7.4	4.9	18.8
Total	44.1	47.5	55.3	98.5	100.4	98.4

Source: Labor Force Survey (various years), Bangladesh Bureau of Statistics.

compared to 8.4 million men in 2010 (BBS, 2010a). Accumulation of this figure into the labor force could substantially increase the unemployment rate. This shows that Bangladesh has experienced a "labor surplus economy" where many women are out of employment.

Emergence and growth of the RMG industry

Bangladesh was formerly part of British-ruled undivided India for almost 200 years (1757–1947), and it came under the rule of Pakistan through the partition of the Indian-subcontinent in 1948. During these regimes, the areas that are now under the sovereignty of Bangladesh faced severe economic discrimination. After the birth of Pakistan, a number of industries were set up under the direct protection of the government, but Bangladesh (then East Pakistan) experienced a mild rate of industrialization due to the discriminated industrial policy of the then Pakistan government run by West Pakistani elites. Only a few industries were established, depending on domestically available raw materials, such as jute, paper, cement, fertilizer, textile and tea, but a majority of these were under the ownership of West Pakistani entrepreneurs. At the time of independence in 1971, only 18 percent of businesses were owned by Bangladeshi industrialists, 47 percent by Pakistani industrialists, 34 percent state-owned and only 1 percent was owned by foreign investors (Rashid, 2006). In the mid-1970s, the government introduced a new industrial policy and nationalized all industries that were banned during the Pakistani rule. In spite of government incentives to promote industrial growth and export earnings, little change was seen in the production of traditional industries. While most of the commodities were produced only to meet the domestic demands, jute and tea continued to be major export commodities. Until 1980, jute and tea were the two dominant export commodities that earned two-thirds of the export income; however, this has fallen drastically in the face of a declining price in the global markets. The country has, however, experienced a steady rise of export-oriented ready-made garment[3] manufacturing during the early 1980s and late 1990s and became a prime source of export earnings. It was a sudden boom during the 1980s that was geared by both local and global factors, which we will explore further in the chapter. Here it should be noted that Dhaka, the capital of Bangladesh, had a long reputation for producing the finest cloths – "Maslin sarees" – during the Mughal Empire era but broke away in later centuries. The RMG production in Bangladesh was evidenced between 1965 and 1968, when The Mercury Shirt, a company based in Karachi, Pakistan, sourced a few consignments of shirts by some tailor companies operated in Dhaka and exported these to some European markets. At that time, there were few tailoring groups in Dhaka who made a minimal amount of export-quality shirts and children's wear on specific orders received from Karachi-based firms (Rashid, 2006).

After independence, the country observed a rapid expansion of the RMG industry during the second half of the 1970s due to the direct impact of a Multi-Fibre Agreement (MFA) on textile and RMG trade (Siddiqi, 2009). Under this agreement, the imposition of quotas led the former industrializing countries to search for quota-free locations to set up garment manufacturing plants and consequently Bangladesh became the promising place to some East Asian countries (e.g., Korea, Hong Kong, Malaysia and China) that were pioneers in garment manufacturing. These pioneers then relocated their factories in Bangladesh. For instance, Korean company Daewoo signed a contract with Desh Garments in 1976. Following the agreement, Daewoo gave free training in production and marketing to 130 supervisors and managers from Desh Garments, but then left production itself to Desh Garments. Within one year, 115 trained people left Desh Garments to set up their own plants or moved to other newly established factories, receiving salaries ten or more times their previous salaries (Kabeer and Mahmud, 2004a). Moreover, tariff and import quota-free access in the EU market under the Generalized System of Preference (GSP), the trade liberalization policy of the Bangladesh government (which attracted foreign investment), and above all, the availability of cheap labor contributed to the rapid enlargement of the RMG sector and women employment (Ahmed, 2009). According to the Bangladesh Garment Manufacturer and Exporters Association (BGMEA), in the year 2013 the RMG industry

Table 4.4 Total number of RMG factories and employed women workforce

Year	Number of RMG Factories	Employment (million)	Women (million)	Women (%)
1983–84	134	0.040	0.034	85
1985–86	594	0.198	0.16	85
1990–91	834	0.402	0.34	90
1995–96	2353	1.290	1.08	85
2000–01	3480	1.800	1.44	85
2005–06	4220	2.200	1.87	80
2009–10	5063	3.600	2.88	80
2010–11	5150	3.600	2.88	80
2011–12	5400	4.000	3.20	80
2012–13	5600	4.000	3.20	80

Source: Bangladesh Garment Manufacturer and Exporters Association (BGMEA).

provides jobs for 4 million people, of whom 3.20 million are women, contributing about 80 percent share of women (Table 4.4).

With the expansion of factories, export values and share in total export, earnings have also increased proportionately. While the total export earnings from RMG were US$14.57 million in 1984, they have reached to US$21,515.73 million in 2013 (Table 4.5) and the total share has increased to 79.63 percent from 4.89 percent in the respective years (BGMEA, 2013; BEPB, 2013).

It is evident that RMG export in various years is in an upward turn, and it is becoming the main source of export earnings for Bangladesh. The other exporting products have a very marginal role in foreign currency earning (Table 4.6).

Table 4.5 Export income and contribution of RMG

Year	Export of RMG (million US$)	Total export (million US$)	% of RMGs to total export
1983–84	31.57	811.00	4.89
1985–86	131.48	819.21	16.05
1990–91	866.82	1717.55	50.47
1995–96	2547.13	3882.42	65.61
2000–01	4859.83	6467.30	75.14
2005–06	7900.80	10526.16	75.06
2009–10	12496.72	16204.65	77.12
2011–12	19089.69	24287.66	78.60
2012–13	21515.73	27018.26	79.63

Sources: Bangladesh Export Promotion Bureau, Government of Bangladesh.

Table 4.6 Product-wise share of export earnings (%)

Products	2007–08	2008–09	2009–10
RMG	75.83	79.33	77.12
Frozen food	4.78	2.92	2.73
Jute goods	2.26	1.73	4.86
Leather	2.02	1.13	1.40
Raw jute/Agricultural products[a]	1.17	0.95	1.50
Chemical products/ Engineering products[a]	1.53	1.80	1.92
Tea	0.11	0.08	
Footwear[a]	-	-	1.26
Other	14.30	12.04	9.21

Notes: [a]Indicates products exported in only in 2009–10, and new items are included in the broader category.
Source: Bangladesh Garment Manufacturer and Exporters Association (BGMEA), 2013.

Shifts from housewives to factory workers: challenges to tradition

The rapid growth of the RMG industry opened the door for the entrance of women into the labor market. The dramatic shift of women employment from traditional agro-based subsistence farming and self-employment to trade and commodity production was facilitated by both supply and demand factors: an abundant supply of women workers and employers' preference to hire women workers – for a number of reasons. First, there has been a transformation in the countryside including the erosion of subsistence agriculture, declines in land holdings and land security, and the advent of mechanized rice milling, which reduced the scope of women employment.[4] Due to the unavailability of jobs, women are pressured to find work, increasingly in the RMG industry. In a poverty-stricken society where large numbers of women, particularly uneducated, divorced or separated who constantly fight against hunger, any employment opportunity is considered to them a viable means of survival. Accordingly, a major part of the women's workforce in RMG industry is composed of the overrepresentation of widows, divorced, separated or unmarried young girls. Their presence in the city is largely pushed by the poverty-stricken conditions in their respective villages (Absar, 2000; Kabeer, 2004). Second, the traditional avenues for employment of women, mainly in the agricultural construction and domestic sectors, which are more laborious and hazardous, are usually done in public places; whereas jobs in the RMG sectors are mainly carried out inside the factory. Thus, RMG employment is seen as a "respectable" form of employment for women of lower-middle-class[5] and landless poor-class families who are somehow forced to work outside of their home (Ahmed, 2004). Third, Bangladesh is one of the most vulnerable areas in the world that frequently faces severe natural catastrophes leaving thousands of people homeless, thus constricting their choices in finding a means of survival (Mathbor, 2007, 2008). Being affected by high incidence of severe natural calamities, rural poor people move to urban areas for subsistence. This migration trend is higher among women than men who are drawn from landless households (Feldman, 1993; Afsar, 2001). According to our estimates, every day more than a thousand girls and women migrate from rural to urban areas in search of works (Ward et al., 2004). Due to the lack of education and necessary skills and having no other suitable options, many of these migrated women are forced to enter into the labor market and get involved in low-paid informal work, particularly in RMG industries to contribute to their family income (Kibria, 1995; Kabeer, 2004; Paul-Majumder and Begum, 2006).

Women workers are the economic and strategic choice to employers for a number of reasons. First, women's labor is comparatively cheap because employers are able to get unpaid labor through extending overtime work (Ahmed, 2004; Muhammad, 2011). Second, women's "natural dexterity" gives them an extra advantage to be employed in garment factories. It is believed that the task that has to be performed in the garment factory is aligned with their traditional work of sewing,[6] which ensures higher productivity (Paul-Majumder and Begum, 2006). Third, women's "natural docility" influences employers to prefer them. Employers always set higher targets and operate coercive rule to get maximum production. Similarly, women modestly carry out orders given by management without raising any arguments. They do not take part in union activities and are less likely to raise their voices against injustices. It is believed that arguing with male bosses is indecent; and organizing activities, such as strikes, are not suited for women (Dannecker, 2002; Khan, 2004). Finally, employers are sometimes more inclined to recruit young and smart girls, a choice which is persuaded by sexual instinct (Siddiqi, 2009; Hossain, Mathbor and Semenza, 2013).

The above description indicates that higher participation of women workers in the RMG industry is fostered by both employers' preference for cheap and "best-suited" labor and urgent need of income generation for survival among women. However, the preference for hiring women is, in fact, an employers' choice (Ahmed, 2004). The justification in favor of this claim is that limited opportunities of employment are not only a reality for women but also are similarly true for men. Still, many men who wish to work in this sector in spite of low remuneration are unemployed. Since employers are inclined to secure a compliant and low-cost workforce, women workers are the strategic choice to reach this goal. Whatever the reasons are, the fact remains that the RMG industry has accelerated a shift in the role of women from being housewives to factory workers. Most of these workers are migrants from the rural areas; and for many of them, this is their first experience of paid employment outside household work (Kabeer and Mahmud, 2004a, 2004b). The garment manufacturing industry has given the opportunity to rural poor women, who are mostly less educated and unskilled, to be included in the national (and global) labor force where previously their unpaid household work was unaccounted for. It is argued that women's employment in the RMG industry is giving them a collective voice to challenge social traditions that restrict women's participation in economic activities (Hossain, 2012). The RMG industry has brought many women to cities to work, at the expense of their male members. Many of them are now self-dependent, and in many cases, they are contributing to family maintenance by sending remittances to their homes in the villages (Naved et al., 2001; Rahman, 2005; Kabeer, 2008). Research data shows that women workers are providing 46 percent of family income; and 30 percent of women are maintaining their family, breaking the norm of the "male breadwinner model" (Amin et al., 1998; Absar, 2001; Ward et al., 2004). Moreover, garment workers are challenging social norms and traditions by delaying marriage, marrying someone of their own choice, and working with their male counterparts outside their home, things that were unimaginable even a few years earlier (Feldman, 2009; Khosla, 2009; Hossain, 2012).

Working conditions and gender relations

The literature shows a paradox about the influence of women employment in the global RMG industry of Bangladesh. The above section lucidly explains that women employment in the RMG industry has wider social consequences, such as the empowerment of women. It is the nascent side of globalization; but on the other side, a much more deplorable aspect can be seen as a number of labor rights are being violated, specifically in terms of wages, overtime payment, leave, labor benefits, workplace safety and job security (Alam and Blanch, 2011). Workers' pay is extremely low in comparison to their counterparts in other countries (Table 4.7) and also below the living wages[7] of the country. They are thus unable to survive in the city area with their wages bordering on the level of poverty. Their low earnings are often supplemented by overtime

Table 4.7 Comparative hourly wages of garments workers in the world

Name of the country	Hourly wage (US$)
United States	8.25–14.00
United Kingdom	7.58–9.11
Venezuela	2.73
Costa Rica	2.19
Colombia	1.29
Honduras	1.02
Philippines	0.94–1.00
China	0.93
India	0.55–0.68
Vietnam	0.52
Pakistan	0.37
Cambodia	0.24
Bangladesh	0.20

Source: Institute for Global Labor and Human Rights (2010).

work thereby incurring a deficit familial cost. The occurrence of overtime does not happen spontaneously and is not initiated by the workers; rather, they are supposed to provide extra hours to ensure the products are supplied in due time (Muhammad, 2011). This overtime work is done after the usual working hours and often causes serious difficulties for women. After walking two to three kilometers home from the factory without any transport facilities, they have to start their "third shift",[8] which is the preparation of food for their families, with the pressure of starting a brand-new shift early the next morning. Working conditions in the factory are detrimental to their health. Cutting and sewing produces dust, but management does not provide any forms of inhalation protection, such as masks, to protect them; and ironing produces heat, but in many cases, all of these tasks are done on the same floor.

Poor lighting and ventilation, unhygienic surroundings, and inadequate toilet facilities have also been reported (Kabeer, 2004; Paul-Majumder and Begum, 2000). Most of the workers face different kinds of health difficulties resulting from these unhygienic working conditions, such as weight loss, fatigue, headache, hearing impairments and eye problems (Rashid, 2006; Kabeer, 2004; Amin et al., 1998). However, garment authorities do not provide any medical facilities contravening the factory rules. The most pervasive but least visible form of exploitation is sexual harassment. Verbal abuse, sexual coercion and intimidation are widely accepted modes of harassment. The highly sexualized vocabulary and body language used by line chiefs, supervisors, production managers and others in management to "discipline" women workers creates a hostile, intimidating and sexually charged environment (Siddiqi, 2004, 2009). Due to shame and social humiliation, victims rarely share their personal traumatic experiences with others; rather, many of them leave their jobs or move silently to other factories if the opportunity arises. In spite of the nonexistence of workers' basic rights and securities in the factory, they are incapable of raising their voices due to, for instance, the absence of any formal associations. Workers cannot join any trade union organization for fear of losing their jobs (Dannecker, 2002; Khan, 2004). The most alarming aspect in all of this is that many of the factories are located in old apartments, which are categorically unsafe and deemed high-risk sites, prone to industrial accidents such as fires or factory building collapses (more on this in Chapter 8).

A gender division of labor and hierarchal gender relations exists inside the factory. Although the Bangladesh garment industry is dominated by women workers, they remain at the lower tiers in the job hierarchy. Tasks are allocated on the basis of gender, which determines many of the working conditions of women workers. Women workers are absorbed in a variety of activities, including sewing, packing, inserting buttons, making holes for buttons, inspecting garments and cleaning threads, while men workers are involved in cutting, ironing and finishing (Paul-Majumder and Begum, 1997). Usually, the tasks performed by women are lower paid than their male counterparts. A survey report prepared by "Wan on Want" shows that 83 percent of women workers are employed as sewing operators and only 10 percent as helpers (Alam and Blanch, 2011). Women are less often hired for mid-level positions (supervisors, floor in-charge, quality controllers, cutting masters) with comparatively higher pay. Women are hardly found in administrative and management-level positions in the factory due to gender differential beliefs and practices (Kabeer, 1991). During the 1990s, women employment in the RMG sector was looked down upon, and the perceived notion was that it was a job for lower-class people. Therefore, educated women were reluctant to start their careers in this sector. Women are viewed as reluctant to take on any kind of challenges at the workplace, while it is men who are seen as able and responsible in controlling and disciplining women.

Legal framework and industrial relations

Workers' rights are not simply a matter in a particular factory or state, but rather a matter of global concern. Producers, buyers, human rights organizations and consumers are integrated in the current globalized production system. Various national, international and multinational economic institutions have also been allied in the regulation of labor. Many transnational institutions (WTO, NAFTA, ASEAN, SAPTA and ILO) have adopted different regulatory systems and every member state of the concerned global forums is principally and legally bound to implement the respective labor standards. Member states also have their own legal and regulatory system that follows the international standard, both equally important in ensuring and promoting the rights of workers. Being a member of various global forums, Bangladesh is theoretically supposed to implement the provisions undertaken by the respective regulatory systems. The main regulatory framework of worker rights in Bangladesh comes through the ratification of ILO conventions and recommendations. Bangladesh has ratified all the conventions except convention No. 138.[9] By ratifying these conventions, Bangladesh has given consent to ensure all the formal rights, such as: the right to get an appointment letter, sufficient and regular pay without any discrimination, reasonable working hours, job security, involvement in trade unions and collective bargaining.

Immediately after independence, Bangladesh declared a labor policy in 1972 recommending the reduction of trade union activities in welfare organizations. Accordingly, the right to strike and collective bargaining were prohibited in welfare organizations for six months by a presidential order in May 1972 and fully withdrawn in 1973. Meanwhile the "Emergency Power Ordinance 1974" was enforced, which completely suspended all the democratic rights of workers by restricting trade union activities such as strikes, lockouts and collective bargaining. This restriction was continued by the subsequent military regime through the Industrial Relations (Regulation) Ordinance of 1975. Through the adoption of the Industrial Relations (Amendment) Ordinance of 1977, the right to freedom of association was restored to some extent and further improvements took place through the adoption of the Labor Policy of 1980. Unfortunately, this situation was further worsened with the imposition of the Industrial Relations (Regulation) Ordinance of 1982, by which the military government suspended trade union activities, strikes and freedom of association. During the military regime, Bangladesh Export Processing Zone (EPZ) started operations under the Bangladesh Export Processing Zone Authority (BEPZA) Act 1980. Through an amendment to that act, EPZs were exempted from operation of certain laws. In 1986, the military government suspended the Industrial Relations Ordinance of 1969, which was the basis of collective bargaining in EPZ factories. The logic of suspending trade unions in EPZs was that by introducing trade unions in such areas, it would jeopardize the working environment. This led to the EPZ workers losing their right to form associations and collective bargaining.

After the fall of military regime at the end of the 1980s, the right-wing political Bangladesh Nationalist Party (BNP) rose to power with the support of the moderate Islamic party, Bangladesh *Jamat-e-Islami*, in 1991 through a democratic election under a caretaker government. During this period, union activities were restored again. Workers and union leaders demanded effective implementation of trade union rights and modification of labor laws to remove all uncertainties and vagueness in existing laws. The government formed the National Labor Law Commission as a response in 1992, consisting of 38 members headed by Justice Abdul Kuddus Chowdhury. The commission held consultations with the workers' representatives, leaders of the Collective Bargaining Agent (CBA), employers' representatives, civil society members and NGOs to get their views and submitted the report to the government within two years of its constitution. Unfortunately, over the next few years, particularly in the regime led by the Bangladesh Awami League (BAL) from 1996 to 2001, this report was not able to come into force. As a consequence, discontented workers, mainly in the RMG sector,[10] started raising their voices outside the factory premises in the form of vandalism, strikes, road blockings and demonstrations, causing a serious threat to the sustainability of the RMG industry itself. At the end of the 1990s and early 2000s, the workers' aggressions spun out of control. Recognizing the detrimental effect of labor unrest on export earnings, the Bangladesh government was compelled to open the door for social dialogue through tripartite and multistakeholder involvement. Finally, a tripartite committee was formed to settle the industrial disputes and minimize workers' discontent. This committee sat in three consecutive meetings to discuss the issues. A landmark outcome of these discussions was the signing of a Memorandum of Understanding (MoU) in June 2006 between the government, the BGMEA and leaders of the workers. According to the conditions of the MoU, the government would take initiatives to reform the labor laws, which later led to the emergence of the Labor Law of 2006. At the same time, many labor NGOs as well as the United States, the main importing country of Bangladeshi garments, exerted strong pressure to ensure collective bargaining rights in the EPZs. In response, Bangladesh issued a gazette notification in 2001, withdrawing the prohibition on freedom of association in EPZs and promised to adopt a new law by the end of 2004. Accordingly, the Industrial Relations Act of 2004 was passed, giving rights to form workers' associations in three stages between 2005 and 2008 (Faruque, 2009), and it was modified later in 2010. Therefore, the Labor Law of 2006 and the EPZ Workers Welfare Association and Industrial Relation Act of 2010 are the two main legal documents to the development of the industrial relations system in Bangladesh. A brief description of these two laws is provided below.

Bangladesh Labor Law of 2006

After the Independence of Bangladesh, the Bangladesh Labor Law of 2006 is the most comprehensive law, which came into effect October 11, 2006, as a result of demands by stakeholders to improve the regulatory framework of trade unions and to modify existing labor laws to avoid overlap and inconsistency. This law recognized many of the labor rights dictated by ILO, such as the right to get an appointment letter, sufficient wages, weekly and occasional leave/holiday, maternity and childcare benefit a, healthcare facilities, work safety and a congenial working atmosphere, transport allowance, food or lunch allowance, bonuses, fringe benefits, pensions and group insurance. The law recognizes, for the first time, the right to associate. Section 176 of the act provides that every worker has the right to form a trade union and to join an association of their choice. It also allows trade unions to establish and form federations and to affiliate with international organizations and confederations or workers' organizations. Similarly, Section 195 states that employers, employers' associations or a person appointed by employers cannot discharge workers for their involvement in unions or motivate them either by offering bribes or threats to not participate or organize workers.

It has also kept the provision of an arbitration council and labor court to settle industrial disputes. However, there are some limitations in the Labor Law of 2006.[11] The main weakness of this law is the failure with regard to the application of the ILO convention on Freedom of Association and Protection of the Right to Organize, 1947 (No. 87). However, in a recent amendment, the right to collective bargaining and workers' share in company profits have been included (Table 4.8).[12]

The EPZ Workers Association and Industrial Relation Act of 2004

The EPZ Workers Association and Industrial Relation Act of 2004 (Act No. 36 of 2004), passed by the parliament in 2004, granted a limited right of trade unionism and gave workers in industrial units within the territory

Table 4.8 Key features of Bangladesh Labor Law of 2006

	Key provisions	Limitations
Working conditions and labor benefits	Provision for appointment letter and identity card Right to minimum wage Maternity leave for 16 weeks with full payment One day per week for holiday/day off, and one day of annual leave for every 18 days of work Working hours: 8 hours a day, 48 hours per week (in exceptional cases, 60 hours per week) Payment made within seven days of the last day of the wage period	Absence of rationing facilities No maternity benefits for workers who already have two or more children Overtime work up to 10 p.m. No provision for accommodation and transport facilities Very weak provisions for punishment of employers in case of labor rights violations (e.g., three months' imprisonment or fines of 1000 taka (US$15)) No job protection and social security benefits for workers
Fundamental labor rights	Right to form associations and collective bargaining No discrimination at work in terms of wage and employment conditions Minimum age of employment is 18 years Freedom from forced and compulsory labor	Unions approved upon 30% minimum worker membership requirement (of total permanent employed workers) Restriction on temporary workers for joining unions Provision of joining only one trade union per worker Only one union per factory

Source: Bangladesh Labor Law of 2006 (Act No. 42 of 2006).

the right to form associations as of November 1, 2006. The objective of this act is to recognize the rights of workers to form associations, to regulate relations and to settle disputes arising between employers and workers in the EPZs and any associated matters therein. According to this act, only one trade union is allowed in a factory, but the union is required to include a minimum of 30 percent of the workforce to form association and over 50 percent of the workforce must at least support its establishment. In actuality, the act was only implemented in March 2008 when 69 industrial units in Dhaka and Chittagong EPZs introduced workers' associations on the back of referendums by workers (Faruque, 2009). This law was adopted as a test case, which ended in 2008 and was subsequently extended until October 31, 2010, by the caretaker government (Daily Star, 2010). After the formation of a new government in 2009, and continuous pressure from trade union leaders, activists and NGO workers, the EPZ Workers Welfare Association and Industrial Relations Act of 2010 was finally adopted, amending the previous one, though both of these acts have similar provisions with the exception of some terminological change. It is worth noting here that the EPZ Workers Association and Industrial Relations Act of 2004/2010 does not contain any provisions for workers' welfare issues. These issues are explained in BEPZA Instruction I and II.

The major provisions covered by this law are the process of gaining registration of a workers welfare association, approval of a constitution and formation of executive body, types of unlawful behaviors of unions and employers and the penalties associated with those behaviors, process of collective bargaining and dispute resolution, formation of labor and appeal tribunal, functions and power, conditions for strike and lockout, dismissal of unions, and so on. However, this law has many limitations that hamper the sound industrial relation system and restrict the core rights of workers for forming associations and collective bargaining (Table 4.9). The main limitation, as mentioned earlier, is the forming of an association: workers need prior approval, and to acquire it, they need written consent from 30 percent of the workers as well as the consent of 50 percent through popular vote. It also restricts unions from communicating with NGOs or other political parties.

Both the Labor Law of 2006 and the EPZ Workers Welfare Association and Industrial Relations Act of 2010 have included many of the rights and have almost similar provisions. The main problem is that, whatever safeguards are made in these laws, there is still a big gap between the ideal provisions and their real practices. Cathy Feingold, the international director of the American Federation of Labor and Congress of

Table 4.9 Key provisions of the EPZ workers' welfare association and industrial relations act of 2010

Key issues/Provisions	Limitations
Right to form Workers Welfare Association	Must obtain prior approval from BEPZA chairman by submitting application with the signature of 30% workers
Right to participate in collective bargaining	Needed support of 50% workers through a popular vote arranged by BEPZA in order to form association
Right to strike and lockout	Does not allow more than one association in one industrial unit
Right to claim in EPZ labor tribunal for resolving industrial disputes	Restricts communication with NGOs, other unions and political parties
	Prevents workers' associations from obtaining or receiving any funds from outside source without prior approval
	Confers excessive powers of approval to the executive chairman of BEPZA

Source: EPZ Workers Welfare Association and Industrial Relations Act 2010.

Industrial Organizations (AFL-CIO), expressed that real change in the fate of workers can only happen if the country improves and enforces its own laws (Urbina, 2013). Massive corruptions in the administration, illegal interference of ruling parties and dodgy pillars have thwarted the promising hope of these provisions.

Global trade, RMG production and labor rights

Labor rights of RMG workers in Bangladesh are directly influenced by globalization of production. The global chain of production and price competition in the global market adversely affects workers' rights in Bangladesh. This is mainly due to the dependence on the developed world for an export market of the products and for importing raw materials and other machineries. Globalization has increased an already tough competition among the producers, and neoliberal trade policy provides the opportunity for firms to relocate to low-labor-cost countries for a cheaper cost of production. Along with cheap labor, FDI-friendly domestic trade policy and the MFA have attracted many foreign investors to set up their firms in Bangladesh, leading to the rapid expansion of the RMG industry in Bangladesh. In order to gain access to the markets in the developed world, Bangladeshi producers and exporters are dependent on lead firms, such as NIKE, Walmart, Kmart, Li & Fung and GAP, that play important roles in organizing activities within the global chain of production. Thus, garment manufacturing in Bangladesh is entirely integrated within the global chain of production. Consumer preference of buying products with lower prices has only increased global competition among multinational retailers and brand companies and extends high-level pressure to producers and exporters to adapt new technologies for high-quality products. Demand fluctuations and price competition in the global market have led Bangladesh and local apparel producers to reduce production costs, with no control except for labor. The local producers then conflate these pressures onto the labor sector through reducing employees, curtailing wages or downgrading labor rights and working conditions. This process encourages the informalization of work and results in workers being more flexible in the form of part-time or home-based workers (Ahmed, 2006). Since consumers have no direct contact with the RMG producers and products are transported to their hands through a series of different intermediate actors, the consumers' demand for maintaining labor standards at the workplace usually does not see any light.

Moreover, recent global economic crises are a great challenge for RMG entrepreneurs. Scholars have expressed their deep concern about the current economic slowdown in a majority of developed countries but it is far from the worst possible state, as people from the developing countries – particularly the poor and working class – will generally suffer the worst consequences (Velde, 2008). The immediate results of recessions are on employment and the labor market. According to ILO, total unemployment is projected to reach somewhere between 18 million and 30 million, and in an extreme scenario, the figure could potentially rise to 50 million. In South Asia, unemployment would increase by up to 2 million where a major share would have come from Bangladesh (Rahman, Moazzem and Hossain, 2009). The Bangladesh economy is largely dependent on FDI and remittances, and these two channels will adversely affect the flow of capital if the global recession continues and job cuts persist. Moreover, a high dominance of RMG export earnings and the entire reliance for RMG exports on the US and EU markets will significantly increase the economic vulnerability of Bangladesh in the near future (BB, 2008b). Although many scholars forecasted that the phasing out of MFA workers' rights would be seriously hampered, Bangladesh has successfully adjusted in the post-MFA period without reducing workers' rights. However, if the global economic crisis persists for a long period, the demand of garment products from consumer markets will fall drastically. Due to the decrease in FDI and capital shortage, imports of high productive instruments, the improvement of productivity of workers and the reduction of wastages will no longer be effective. As a consequence, many factories will be forced to shut down and producers may search for new ways for reducing cost for their own sustainability (Rahman, Moazzem and Hossain, 2009). The burdens will ultimately go to the workers as illustrated earlier in this book (Figure 2.1).

Conclusion

Bangladesh has a labor surplus economy, mostly constituted by women workers. Traditional sociocultural beliefs and practices refrain women from labor-force participation and provide the fuel to maintain the myth of a reserve labor force. However, the rise of RMG factories is a breakthrough in the history of women's involvement in paid work. The industry is making a worthwhile contribution in the empowerment of women by employing 2.8 million women workers who are otherwise unemployed and unskilled. At present, many women have found a way to survive. They are no longer dependent on family members for their daily needs; rather, they are carrying out the role of the breadwinner by remitting money to their family members living in villages. They are able to make their own choices and execute the decisions that they think will be valuable for their lives. Their vivid presence in the public spaces for shopping, refreshments or for other official purposes is a remarkable achievement in negotiating and challenging the patriarchal norms. Women workers have experienced the violation of workers' rights, but this is not happening solely due to indigenous reasons as extraneous factors resulting from the global changing economy have also accelerated this process. In addition to global crises, positional vulnerability of women workers in the labor market provides little space to raise their voice against injustices. They hardly reap benefits from existing laws and regulations due to weak enforcement. At the same time, the increased concerns of consumers, NGOs, labor unions and other human rights and social justice activists have geared movements against sweatshop conditions at global factories around the world, which forces global retailers and MNCs to ensure labor justice at the factory. Therefore, there has been a gradual change. With the continuous pressures from buyers, consumers and different international bodies, factory owners are focusing their attention on improving labor conditions and providing space for workers to organize. As a result, employed women are no longer passive victims of gender-based discrimination; rather, they are actively participating by learning how to organize, share experiences and raise their voices. They are now able to foster an identity beyond the traditional care provider – the identity of a productive labor force.

5

Third World Industrialization: Women Workers between Exploitation and Survival

Introduction

Many scholars have argued that the expansion of global manufacturing is enhancing social justice through providing employment opportunities for women; on the other hand, others have claimed that economic globalization is less likely to expand freedom and labor justice since global manufacturing enterprises are mostly characterized by violations of labor rights. This chapter will address this debate and substantiate with empirical evidence from Bangladesh readymade garments (RMG) industries. We will first highlight how Third World industrialization became rooted in new forms of global production systems such as the "World Factory" and the export processing zones (EPZs), giving rise to a gendered division of labor, and then engage in scholarly debate on flexible accumulation and patterned outcomes.

In our discussion on labor patterns and practices in the RMG industries, we will delineate not only the labor conditions but also the available scopes for improving labor justice, focusing on the well-being and agency freedom of the workers. The chapter concludes with a discussion on how women workers negotiate between their survival and exploitation, as well as a way forward in order to confront the precarious labor conditions.

Third World industrialization

In the postcolonial world, the proliferation of the export-oriented industrialization (EOI) model in the Third World gave rise to changes in the strategies of industrialization and a burgeoning presence of transnational corporations (TNCs) within the national economy. With export production selected as the primary strategy of development, Third World states welcomed new investments from First World firms that were looking to relocate their manufacturing plants. As more Third World states jumped on the bandwagon, the mushrooming of export industries paved the way for the advent of the "World Factory" that focused on the production of world, rather than national, products. According to McMichael (2008), this global production system is often characterized by the separation and dispersion of production stages of a singular product in different geographical areas, utilizing diverse labor and material inputs from each site, thereby accentuating the commodity chains that are embedded within the World Factory. The formula for the success of the World Factory was largely built on sexist assumptions that females were more docile, passive and therefore less of a security risk.

As the growth of industrial capitalism among industrialized countries continued, it gave rise to the relocation of manufacturing businesses from industrialized countries to Third World ones such as Indonesia, Bangladesh and India. This created, along with World Factories, the export processing zones (EPZs) in these countries. EPZs are specialized manufacturing export areas with nominal customs regulations, frequently exempt from labor regulations and domestic tariffs. They were established for the purpose of obtaining imported raw materials and to ship or freight the output directly. EPZs led to the increase in demand for women's paid work. In the mid-1980s, approximately 1.8 million workers were working in a total of 173 EPZs worldwide; 80 to 90 percent of these workers were females aged 16–25. In Bangladesh, women occupied 80 percent of the 1.2 million jobs created in EPZs in the garment factories (McMichael, 2008: 93–94).

This globally organized production system was made possible by information technologies, which enabled the coordination of production tasks distributed across several countries. One of the reasons why newly industrializing countries (NICs) were successful in exploiting the advantages of global integration was due to its understanding of the strategic characteristics of information technologies. In countries such as Singapore, Taiwan and Korea, the informatics industry led the growth and technological transformation of the entire economy. Information technology not only bears on the extent of global integration but it also influences the form of competition taking place within the system. There has been a shift from the focus on low-cost production to a need to produce high-quality products at attractive prices together with timeliness of service, continuous innovation and flexibility (McMichael, 2008). This new system can be illustrated by the clothing and textile industry, such as the case of Liz Claiborne's international network that links clothing factories in countries spanning the globe, such as China, Hong Kong, Korea, the Philippines, Singapore and Taiwan, through an electronic document interchange (EDI) system connected to its headquarters in New York. Thus, we can observe that participation in the global market is to a great extent predicated on the availability of information technology, and it is a significant driving force behind the globalization of production.

TNCs play a major role in the labor relations of Third World industrialization. One of their defining characteristics is their move toward "vertical integration and contracting their production to third-party manufacturers, which may likely turn over these work assignments to other subcontractors" (Klein, 1999: 198). At each stage toward the bottom of the production hierarchy, wages get lowered. The sale of these "contracts" by the TNCs is a significant attribute that gave rise to the World Factory. The drive toward capital accumulation means that these corporations are quick to flee escalating wages, taxes and environmental regulations. Klein terms these "migrant factories", citing countries such as "China, Indonesia, India and the Philippines where the threat of plant closure and job flight are more pronounced" (1999: 224). The temporal nature of these TNCs has a significant impact on labor relations. For instance, in 1985, Reebok produced almost all their sneakers in South Korea and Taiwan. However, when they were faced with strikes in those countries, the factories took flight; by 1995, 60 percent of Reebok's contracts had taken root in Indonesia and China, thereby changing the labor force behind the manufacture of their products (Klein, 1999). As we will see below, women workers that dominate World Factories, EPZs and other sweatshops are caught between exploitation and survival.

Labor patterns and practices

Female share in total manufacturing employment in EPZs worldwide has always been largely disparate compared to their male counterparts. In the 1980s, women aged 17–25 predominated with an 80 percent representation of the total EPZ labor workforce (McMichael, 2008). In Bangladesh, female share of employment rose from 39.3 percent in 2003 to 64 percent in just a matter of half a decade (Murayama and Nobuko, 2009). Women were regarded to be better equipped in handling manufacturing jobs due to their perceived "natural patience" and "manual dexterity" (McMichael, 2008). While it can be argued that EPZs have constructed a platform enabling women to be engaged in formal employment and earn higher salaries than in agricultural industries and domestic services, it is also important to consider the detrimental effects EPZs have inflicted upon women.

In EPZs, women are exposed to glaring discrimination and inequality with respect to employment rights and civil liberties. Most employers do not practice equal remuneration, and wages are fixed according to gender-related barriers. Women are typically paid wages up to 20 percent lower than male workers, in spite of working the same number of long hours and overtime (Waters, 2013). Furthermore, men are widely preferred for career development opportunities and job training, relegating women to their stagnant positions in cheap, low-skilled labor work. Women in EPZs are also subjected to discrimination and lack of accommodation as a result of pregnancy. Compulsory pregnancy tests are required for women during a job application, and routine checks are made throughout their period of employment (Murayama and Nobuko, 2009). They are denied work and may be automatically retrenched if found pregnant. In certain cases, pregnant women are exposed to even more dangerous and hazardous working conditions, such as having to transfer heavy loads and work in poorly ventilated areas, to compel them to resign, thus allowing their employers to avoid paying for maternity leave (Smith, 2013).

Closed off from the rest of the world, a separate set of rules and regulations may apply in EPZs, enabling extensive manipulation and exploitation of the labor workforce. As established earlier, EPZs operate on a quid pro quo basis; hence, Third World countries must ensure that they offer substantial incentives in order to attract foreign investors. Investors constantly relocate their businesses in search for cheaper labor and better economic policies. Thus, Third World countries constantly compete among one another to offer the most favorable economic, political and social climate, which allows manufacturers to save considerable amount of costs and accumulate the maximum level of profits for their products. This intense competition among Third World countries is commonly referred to as the "race to the bottom". The amount of savings obtained may be highly significant; it has been reported that companies may glean up to US$20 million in just income-tax savings alone (Waters, 2013). However, in order to ensure such financial benefits, incentives provided by host governments may render corporate accountability unattainable and stimulate widespread labor abuse and discrimination. It has been asserted that labor workforce in EPZs are subjected to "super-exploitation", where they are expected to keep up with a labor intensity beyond normal human physical and mental capacity, as well as eke out a living based on wages below the level of physical subsistence (Murayama and Nobuko, 2009).

Wage prices of workers may be curtailed regularly in order to retain a degree of competitiveness and attractiveness for foreign investors. Workers in Honduras and Mexico survive on meager wages as low as approximately US$3 daily while being exposed to deplorable and dangerous working conditions (McCallum, 2011). Furthermore, they may also be forced to work overtime for up to 20 hours a day to meet demands of rush orders and shipping deadlines (McMichael, 2008). In Honduras, 70 percent of its workforce is reported to be suffering from lower back complications and respiratory ailments due to rigid and inflexible working positions in stifling and suffocating halls (McCallum, 2011). Exposure to such dire and distressing conditions over long periods, in turn, affects the health and productivity of workers over time. This is exemplified by the average career period of only five years and the high turnover rate among zone workers who are swiftly swapped for younger, more able-bodied individuals as their well-being deteriorates (International Labor Office, 2003).

There is also a general agreement that employers lack both the resources and desire to ensure that the civil rights of workers are accorded to them (McCallum, 2011). In Honduras, employment laws applied to EPZs are remarkably lax and negligent compared to those in non-EPZs. Even when there are labor legislations, responsible enforcement and implementation of such laws are rarely maintained by the government. Local state elites may be unlikely to administer pro-labor regulatory practices due to fear of capital withdrawal (McCallum, 2011). Furthermore, some EPZs in Mexico have also banned the creation of workers' organizations and trade unions, as union-free zones are more widely preferred by foreign investors (International Labor Office, 2003). Hence, workers are prohibited from their right to strike, freedom of association or collective bargaining for more favorable working environments and higher wages (Engman, Onodera and Pinali, 2007). To discourage unionization, some employers have resorted to unfairly retrenching, suspending and blacklisting members of trade unions (McCallum, 2011). Thus, most impoverished workers have no choice but to succumb to being exploited in order to attain some livelihood for their families.

Here, we will delineate our empirical findings of the labor patterns and practices in the readymade garments industry in Bangladesh, focusing on capability for work and capability for voice – two central ingredients of the capability approach to social justice.

Capability for work

In our study in the Bangladesh RMG industry, the capability for work is assessed based on wages and working hours, occupational health and safety, access to maternity leave and childcare benefits, and other structural factors and barriers affecting this freedom.

Wages and working hours: The most important factor that determines the well-being of the workers is wage. According to international standards, workers are entitled to living wages. In explaining the purpose of living wages, the Los Angeles Living Wage Ordinance, for instance, recommends "to establish an hourly wage that, on a full time basis, would provide [a] worker with sufficient income to support a family of four above the federal poverty line" (Fairiss, 2007: 2). The RMG industry in Bangladesh is unfortunately the lowest-wage-paid sector in the world (Muhammad, 2011). The study shows that the minimum wage of the workers is "absolutely insufficient" for subsistence. To quote one worker, "As a machine operator, I earn 4800 to 5000 taka [US$60–65] per month. This is not sufficient to run our family. With my husband's income, our monthly income does not go over 10,000 taka [US$125]. After paying our house rent, we're unable to bear all other expenses". While wages in different factories may vary, our findings show almost similar trajectory where a worker is not paid enough to even support herself let alone her family of four or more.

Since workers' wages are too insufficient to cover their daily costs, they are often forced to do overtime work, leading to long working hours, which has other serious negative consequences to their lives. Most workers leave their homes early in the morning and return home at midnight. After returning home, they cannot avoid the usual household chores such as preparing food for their family with an intense pressure and anxiety of having to get up for the next day's work. Workers with young children are "deeply concerned", "too worried", "awfully frustrated" and "extremely sorry" – to quote some of their expressions – for not being able to spend time with their children. With no proper childcare facilities in their villages and slums, the younger children are usually left with the older ones. In spite of severe hardships, the compensation for overtime work is often below the minimum. Many workers, during their interviews with us, complained that their work hours are not counted properly, leading to many hours of unpaid work.

Occupational health and safety: Working conditions of most factories, as observed and alluded to by the workers, are unfavorable and unhygienic, which has adverse effects on labor productivity in the long term. During our factory visits, it was found that the factories were overcrowded with little or no space for the workers to stand upright. All of the sampled factories, irrespective of size and location, were hot and dusty because a long array of activities, including sewing, cutting, and ironing, are all done on the same floor. In addition to poor working conditions, poor living conditions also contribute to the workers' ill health. Along with other studies (Paul-Majumder and Begum, 2006; Muhammad, 2011), we found that the workers suffer from malnutrition and ill health caused by overwork, and a suffocating and clumsy work environment. As reported, they are inflicted with various kinds of health hazards, such as skin problems, headaches, gastric ailments, back pain and fatigue (see also Khatun et al., 2008). According to the view of the workers, employers place "little attention" on working environment and health safety but "strong attention" on their work. According to a worker:

> If you suddenly visit our factory, you will see how we work there. Although the work floor is equipped with lights and fans, it is always too hot and overcrowded. The emergency exit room is too narrow, just as a show case. During the visit of buyers, all floors are kept neat and clean; toilets are equipped with towels and soaps. Unfortunately all are taken away as soon as they leave the factory. If we ask for soap or towels, our bosses will be furious to us and will say, "Have you ever seen these items at your home throughout your life?" What is important to them is our work, and not our lives.

Due to poor working conditions, lack of safety measures and ill health of the workers, accidents and deaths are common. Two recent tragic accidents in Dhaka that caused the deaths of over 1000 workers highlighted the hazardous and insecure work environment in the Bangladesh RMG industry. The first incident was a fatal fire at Tazreen Fashions, which led to the deaths of at least 112 workers in October 2012 (Theuws et al., 2013), while the second was a factory building collapse at Savar (near Dhaka) on April 24, 2013, killing at least 1127 workers, making it the deadliest factory disaster in RMG history (Greenhouse, 2013). We will examine these further in Chapter 8.

Access to maternity and childcare benefits: The Maternity Protection Convention of 2000 (No. 183) states that on production of a medical certificate stating the presumed date of childbirth, a woman shall be entitled to a period of maternity leave of not less than 14 weeks (ILO, 2000). Following this convention and recommendation, Bangladesh Labor Law (2006) adopted 16 weeks of maternity leave with full employment benefits. Unfortunately, very few workers can actually enjoy these maternity benefits. Workers' testimonies appear to support previous research claims that despite having a legal provision in place, workers have little or no access to maternity leave in most factories in Bangladesh (Absar, 2001; Paul-Majumder and Begum, 2000).

One most persistent problem reported by workers is that of having to care for their children during work hours. Although there is a legal provision for child care, very few factories actually have it. Among the factories visited, only two were found to have childcare rooms. Notwithstanding the availability, the conditions of these rooms are not even suitable for children's health. Working mothers are reluctant to bring their children there. They bring their children only when they cannot find any alternative arrangements. All workers interviewed expressed their dissatisfaction for the childcare facilities. The childcare rooms – although poor and unhealthy – have, however, some strict regulations. A working mother, for instance, revealed: "Although there is a baby care center, children below two years are not allowed. As a result, workers have their close relatives take care of their infants. If anyone does not find alternatives to child care, she leaves her job."

Both physical dexterity and maternity play a critical role in determining employability. Young girls with good physiques are usually preferred, as reported by the workers, and mothers with infants are often refused employment. Therefore, many young married women are in a constant struggle between keeping their jobs and having children. This dilemma between the economic and reproductive roles of young women often ends up in a one-way exit, causing sometimes severe psychological stress. A young married woman expressed her anxiety as follows:

> After three years of marriage, I still have no child. I aspire to have a child, but I am afraid of losing my job. There is a greater possibility to get fired during my pregnancy. No one likes to employ pregnant women because it may hamper the production. And even if I have a baby, I will not be able to keep my [baby] in daycare center because it is too costly. So, who will take care of the baby if I continue factory work?

In many cases, working women resume work, leaving the children behind in the care of their grandparents or other family members in the slums and villages. The main cause for not bringing their children with them is their low income. They are unable to afford education for their children in the urban areas.

Arbitrary punishment and workplace harassment: Coercive and punishment-oriented disciplinary techniques are employed inside the factories to ensure labor productivity. This study has found evidence of hard and rude behavior from middle management toward the workers. The management justified the strict and hard rules as inevitable and necessary for disciplining women workers. All interviewees expressed their dissatisfaction at being physically molested or verbally abused by senior staff (supervisor, line chief, production manager) with abusive words or physical assault as punishment. Sexual harassment was echoed by a female worker in the following way:

> If any worker makes a mistake or becomes unable to fulfill the quota, bosses misbehave with her. Many of them use very abusive words. This harassment [does] not always happen for the failure of achieving target but for their bad intention. Bosses (line chief, supervisor) very often come and stand beside us. Within a moment, they mildly touch our neck and shoulder and blow their hands on our back. Male bosses touch the body of female workers persuaded by sexual intention. This is more frequent for relatively beautiful and smart workers.

When asked about the harsh discipline in factories, middle management staff members did not directly refute the claims made against them but justified their actions. One of them said, "Workers do not feel any obligation for their tasks until they receive pressure from the bosses". On touching workers' bodies, they argued that workers are treated as sisters or daughters. "By blowing hands in their back, staffs show their love and care and encourage them for better performance", argued one management staff. "No ill motives persist there", he added. Differing from this view, a female union organizer said, "the touching of a female body is not simply a matter of love and care, but males fulfill their bad intentions and feel enjoyment". The most severe form of harassment in the workplace is rape. Although not common or open, women workers risk being raped by coworkers or senior bosses. Very often it remained undisclosed due to fear of possible economic (e.g., job loss) and social (humiliation) sanctions (see also Siddiqi, 2000). Sexual harassment of women workers also occurs on the streets, to and from work. Young or not so young, married or unmarried, pretty or not so pretty, smart or not so smart – all women shared their fear of being molested.

Forced and compulsory labor: The fundamental right of freedom from forced labor is not well protected in the Bangladesh RMG industry. Overtime work is mandatory for all workers. Entry and exit of workers is allowed only during the opening and closing hours of the factory as determined by the management. The main entrance of the factory is always kept locked and controlled by security personnel (see also Danneker, 2002; Muhammad, 2011). Although workers have the freedom to move to other higher-paid factories, they usually cannot do so since they get their wages in the second or third week of the month. If any worker wants to move to another factory, she has to move without salary. This delayed payment, a tactic of employers, hinders occupational movement, as disclosed by a female worker during a focus group discussion:

> If I switch over to another factory, I have to lose salary for seven to fifteen days, or even for a month. We can claim our dues provided that [a] resignation letter is submitted at least 30 days in advance with the clearance from the line chief, supervisor and production manager and approved by the final authority. It is very difficult for us to get clearance from different persons by proving satisfactory explanation for resignation. Moreover, there is no certainty of getting a job after one month. Thus, we do not take the decision to leave unless an unusual event tremendously forces us to do so.

Persisting workplace discrimination: Although there is no direct discrimination in wages, gender and other indirect discrimination persists. Women workers are segregated in some sections, particularly in sewing, which are low-paid as compared to other sections such as cutting and ironing. This phenomenon, known as the "feminization of workforce" (Islam, 2008; Standing, 1999), is justified by some gender-biased beliefs of women having nimble fingers, and that they are more calm and patient. Employers, who are all males, argue that women are more efficient and experienced in sewing. Challenging this view, workers revealed that no one had prior experience before entering this sector; it is the employer who decides where to place a new entrant. Usually, female entrants are recruited as helpers in the sewing section where they achieve their skills in sewing and remain in that section throughout their working lives.

Capability for voice

In the case of workers in global production enterprises, the capability for voice asks to what extent workers are able to participate in the collective decision-making process. The capability for voice adequately equips the worker to achieve processional freedom of exit or voice, among the three alternatives of workers' responses against injustices (Hirschmann, 1970). It is the key component of job quality. Capability of voice provides a space for the workers to transform the resources that expand the opportunities for valuable work. The four main conditions of capability for voice (Bonvin, 2012) have been discussed, as follows.

Availability of political resources: The issue of political resources encompasses the workers' ability to constitute a collective body or build strategic alliances. It is also a process of recognition of workers' association or trade union legitimacy. The field data shows that there is no viable existence of workers' unions at the factory level. Workers cannot form or participate in any associations or organizations due to the fear of losing their jobs[1] (see also Danneker, 2002). During our focus group discussions, a woman worker reported,

> We never try to form associations inside the factory because our employers do not like it. They don't allow us to form any association. If anyone takes initiative to organize workers inside the factory, employers will take immediate action to discharge him or her from the job.

While there are no unions at the factory level, some unions are active at sector level and there are some federations both at the sector and national level. These unions, however, cannot impose any effective pressure onto the employers in order to protect labor rights. Unions lack sufficient power and efficiency to negotiate with employers, and union leaders are seen to be concerned about their own narrow interests rather than the interests of the community. Some corrupt practices of certain union/worker leaders have also contributed to a loss of credibility and decline of the strengths of the unions (see also Muhammad, 2011; Khan, 2004; Clarke and Pringle, 2009). Similar to other studies (Taher, 1999; Absar, 2012), we found that political affiliation of the unions is the main obstacle to upholding the workers' interest. Employers are often antagonistic and are unwilling to negotiate with union leaders. Unequal power relations play a vital role.[2]

Availability of cognitive resources: The ability of workers and their representatives to produce their own information and descriptions is a key tool of capability for voice (Bonvin, 2012). If workers at the firm level are not competent enough to press their demands and to express their views about "valuable work" efficiently, they should resort to their representatives. Unfortunately, workers have not found any leadership for their representation on the negotiation table. Due to the absence of trade unions inside the factory, efficient leadership has not been developed. In many cases, the so-called workers' leaders do not belong to a particular group; rather, they represent the workers as an outsider and are very often motivated for their own vested interests. Corrupt practices and unethical roles of leaders are often reported by the workers. At the same time, employers are not inclined to arrange any training programs to increase labor power.

Available entitlements: Local labour laws of Bangladesh, both 'Labour law 2006' and 'EPZ workers welfare association and industrial relations act 2010' have given the right of collective bargaining and other labour benefits but in practice workers' can't claim these legitimate benefits and entitlements. Legal guarantee and enforcement of mechanisms such as the right to strike may significantly contribute to a more balanced power relationship within a firm. For lack of collective bargaining and efficient leadership, the labor benefits and entitlements are at the minimum level. The workers cannot force the employer to comply with the legitimate entitlements and their enforcement. Formulation of a good labor law and its implementation is a prerequisite to this end. However, still we are unable to enact a labor-friendly law. The main barrier comes from the industrialists. A significant number of industrialists are the legislative members who influence the government from enacting or enforcing a new labor law.

Weak or no enforcement of labor law is also responsible for the low standards of labor rights in the factories. Union leaders and labor scholars strongly believe that if an enforcement mechanism of labor law is strengthened, labor rights would be improved significantly. Workers and union leaders claim that the industrial police very often work in favor of employers. Employers use this force to suppress workers' voices. Union organizers also reported that monitoring and inspection by the concerned authority is very weak and corrupt. They think that for ineffective inspection, the key responsibility lies with the corrupt and inefficient personnel. A union organizer said:

> Owners of the factories have good linkages with the ruling political parties that influence the concerned persons [in the government agencies] to release the NOC [no objection certificate], although they do not comply with the rules and regulations for establishing and running a factory. Corrupt practices of the government officials in the form of, for instance, bribes are also responsible for issuing NOCs without proper inspection.

Readiness of interlocutors: Any process concerning the definition of "valuable work" involves a collective decision of different stakeholders such as employers, shareholders or other corporation members engaged in the global chain of production. The workers' well-being is dependent on goodwill and the legal framework and duties (voluntary or compelled) imposed on employers. It is evident that employers' reluctance to listen to the concerns expressed by workers is a great barrier to the path of transforming into "valuable work". Employers and shareholders do not want to sit together with the workers, and the decisions are taken unilaterally by employers. Employers strategically keep workers from joining any trade union, since an organized workforce may potentially induce more pressure on the owners to execute their demands. In case of a potential association or union, punishments and panic are common methods used by employers, as echoed by a union organizer:

> In the absence of workers' unions or associations, owners can easily ignore the rights of individual workers. Thus owners always follow ways so as to make sure that workers are not organized. By firing the organizers, employers often create panic among the workers, thus refraining general workers from joining any association.

Employers' association can undertake many welfare schemes for the welfare of the workers, including raising wages and other labor benefits. In practice, however, they try to make a consistent effort to keep the production cost down by paying the minimum below the subsistence level (see also Yan and Weiqing, 2006; So, 2010). Employers try to justify it by arguing that, to quote one, "it is very difficult to survive in the competitive market by paying higher wages and other labor benefits if global buyers do not take any responsibility". During interviews, it was reported that employers take an oppressive stand against workers' unions. Some employers lodge false cases against union organizers, which often leads to jail, torture or even being murdered. A recent killing of labor activist Aminul Islam, who was arrested and tortured by law enforcement a few years ago for his role in organizing a protest against low wages in the Bangladeshi RMG industry, demonstrates a gloomy picture of workers' oppression in Bangladesh (Manik and Bajaj, 2012).

MNCs can play a vital role in addressing the structural injustices prevalent in the production segments of the global commodity chain (Yong, 2006). Pressures from trade unions, NGOs and consumer groups have led MNCs to develop their own "code of conduct" and a variety of mechanisms aimed at enforcing labor rights at their supplier plants (Bulut and Lane, 2011; Locke et al., 2007; Schrage, 2004; Mamic, 2004). For this aim, buyers and/or global suppliers have identified some key issues combining core conventions of ILO and local labor laws that are recognized as buyers' "code of conduct" (Kaufman et al., 2004). MNCs deploy a monitoring system at their supplier plants to inspect the "code of conduct" either by themselves or by a third party, such as NGOs or labor groups. Leading MNCs, such as Walmart, Nike, Reebok, Levi Strauss, Disney, Li & Fung, Sears, Hallmark, GAP, Hasbro and Tommy, and Haines & Martinez, have offices or full-time compliance officers to monitor labor rights, workplace safety and environmental protection. If producers fail to comply with their codes of conduct, the contract of buying products may be canceled or discontinued. One representative from Tesco, a brand-name company buying clothes from Bangladesh, reported: "We regularly inspect codes of conduct at the factory. If the producers do not follow the codes of conduct, we refuse their products and do not make any further contact with them".

Despite making some positive changes in labor rights, the role of multinationals and compliance monitoring is not beyond criticism. Our study shows that buyers' monitoring is not sufficient. Similar to other global factories around the world, the effectiveness of factory inspections still remains a subject with considerable debates. During focus group discussions, one worker expressed her view in this way:

> We do not get any opportunity to talk to the buyers. When buyers want to speak with workers, they directly come to the manager's office and management calls its preferred workers. If we fortunately get any chance to be here, we can't tell them the truth as we are afraid of losing our job. If we tell them our real picture, certainly we will [be fired].

Although the representatives from brand companies and local buying houses place considerable emphasis on ethical business, they are also subjected to criticisms. A remark made by a commercial manager, for instance, shows a surprising note to this issue: "Buyers monitor code of conduct for their own interests. Finding any fault in the product may induce pressure on the producers to sell the product with a half price of the original contract".

Conclusion

The study shows that the Bangladesh RMG industry apparently practices unjust labor conditions. Workers' rights and labor benefits are not in line with international standards. Workers – women, in particular – accept these exploitative labor conditions due to the lack of other opportunities and an abundance of cheap labor. These local dynamics certainly provide the local capitalist state and the global buyers a "comparative advantage" but at the cost of "women's disadvantage." Despite hyperexploitation, most workers consider the RMG industry an "exit point" to enter the public spaces from their confined space at home, providing a possibility to become self-reliant.

Despite bizarre and precarious labor conditions in Bangladesh, the study shows that labor rights in Bangladesh are increasingly influenced by the role of transnational actors. International and local NGOs can play important roles for improving the labor rights situation in Bangladesh through organizing workers and networking with corporate buyers and human rights organizations. For instance, Bangladesh Independent Garment Workers Union Federation (BIGUF) supported by American Center for International Labor Solidarity and *Karmajibi Nari* (KN) (organizing workers), Change Associate (health awareness), *Ain O Salish Kendra* (legal aid), Bangladesh Legal Aid and Services Trust (legal aid), *Odikar* (documentation, fact finding, training and advocacy) and *Nari Uddog Kendra* (low-cost accommodation) are working to improve the labor justice. One structural barrier in enhancing labor justice is the workers themselves: RMG workers are mostly comprised of rural poor women who are mostly illiterate and unaware of their rights. "Capabilities to function" (Sen, 2009) is therefore a vital element in ensuring broader labor justice that includes, for example, creating awareness among the workers, employers, and civil society through individual contact, organizing workers' conventions, seminars and even mass processions. Deployment of the "codes of conduct" may not work well unless there is awareness and structural arrangements at the grassroots level.

Consumers, on the other hand, can also play a pivotal role in enhancing labor justice. All union leaders, labor experts and labor welfare officers in the factory interviewed for this study think that consumer pressure upon MNCs through boycott and movements against unjust labor practices can have a significant contribution on the improvement of labor rights in the local supply chains; although it may also exacerbate the labor conditions in cases where global buyers stop buying commodities. After the factory building collapse in Bangladesh, agitated consumers chanted slogans in front of retail shops carrying a placard: "No clothes with blood". As a result, US retailers, such as GAP, JCPenny, Sears, Target and Walmart, announced a "new plan" for safety at garment factories (Greenhouse, 2013). Therefore, consumer pressure as well as citizens' movements can be an effective instrument to persuade the MNCs to act as responsible agents.

6
Globalizing Food and a Tale of Two Revolutions: Labor, Gender and the Environment

with Iris Carla De Jesus

Introduction

The process of local and regional integration into global markets was intensified during a time known as the "first green revolution", characterized by a technical package of bioengineered hybrid seeds requiring chemical and mechanical inputs, designed to improve agricultural productivity in basic grains such as wheat, maize and rice. Gradually, the green revolution technology was extended from basic to luxury foods, known as "high-value foods" (HVFs). This extension has been called the "second green revolution" (McMichael, 2008). Like the green revolution of the 1960s, the global aquaculture sector embraced a similar shift, known as the "blue revolution". It aimed at increasing global aquatic production in order to stave off widespread hunger in the tropical nations. By 1985, the World Bank, the Asian Development Bank and a variety of other international aid agencies were pouring $200 million a year into aquaculture projects. Mangrove forests in the Philippines, Thailand, Bangladesh and Ecuador were chopped down to make way for shrimp ponds. Carp and tilapia farms were staked out on the flood plains of the Ganges, the Irrawaddy and the Mekong rivers. As a result, the production of pond-raised fish has boomed. While the blue revolution was driven and accelerated by neoliberalism to quench the appetite of wealthy consumers in the North, it came with a price. The current blue revolution has been characterized by many writers as a transformation of agrarian landscape in the South to large farms in the hands of the few, ecological devastation, displacement of rural subsistence farmers, rural tensions and violence, peasants' movements and resistance, exploitative labor relations and so forth (Islam, 2014). This chapter will examine these revolutions that significantly shape the globalization of production and their roles/power in transforming both ecological and social landscapes in the global South, focusing on labor, gender and the environment.

The green revolution: boon or bane?

Mankind's inevitable coexistence with science and technology owes much to the fact of food problems that have haunted our world since time immemorial. Science and its associative agricultural technology are solutions applied to these problems in the hope of reducing massive poverty and strengthening food security that, until today, predominantly plagued the global South. U.S. Agency for International Development (USAID) Administrator William S. Gaud has termed this phenomenon the "green revolution" (IFPRI, 2002), which was supposed to improve the farming processes that produce the food we eat. The first investments were on rice and wheat, and the initial goal of the green revolution was to breed improved varieties of these in conjunction with an expanded use of fertilizers and other chemical inputs, aided by systems of irrigation, to decrease the farmers' dependency on today's erratic weather patterns. New varieties were developed to be more responsive to nutrients and had shorter, stiffer straws to support the weight of the subsequent heavier heads of grain. Another variation was quick maturing varieties that could grow regardless of the season, hence, allowing the farmer to grow more crops annually on the same land. These new varieties were also more resistant to pests and diseases and retained desirable cooking and consumption traits. Asian countries such as the Philippines, Thailand and India soon adapted to this new knowledge and technology. Moreover, high-yielding varieties (HYVs) have also been developed for major food crops that suit the cultural diet and taste of Asian and other developing countries (ibid.). Institutions have since been built to focus on the research and development of food crops to strengthen their resilience.

The fundamental aim of the green revolution was to improve farmer productivity through a faster rate of output growth than input use. Many scholars have agreed that agriculture and the industry play a key role in poverty reduction. According to the Food and Agriculture Organization of the United Nations, households in the lowest expenditure categories still derive a large share of their total income from agriculture, and the lowered production costs per ton of grain led to an outward shift of the supply curve, thereby lowering food prices. Furthermore, a productivity-induced agricultural expansion can "pull" other sectors with it and increase economic activity and employment opportunities in rural areas (FAO, 2008). To elaborate, the increased standards of living of farmers provided them more disposable income that stimulates the non-farm economy by their consumption of non-farm products such as retail goods. In turn, the non-farm economy grew and created job opportunities for many. Hence, it suggests that more attention and resource allocation is needed by the agriculture sector for the long term.

Since the advent of the green revolution, about 20 percent of the wheat area and 30 percent of the rice area in developing countries were planted with HYVs, and by 1990, this share had increased by 70 percent for both crops (IFPRI, 2002). This means that even though the world's population had increased by 60 percent, cereal and calorie availability per person increased by nearly 30 percent in comparison. Technological innovations due to the green revolution have also benefitted many farmers – there is an average 2.3 percent annual growth rate of agricultural area equipped for irrigation in Southeast Asia alone, and 1.2 percent in South and Southwest Asia (FAO, 2011: 35). In South and Southwest Asia, the average percentage of irrigated land as a proportion of agricultural land had increased from 40.5 percent in 1999 to 45.9 percent in 2009 (2011: 36). Studies done by the IFPRI have shown that the green revolution increased returns for farmers, as they were able to grow more crops per year. Hence, this had raised their standards of living, leading to a steady decline in poverty in the global South.

The green revolution did not prove to be beneficial for all though. Sociologists believe that the green revolution disguises itself in the name of industrial and economic development to hide neocolonialism that shrouds the reality of the development of many Third World or ex-colonial countries. First, with the advent of the green revolution, the United States saw the need to dispose of agricultural surpluses in the form of economic "food aid" to developing nations with a view of improving diplomatic and foreign relations under the Public Law 480 Program (McMichael, 2008). Second, this in turn created food dependency among Third World nations, as cheap – almost free – food such as wheat was imported to urban cities, supporting the growth of government industrial plans. Hence, the issue of food security was ignored by Third World nations in the name of development, resulting in the displacement of small-scale farmers from their trade while these societies saw the collapse of their agricultural sector. We have to take into consideration that these imported food surpluses from the US were not the best quality either. Third, the rise in demand for petro-farming (industrialization of agriculture) undermines nature's intrinsic qualities over time and in the process, intensive agriculture annually loses 2 million acres of farm land to soil erosion, soil salinity and flooding (Islam, 2013; McMichael, 2014).

The development project that fueled the need for industrialization of many agricultural countries led to major changes in the rural economy. Farmers adopted monoculturalism by producing one type of profitable crop in large numbers, with the help of new technologies and unnatural agricultural inputs to hasten crop growth. Guha (2000) argued that the demands of cities and factories for materials to process and consume led to this transformation of agriculture through the adoption of more capital-intensive, market-oriented methods of production. Simply put, monoculturalism led to diminishing agricultural biodiversity. In the name of economism, what was once a staple is no longer being grown. Similarly, the growing demand for biofuels as an alternative energy source displays another form of monoculturalism. Instead of rice paddies and fruit trees, land is largely being used to grow inedible cash crops such as oil palm trees and *Jatropha*. White (2010) asserted that a Norwegian agro-fuel company took advantage of Ghana's traditional system of communal land ownership in an attempt to claim and deforest large hectares of land intended for planting the largest *Jatropha* plantation in the world. Many scholars and capitalists at the time had argued that biofuels were a good alternative to fossil fuels and that they decreased the need for the latter and prevented natural resource depletion. In actual fact, recent studies suggest that agro-fuels might actually have a greater aggregate environmental cost than fossil fuels and yield less energy than they consume in production. Although the demand for biofuels is fundamentally not a direct consequence of the green revolution, and being driven by an increase in oil prices, the technological advancements for the green revolution are being used to efficiently conduct biofuel production. Another consequence of the green revolution is environmental degradation. Rachel Carson's book, *Silent Spring*, ushered a public awareness of the harsh consequences of new technologies and innovations on farming activities done to the American environment. It is dubbed the "founding event" of modern environmentalism (McMichael, 2008). The book concluded that the green revolution might not necessarily be good for us or our environment. It portrayed the harsh realities of the use of chemicals as fertilizers and the pesticide pollution that invaded farms and neighborhoods. In addition, many farmers were displaced or forced out of the industry to look for odd jobs that required no qualification in the cities because they could not afford the new technologies invented by capitalists, while those who could afford them remained competitive in the global market.

What better way to discuss the harmful effects of the green revolution than through a documentary that captures real life experiences of farmers? *The Future of Food* (Garcia, 2004) depicts the industrialization of food production and agriculture in the United States. It portrays multinational companies, such as Monsanto, as using the green revolution as a tool to proliferate the agricultural industry, and the political scene, to increase profits. The green revolution was intended as a saving grace for organic farmers, but due to the base nature of greed, companies like Monsanto, possessing vast resources, appropriated technologies that would have otherwise helped the farming community. Although genetically modified (GM) seeds may seem beneficial in the way that they increase food production and increase resilience to harsh conditions, not many organic farmers can afford them. Furthermore, these seeds need vast amounts of pesticides for sustenance, which in turn deteriorates the environment due to excessive use. In addition, large MNCs like Monsanto utilize their political power to patent their seeds and many other entities. Hence, this led to the demise of many organic farmers who faced multiple lawsuits against them.

The discussion of the negative consequences of the green revolution abounds in literature, scholarly debates, and conferences and forums. However, we cannot ignore the positive effects it has on our world's food security because it is re-revolutionizing itself once more to adapt to the changing demands of consumers and the persistent problem of food insecurity. Currently, the estimated number of undernourished people in the world is 1.02 billion and it was expected to decline by 9.6 percent. In 2010, it did decline but only to 925 million; Asia and the Pacific alone accounted for 578 million (FAO, 2010). Empirical evidence shows that the success of technological advancements and know-how from the green revolution is being carried on to a relatively new phenomenon that is realized through the efficient production of seafood to meet consumer demands. The next section of this chapter will discuss the factors for decreasing demand of staple foods such as rice and increasing demand for high-value foods like salmon, tuna, shrimp and red meat.

The world's consumption trend

As agricultural systems are increasingly linked to global commodity networks and generate complex intersections (Islam, 2008), farmers become increasingly aware of the changing diets of consumers, especially those from developed countries, and are compelled to switch to the production of high-value foods to meet global market demands. High-value food or agricultural product is defined as agricultural goods with a high economic value per kilogram, per hectare or per calories, including fruits, vegetables, meat, eggs, milk and fish (Gulati et al., 2005). This transformation has been called a "silent revolution". Gulati et al. (2005) argued that the causal factors of the green revolution and the "silent revolution" are quite different even though both represent a change in the patterns of agricultural production. The former was driven by technological innovation while the latter was driven by shifts in international and domestic consumer demands. It is important to know this difference in order to conceptualize the factors that have given rise to the increasing demand for HVFs. Gulati et al. (2005), in a comprehensive study that was presented to the World Bank in 2005 called "Growth in High-Value Agriculture in Asia and the Emergence of Vertical Links with Farmers", explicated four factors for the increasing demand of high-value foods in Asia. The first factor is income growth. As incomes rise, the state of expenditure allocated to food tends to decline. In other words, the budget allocated for food declines from over 65 percent in the least-developed countries to less than 10 percent in most industrialized countries (Gulati et al., 2005: 3). Furthermore, the majority of this decreased budget for food is increasingly allocated to relatively more expensive sources of calories such as meat, fish, eggs and vegetables. It is also asserted that income growth is a key factor to people's changing diets. The second factor is demographic factors like urbanization and population growth. In India, the urban population has increased from 15 percent of the total population in 1980 to 26 percent in 2002, whereas in the Philippines, urban population has increased by 23 percent in 2002. Gulati et al. (2005) stated that urbanization does indeed affect food consumption even though this connection is not well documented. However, studies by Huang and David (1983) have shown that urbanization is associated with lower rice demand in India after controlling the variables of income and food prices. The third factor is outward-looking trade policies. Policies to promote trade, including lower tariff barriers, market-determined exchange rates, and deregulation of international trade, have created opportunities for developing countries to export agricultural commodities to high-income countries and other developing countries. Gulati et al. (2005) noted that through trade liberalization, it is advantageous for farmers to be more exposed to trade competition and the global market. However, some farmers who lack the resources may likely be ostracized from high-commodity agricultural trading in the global market. In addition, this exposure compels farmers to shift production from staple crops to high-value agricultural commodities, thereby neglecting their local rural diet, which heightens food insecurity within their region. The fourth and final factor that Gulati et al. (2005) introduced is foreign direct investments (FDIs). FDIs promote the growth of high-value agricultural commodities by linking farmers in developing countries with high-value export markets, thereby creating a new market high-value agricultural commodities by preserving perishable goods and supplying them to high-income markets; and by utilizing foreign expertise and the scale of operations to reduce market margins in the processing and/or retail sector. The World Health Organization (WHO) has also voiced similar trends when explaining the increasing demand for the consumption of HVFs. The WHO asserted that the increasing pressure on the livestock sector is due to urbanization as it stimulates improvements in infrastructure including cold chains, which permit trade in perishable goods (WHO, 2012).

In terms of dietary patterns of fish, average consumption of fish declined in developed countries from an average per capita consumption of 24.3 kg per year in 1985 to 21.7 kg per year in 1997. This may be attributed to the fact that human population growth had been stagnating in developed countries, and hence it led to stagnated fish consumption in the North. Interestingly, income growth in developed countries led to more people preferring to consume high-priced fish-based calories such as salmon, bluefin tuna and cod, as compared to the cheaper fish-based calories like tilapia (Delgado et al., 2003: 5). This change in preference has led to a 13.4 percent growth rate of high-value finfish aquaculture – a majority of which are salmon and bluefin tuna – from 1985 to 1997, while low-value finfish only saw a growth rate of 10.9 percent. Crustaceans such as shrimp are increasingly becoming popular among Northerners, with a growth rate of 13.3 percent between the same years (ibid.: 19). This growth trend continued until today and has caught the attention of many scholars, therefore dubbing this new phenomenon the "blue revolution".

The implication of this new consumer trend is phenomenal. The modes, means and relations of production have changed tremendously, partly also due to globalization and the advancement in science and technology. What was once a local production to feed local diets has now become a global agro-food production to meet consumer demands in the North. The next section focuses on the aftermath of this changing trend and the birth of a new revolution that has affected local food production in the global South. Several case studies, such as tilapia farming in the Philippines and shrimp cultivation and production in Bangladesh, will be brought forward to explicate the effects and consequences of this new phenomenon on both the ecological and social landscapes of these countries.

The blue revolution

The blue revolution is an aquacultural revolution. As mentioned, it is similar to the green revolution, which allowed dramatic increases in crop production, increased mechanization, and improved pest control and soil fertility through the addition of herbicides, pesticides and non-natural fertilizers. Similar processes are being done in the water. In other words, the blue revolution is merely mirroring developments in the green revolution. According to *The Economist* (2003), as people get richer, they tend to eat more fish, and the average consumption per person has doubled within 50 years. Unfortunately, as demand increases, the ocean's supply of fish declines. People are eating more than the natural process of replenishment. Furthermore, prices are increasing over time and the population of farmed fish is currently insufficient to stem this incline. Nikolas Wada, a researcher with the International Food Policy Research Institute, stated that the rise in seafood prices is even more remarkable when set in the context of prices for other animal products that have plummeted over the past 30 years. He further asserted that despite the price inclination, people have been able to continue eating fish, and this is largely due to the booming aquaculture production. The aquaculture industry had been growing steadily, especially in Asia. In 2000, the industry produced 36 million tons of fish and shellfish; and since 1990, the industry has been growing at an average compound rate of around 10 percent a year (ibid.). Attention is now focused on this industry vis-à-vis food production because scholars agree that aquaculture makes a significant contribution to food security. It helps fill the gap between the rising global demands for fishery products and the limited increase in captured fish production (FAO, 2003). According to the FAO, the global fish supply has increased from 5.3 percent in 1970 to 32.2 percent in 2000. Furthermore, the aquaculture sector is able to breed and farm over 200 different species of fish and crustaceans, which contributes to important sources of nutrients for many, like high-quality protein and vitamins A, D and E. Scientists have also asserted that the consumption of fish enhances brain development and learning in children, protects vision and eye health, and offers protection from cardiovascular disease and some cancers. These facts strongly promote the growing industry worldwide (ibid.).

Delgado et al. (2003) asserted that numerous studies have warned of potentially negative effects of escaped farmed fish on wild populations. There have also been significant environmental trade-offs, and the World Wildlife Fund argued that some forms of aquaculture actually place pressure on wild fisheries through demand for wild-caught fish as feed. Unfortunately, in response to these problems, many industry advocates and policymakers have strongly defended the aquaculture industry as an environmentally sustainable means of contributing to the world's fish supply. Hence, Delgado et al. argued that these problems persist while the industry grows because economic factors are the crucial driver of these changes in fisheries. It is imperative that audiences beyond the fish sector – such as sociologists, environmentalists and policymakers – also contribute to the fisheries dialogue and have a better understanding of issues vis-à-vis policy issues in world food and agriculture. Fortunately, some studies have already been done in Asia, particularly in Bangladesh and the Philippines, on their aquaculture industry and its effects locally.

Case study: farming genetically modified tilapia in the Philippines

The breeding of genetically modified tilapia represents the achievements of the fastest-growing, food-producing aquaculture. Yosef (2009) stated that after the breeding of improved tilapia in the already substantial tilapia industry of the Philippines, tilapia became affordable for the poor. This project in the Philippines is called the Genetic Improvement of Farmed Tilapia (GIFT) and it operated from 1988–97. This project was succesful, compared to aquacultural projects in other Asian countries, because of the proper, effective institutionalization of its developement and research. Futhermore, the GIFT project has maintained low prices of tilapia to make them more accessible and affordable to people from low-income status groups. In addition, the creation of fish farms have benefitted, directly and indirectly, approximately 280,000 Filipinos with employment opportunities. Occupations like fish farmers and hatchery operators were the available positions they could apply for. Aquaculture began on a very positive note. There are two main causal factors for the development of this industry in the Philippines. The first is that, as with many other countries worldwide, the Philippines is facing a demersal fish stock decline of up to 44 percent since the 1970s. Due to this depletion of fishery resources, coupled with population growth, aquaculture was seen as a sustainable alternative to traditional capture fisheries. Second, fish is an integral part of the national diet of the Philippines. An average Filipino consumes 28 kg of fish annually, as compared to the world average of 16 kg. Hence, Yosef (2009) concluded that the demand for a reliable source of fish constantly drives new technologies that can raise yields and meet the nutritional demands of a growing population. Its fisheries sector has already employed more than 1 million people (12 percent of the rural labor force) in 2000. The Philippines fisheries sector is divided into aquaculture and capture fisheries, where the latter is in turn divided into commercial and municipal fishing.

Tilapia was the chosen fish for genetic modification and breeding because it is considered verstaile across different environments. This characteristic has earned it the nickname "aquatic chicken". However, as versatile as it may be, farmers need to be equipped with the right knowledge and technology in order to harness the versatility of this fish for breeding. In order to do so, the government of the Philippines launched a two-year research program at the Freshwater Aquaculture Center of Central Luzon State University and discovered a line of technologies, such as floating net enclosures for breeding and floating cages with feedings, suited for commercial tilapia production that would be sustainable and developed over the next few decades. It did not stop there. Upon discovery, the government transferred the finished products to resource-poor rural communities and potential large-scale commercial farmers via three main programs: Inland Fisheries Project (1971–76), Freshwater Fisheries Development Project (1979–83), and National Self-Reliance Movement (1980s) (Yosef, 2009: 7). These programs were successful in transferring tilapia technologies because they provided technical assistance, workshops, credit from government banks and training for beneficiaries. The farmers and researchers maintained the momentum of the programs despite their completion by establishing two-way linkages between them through collaborations, workshops and seminars, demonstration of technologies, and dispensing fingerlings (Guerrero, 1994). Dr. Rafael D. Guerrero III, Executive Director of the Philippine Council for Aquatic and Marine Research and Development, asserted that the secrets of success to tilapia farming and the GIFT project in the Philippines have mainly been government support; government moratorium on tilapia price and market intervention; cooperation between the government and the private sector, along with many other international organizations such as FAO, UNDP and USAID; and cooperation among researchers (ibid.: 11). It is evident that the Philippine government emerged as a central player to this development. They extended their support through the creation of the Agriculture and Fisheries Modernization Act (AFMA) in 1997 and the Philippines Fisheries Code of 1998, which created a National Fisheries Research and Development Institute with the aim of elevating the Philippines as one of the top five fish producers in the world (Yosef, 2009: 25). Thus, government support is definitely one of the most important factors for a successful aquacultural industry and the reduction of poverty through maintaining lower fish prices and allowing fish stocks to be accesible to the poor. Political support has also placed the Philippines at a very competitve level in terms of trade and export in global aquacultural markets.

Case study: shrimp cultivation in Bangladesh

Contrary to tilapia farming in the Philippines, the growing shrimp cultivation sector in Bangladesh is attributed to the growing demands for high-value crustaceans by consumers from the global North. Over the past few decades, classical export commodities, such as coffee, tea and sugar, have largely been in decline and displaced by "high-value food" that includes shrimp. Apart from dietary change, trade reform and technical changes in the food industry, shrimp became one of the major high-valued transnational commodities because it is promoted by the FAO and similar institutions as central to replacing the protein lost due to exhaustion of global fisheries (Islam, 2008: 210). Since then, Bangladesh became one of the major shrimp-producing countries of the world, primarily because it houses the largest mangrove forest in the low-lying area of the Sundarbans. Therefore, the export of cultivated shrimp in Bangladesh has undergone rapid expansion over the last two decades. Between 1980 and 1995, the area under shrimp cultivation increased from 20,000 hectares to 140,000 hectares. The Department of Fisheries estimated that there are approximately 203,071 hectares of coastal shrimp farms producing an average of 75,167 metric tons of shrimp annually and an average of 370 kg/ha/year (ibid.: 214). A majority of the percentage of earnings in terms of value of Bangladeshi shrimp export come from the United States (34.78 percent) and European countries (48.74 percent) specially Belgium and the United Kingdom. Although the shrimp cultivation sector in Bangladesh seems to be developing fairly well, scholars argue that more needs to be done to improve the industry's system of trade and export, certification, quality, and standards of production, social benefits and workers' rights. According to Islam (2008), shrimp aquaculture in Bangladesh – linking the European Union, the US and Japan – exhibits several characteristics of a buyer-driven global commodity chain (GCC). A global commodity chain consists of sets of interorganizational networks clustered around one commodity of product, linking households, enterprises and states to one another within the world economy. These networks are situationally specific, socially constructed and locally integrated, underscoring the social embeddedness of economic organization (Gerrefi and Korzeniewicz, 1994: 2). Instead of other scholarly approaches to analyze different shifts in global capitalism – including the recent shift from public to private regulations in global agro-food system – Islam (2008) further argued that the GCC is a more appropriate approach to adequately capture both the special features of these transformations across the world economy and the relationships that link these processes together. So, this approach explores how production, distribution and consumption of products are globally interconnected along commodity or value chains (Islam, 2008: 210). The importance of understanding the dynamics and impact of the placement of the shrimp cultivation industry in the GCC offers us a comprehensive understanding of the implications the shrimp industry has on its relations of production and its various stakeholders.

Gender and employment at the bottom of a global commodity chain

A study conducted by Islam (2008) on shrimp processing factories in Bangladesh shows that, along with the effects of local conditions, buyers' pressures transmitted through the global commodity chain and the rapid process transformation of the global agro-food production affect gender and employment relations in the lower segments of the chain. It has been found that the feminization of the workforce in aquaculture is accompanied by the marginality of females, who receive lower wages and social prestige than their male counterparts, and who are mostly concentrated at the beginning and end of the local supply chain, with very limited access to other important nodes of the chain (Islam, 2008: 211). His study has discerned two main patterns in the workforce: *feminization alongside masculinity,* characterized by an increasing female workforce in the processing factories but the continued dominance of male worlers; and *flexibility and informality alongside rigidity,* in which an increasingly casual, temporary and part-time workforce that is precarious and vulnerable works in an inflexible and formal workplace with various codes of conduct (ibid.: 212). Unfortunately for workers in South Asia, good jobs are hard to find and even harder to keep; while bad jobs, albeit plentiful, offer terrible working conditions and are increasingly becoming informal and temporary. This bitter reality is encountered almost every day by countless cheap laborers in the global South who mostly produce for wealthy buyers' consumption in the global North. And because shrimp factories in Bangladesh are linked within the GCC as an agro-food production system, it is exposed to power relations within the chain that influences the production system of these factories. Most large corporations that control the production in factories in Bangladesh strive to lower costs of production by subcontracting. Subcontracting is a common procedure done in Asia by large corporations from the North to lower labor costs, and it allows them to control labor power while evading responsibilities for exploitation.

Through his field work in three districts of the Greater Khulna region – Satkhira, Bagerhat and Jessore – Islam (2008) found that there is a significant degree of female participation in the shrimp sector of Bangladesh. These women, however, are located at the lower end of the supply chain: sea (fry collection) and processing factories for peeling, de-heading and cleaning of shrimp. A few women own shrimp farms or are self-employed, and none of them have been involved in fry trading. The study found that 70 percent of the workers who are collectors of shrimp fry from the sea are women, 40 percent of shrimp pond owners are females and only 3–4 percent of traders, contractors and middlemen are women. Simply put, most of the women are employed in low-wage positions away from the managerial level, which is mostly comprised of men. When asked for the reason for the number of women in low-wage positions, a CEO of the factory asserted that administrative and managerial jobs were not suitable for women because it "requires them to do duties throughout the day and night". Evidently, there is patriarchal bias being practiced in human resources management. The study shows that in the processing factories, a gendered construction of culture dominates the hiring process and becomes a preamble to the differential treatment of men and women. As of 2006, there were 130 processing factories located in different urban and semi-urban areas of Bangladesh. Of these, 65 were in operation. It is estimated that more than 20,000 women work in the processing factories, representing 60 percent of the labor force (ibid.: 222).

Over time, since the workforce is highly feminized, lowly paid, informal in nature, and without any employment contract, subcontractors are seen to leverage on this "advantage" to reduce risks of production and costs by the externalization of firm labor – the reduction of direct employment through labor contractors. This casualization of labor, especially experienced by female workers, robs them of basic workers' rights that benefit permanent staff. Job stability is hence an important aspect of a job that these female laborers do not get to enjoy. The casualization of labor is due to the upstream and downstream pressures that converge within the shrimp processing factories. These pressures include supply failure due to adverse weather conditions, weak infrastructure, political instability and, most grievous of all, the complex demands exerted by buyers such as deadlines, quotas and standard compliance. Processors and exporters, in turn, drive all these pressures onto the laborers (ibid.: 225), against rigid rules and regulations with regard to hygiene, work time and other quality requirements. Most of the laborers are paid extremely low wages, which are usually not even paid on time. Apart from the casualization of labor that Bangladeshi workers experience in factories, they also experience exploitation and are frequently taken advantage of. Most of the workers that were interviewed during Islam's (2008) field work complained of the lack of safety gear, such as gloves, that should be provided to them during the de-heading and peeling of shrimp. Workers are only given gloves during the final stage of packing, where they do not really need them the most. Hence, many suffer from severe hand infections, and as they have no medical benefits, they face the full brunt of purchasing medication for these factory-borne illnesses on their own. Maternity leave is nonexistent, and if women workers fail to show up for work, they simply do not get paid. The laborers are conscious of the poor working conditions they are subjected to; however, they are deprived of the platform to raise their concerns or express their grievances in public. Since there is an absence of other income-generating acitvities for women in Bangladesh, part-time work becomes highly in demand and competitive, and voicing their grievances would only result in lost jobs. The people's vulnerability becomes the capitalists' property and advantage (Islam, 2008, 2014).

Ecological consequences of commercial shrimp

As reiterated in earlier sections of this chapter, aquaculture is becoming a strong industry to boost an Asian country's economy as the demand for both low-value food to feed local diets and high-value food to meet the demands of the North is generally increasing. Benefits that this industry brings to host countries include employment opportunities, transfer of research knowledge and technology from the West, new infrastructures, and foreign investments to boost the local economy. However, the ecological consequences of these industries abound and have a tremendous impact, not only on the environment but also on locals working in and living around these factories.

Aquaculture, specifically shrimp aquaculture, causes water polllution and is also affected by it. Shrimp aquaculturalists assert that their crop failures are attributed to the organic and inorganic pollution coming from other industrial sources such as sewage wastes from urban and industrial centers and from other forms of modern agriculture; but little do they know that shrimp farms are also responsible for the considerable self-pollution and bacteriological and viral contamination that infects the environment (Barraclough and Finger-Stich, 1996). Each hectare of pond produces tons of undigested feed and fecal wastes every crop cycle, and these ponds discharge unfavorable chemicals like ammonia, nitrates and nitrites that are fatal to fish in the sea. Other water pollution sources include the overuse of fertilizers and veterinary and sanitary products such as antibiotics, as well as waste-laden water that sloshes between neighboring ponds within a densely populated mangrove swamp full of shrimp processing factories. Large amounts of sedimentation are also an environmental issue that is posing serious problems of disposal. These consequnces have detrimental implications for other water users as well as for the environment. Salinization of freshwater sources and soil is a common problem associated with shrimp farming, not just in Bangladesh but in other countries such as Thailand and Taiwan. Shrimp farms, in order to run their production, have to pump fresh water from ground water aquifers into ponds and this causes the lowering of water tables, which in turn, causes sea water to flow inland into freshwater sources. In addition, the pollution of agricultural land can also be attributed to this effect. These, among other implications such as decreasing biological diversity, are truly adverse. For instance, Thailand houses many intensive shrimp farms covering many hectares of land. An average 33 cubic meters of fresh water per day is pumped in for each metric ton of shrimp produced. The area's average ground level, in turn, decreased from 3 meters below the surface in 1989 to about 7 meters in 1991. These sinking water tables are also reportedly the cause of shrinking land levels in Taiwan, causing rice fields to become lakes and buildings to collapse (ibid.: 25).

Biodiversity loss is also a serious aftermath of not only shrimp aquaculture but many types of aquaculture for that matter. For example, salmon is one of the most sought after high-value seafoods on the market, especially among Western countries. Unfortunately, for every kilo of farmed salmon or other carnivorous fish, five kilos of wild fish must be caught as fish food to breed salmon (Naylor, 2012). Shrimp ponds cover huge tracts of land, and they pollute large volumes of water. This modified water circulation system is altering wild fish and crustacean habitats, and diseases are spreading over to wild stock. Pollution from shrimp farms also contributes to the increasing frequency of estuarine water algae accumulating rapidly in water columns, resulting in the discoloration of the surface of the water, thereby endangering other native flora and fauna (Barraclough and Finger-Stich, 1996).

Mangrove deforestation is also a serious issue when it comes to aquaculture. Mangrove forests constitute an important component of the coastel ecosystems in tropical regions. These areas were regarded as worthless by colonial settlers and urban dwellers but are regarded as important and vital to the coastal indigenous population, who have been using them sustainably for sources of food, materials for construction of houses, nurserybeds for fish and crustaceans, and as protection against storms and floods. However, during recent times, these mangroves have been disappearing quickly to make way for the development of cash-crop farming, urbanization and shrimp pond construction. A study by the Network of Aquaculture Centres in Asia-Pacific (NACA) reported that in Thailand, mangroves were reduced by half in the 1980s, by 20–25 percent in Malaysia, and by 50–60 percent in Manila, and they were all for aquacultural use (Barraclough and Finger-Stich, 1996: 30).

The discussion in this section sheds light on most of the problems attributed to the development of aquacultural farms for shrimps and other fisheries in Asian mangroves. Apart from the harmful effects of the blue revolution to the environment and ecology in Asia, stakeholders in this project are also experiencing two types of displacement. The first is displacement due to the casualization of labor – as discussed in the previous section on the case study of shrimp processing farms in Bangladesh – and the other is displacement from their natural habitat. McMichael asserted that the former causes the redundancy of people (McMichael, 2008). The casualization of labor causes jobs to be temporary and unstable for the locals as subcontractors aim to cut production costs and risk. He stated that the development project, mandated by international financial institutions and organizations, such as the World Bank, the United Nations and the International Monetary Fund, destablizes rural communities through market forces and internal colonialism by developing farms to meet consumer demands, thereby forcing them into casualized wage labor.

The latter, on the other hand, is due to the encroachment of mangrove swamps in Asian countries, such as India, for the development of shrimp ponds and other aquacultural activities. Swamps are increasingly being taken over by shrimp ponds, while also displacing other important agricultural industries, such as rice fields, thereby contributing very little to the food security of the country and denying locals land for their routinized customary rites and rituals. This effect disrupts the livelihoods of the mangrove dwellers through de-peasantization, forcing them to evacuate from their habitat and go into wage labor.

Optimism toward a sustainable aquaculture?

Despite all of these problems caused by the blue revolution and its associative aquacultural projects, governments and organizations still continue to invest in them. It is undeniable that this budding industry stimulates local economies and provides employment opportunities for the masses. The aquacultural industry still has a lot of room for improvement and can be sustainable, provided that there are adequate checks and balances, strong government support, strict certification regimes and external pressure from consumers and buyers. Thankfully, many nonprofit organizations are fully aware of the variety of harmful consequences of shrimp farming, and many other capitalistic activities, evident by the sheer number of civil society groups such as environmentalists, activists and sociologists who constantly push for change in terms of human rights and environmental protection in our world. These communities of people and scholars continue to pressure capitalists and governments to change their systems and modes of production so as to make our earth a more sustainable place to live in, and to save others who are most affected by these activities from environmental impacts and unjust treatment. Ever since the publication of Rachel Carson's revolutionary book *Silent Spring,* people are increasingly choosing to lead sustainable lifestyles over time. Changing a lifestyle is not simply choosing to consume a product that is produced sustainably; it also incorporates sustainable production by the producers (Scott, 2009). This ideology permeates many environmentalist projects such as the Earth Summit and the World Summit on Sustainable Development, when Agenda 21[1] by the United Nations was reaffirmed by many nation-states in 2002 (UN, 2009). Agenda 21 recognizes that fundamental changes in the way societies produce and consume are indispensable for achieving global sustainable development. It is not just consumers changing their consumption patterns but producers changing their consumption of resources and cutting down on their pollution emissions in the production process (Scott, 2009: 4). Globally, unsustainable patterns of consumption and production continue to warrant attention and action, which has prompted UNEP to contribute to increasing the body of knowledge and experience through another project that would encourage governments and people to live a sustainable consumption lifestyle. The Marrakech Process is a global effort to accelerate progress toward the 10-year Framework of Programmes (10YFP), a report on sustainable consumption and production (SCP). Through the development of task forces that national governments have taken on voluntarily to support a shift toward SCP, this report is said to be contributing toward the Task Force on Sustainable Lifestyles led by Sweden (ibid.: 6).

With specific reference to shrimp farming, the World Wildlife Fund (WWF) is also raising awareness on global concerns regarding its unsustainable production by imploring shrimp producers to comply by the standards or the Shrimp Aquaculture Dialogue (ShAD). Created in 2007 by WWF, ShAD meetings have been attended by more than 400 people from a diverse spectrum of stakeholder sectors including: shrimp producers, environmental and social NGOs, development organizations, retailers, wholesalers, aquaculture associations, academics, researchers, government representatives and independent consultants (WWF, 2011: 5). The Shrimp Aquaculture Dialogue has developed a performance-based set of standards that define the acceptable levels for the major social and environmental impacts of shrimp farming. The ShAD Global Steering Committee (GSC) has attempted to create a series of performance thresholds that can currently be met by the top-performing producers, in an attempt to reward those producing to the specified target levels and to create an incentive for other players to improve performance. The GSC believes that this represents a sufficient proportion of producers and ensures that only those who are actively achieving the target levels are rewarded (ibid.: 4). Hence, the certification can only be attained if the standards set by ShAD are met. It is rewarding because consumers are increasingly becoming fond of WWF certified products.

In a comprehensive study on shrimp cultivation in Bangladesh, Islam (2010) asserted that producing countries are facing increasing challenges in international trade concerning the quality of shrimp they export. Since consumers in recent times divert their trust toward private certification schemes rather than those certificates issued by local governments, producers are pressured to meet the shifting privatizing regulations in order not to lose out in the market. This trend, fortunately, offers an opportunity to develop a more sustainable aquaculture. For example, the Bangladesh Standards and Testing Institution (BSTI), a public certification agency of the Bangladesh government, used to certify Bangladeshi shrimp before it was exported. However, because of global competitive pressure for "quality shrimp" – pressure that is coming from buyers as well as environmental groups – this form of regulation has shifted from the public to the private sector. At the same time, other big buyers, such as the United States and Japan, created pressure via the commodity chain to use a private system of regulations called the hazard analysis critical control point (HACCP) to maintain shrimp freshness and quality. Through the HACCP, many shrimp factory owners had to renovate their facilities and convert them into modern plants. Even political institutions that oversee the fisheries industry in Bangladesh were created and were equipped with modern facilities, just to meet the HACCP requirements (ibid.: 47). There were further shifts from public to private governance of the shrimp processing industry with the emergence of a third-party certifier called the Shrimp Seal of Quality (SSOQ). SSOQ aimed at certifying shrimp on the basis of five factors: (1) food safety and quality assurance, (2) traceability, (3) environmental sustainability, (4) labor practices and (5) social responsibility (SSOQ, 2002). All are among the key issues of concern for the environmental groups, labor rights movement, and finally the buyers, such as Walmart, Darden and Lyons (ibid.: 48). Its stated objective is to achieve sustainable improvement in the volume and value of Bangladeshi shrimp exports, and it is aimed at intervening in the shrimp farming sector by introducing "better management practices".

Conclusion

This chapter has succinctly dicussed the green revolution and its consequnces, as well as the phenomenon that has brought about the emergence of fish farming aided by green revolution technologies to increase the supply of finfish and crustaceans, such as tilapia, salmon and shrimp, to meet the consumer demands for high-value food. Although many scholars have argued for the blue revolution, claiming that it has brought about great changes in terms of strengthening the food security of our societies and boosting the economy of food-producing countries, such as Bangladesh and the Philippines, many scholars (e.g., Islam, 2008, 2010, 2014; Guerrero, 1994; Delgado et al., 2003) have elucidated the reality of fish farming and what it does to the environment and certain stakeholders who are situated at the bottom of the global commodity chain. These problems can still be rectified as consumers now shift toward a sustainable consumption lifestyle due to the persistent efforts of nonprofit organizations, such as the FAO and WWF, and environmentalists to raise the awareness of the ecological footprint created by the foods people are consuming. Certification regimes are created in response to this growing demand of sustainability and the protection of workers' rights, and these regimes pressure farmers and capitalists to change the standards and quality of their modes, means and relations of production, so as to remain competitve in the current market. Hence, there is still hope. Aquaculture is a budding industry with a lot of room for growth, and it can be sustainable so long as stakeholders at the top of the GCC cooperate.

7
Migrant Labor: Conditions, Contradictions and Confrontations

Introduction

With the advent of the neoliberal globalization project following the debt crisis in the 1970s, the meaning of development was changed and reframed as "successful participation in the world economy" (McMichael, 2008: 151), characterized by *liberalization* that includes "privatization of public functions and the 'freeing' of markets for labor, money, goods, and services" (ibid.: 152). This led governments to open up their markets and find their "niche" in the global economy in order to survive. Underlying this strategy is the theoretical justification, by English political economist David Ricardo, of the *comparative advantage* (Maneschi, 1998). Economic growth could only be achieved when countries maximize their trade advantage through economic specialization. Global governors like the World Trade Organization (WTO) made sure that conditions were put in place for the opening up of markets, easy movement of labor and economic specialization to occur. Neoliberalism guarantees not only the mobility of capital but also that of labor. Labor now becomes "the new export" that increasingly circulates, seeking employment opportunities – whether legal, illegal or slave/bonded labor. Migration is not new to this century; the separation of people from their land is etched into the making of the modern world. During the 1980s, spurred by debt regime restructuring, there was an internal migration states of between 300 and 400 million people. However, global migration is feminized: 75 percent of displaced people are women and children. Foreign remittances, sent by labor migrants, not only support over 100 million people, they supplement or subsidize public ventures in many developing countries (McMichael, 2008: 205). Under neoliberalism, "labor exports" are a significant way to earn foreign currency. Migration has thus become a "private solution to a public problem" (Hochschild, 2001: 18).

The "commercialization of care" through the displacement of love lies at the heart of globalization, wherein migrant female workers are the cog in the wheel of capitalism; the perpetual exploitation of their labor drives the vehicle of neoliberalism forward. In the neoliberal economy, love and care are treated as distributable, commoditized resources that are extracted from the Third World, and displaced to the First World, arguably alluding to the neoliberal paradox of accumulation through dispossession (Harvey, 2005). In this chapter, through different case studies, we will uncover the working conditions of migrant workers and their links to some of the characteristic practices of the globalization project: outsourcing, displacement and informalization. We seek to document their living and working conditions, how they are denied very basic human rights, and how they are viciously exploited.

Migrant labor in export processing zones

The WTO achieved liberalization of markets through various means including trade-related investment measures. Under such a strategy, countries that were under the governance of the WTO had to implement measures such as a reduction to "performance requirements" imposed on foreign investments. The goal of such a measure was to enable investors to shed the excess burdens of regulations that benefit the host country and free them to compete in the local economy. The idea was that "performance requirements" would dissuade foreign investor presence. Consequently, countries started competing for the businesses of TNCs through concessions, giving birth to the first export processing zone (EPZ) in Ireland in 1958, followed by EPZs in Puerto Rico in 1962, Mexico in 1964, and Canada in 1965. From there, the movement spread to Asia, with EPZs in Taiwan in 1966, South Korea in 1971, and the Philippines and Malaysia in 1972. Today, there are over 1000 EPZs or special economic zones worldwide (Frank et al., 2012: 213).

According to McMichael (2008), outsourcing involves the relocation of goods and services production as a cost-reduction strategy. EPZs are, according to Klein (2009), tax-free economic zones within a country that is sealed off from the local government. The concept is that a country would create a special zone investors may use that is free of economic, environmental and labor regulations. The hope is that, eventually, investors will see the value of producing in the country, settle down and turn into a lasting development. While EPZs attract some foreign investments, they also allow quasi-bonded or slave-like labor relations.

We will see now a case in the Philippines where migrant labor from the countryside experiences a dire condition in the EPZs. Cavite is an EPZ situated in Rosario, in the Philippines. Naomi Klein (2009) documented the situation of Cavite in her book *No Logo* really well. The rent in Cavite is ridiculously cheap at 11 pesos (US$0.24) per square foot and corporations are treated to a five-year tax-free stay. Wide arrays of products are assembled in Cavite, ranging from Nike shoes to IBM CD-ROM drives. The streets in Cavite are orderly and clean. Workers shuffle in and out every day in factory uniforms resembling those of schools. But according to Klein, outside of Cavite the "bubble bursts". The town of Rosario remains a mess, water is lacking and garbage overflows in the streets. Lastly, the area is cordoned off from the local population and is well guarded by the military that are willing and able to crush any labor unrest. The majority of the workers in Cavite are comprised of migrant workers; they are workers that come from the rural parts of the Philippines, most of them distant places from Cavite. In fact, 80 percent of all workers in Cavite have migrated from other provinces in the Philippines. The irony of this is that many of these workers are farmers or children of farmers, whose farmlands were lost to even more EPZs. These people were displaced from their own lands and now neither own property nor a job.

Having no land or work, these vulnerable people presented EPZ recruiters with an excellent opportunity to recruit cheap labor. Recruiters often went to the villages of displaced farmers with the promise of a high enough income to remit back to their families. Parallel to the women of Barbados, who found "pink collar" jobs attractive because they offered identification with office work even though they paid lower than cane field work, these workers saw working in a factory as attractive and associated with modernity. As McMichael (2008) writes, the development narrative sustains the unsustainable assumption that peasants are redundant in the modern world. Thus, displaced peasants move to urban areas or zones such as Cavite in hopes for a better, more modern life.

Yet, as Naomi Klein has found, these promises are but castles built on air. The fierce competition for investors means that wages in such EPZs are extraordinarily low. Klein notes that most of the money workers earn is spent on dormitories (because they are migrant workers) and on food. If one thinks that the accommodations are at least decent since they are paid for, the inverse is true; the rooms are so crowded that white lines have to be painted on the floor to demarcate where each worker sleeps, almost like an actual parking lot. Working conditions as well are terrible. Apart from the poorly ventilated factories that turn into ovens in the day and become damp at night, causing a rise in pneumonia cases, workers have to endure long shifts with only two 15-minute breaks. The point is to squeeze every single working second out of the worker. Regular shifts last for about 15 hours and mandatory overtime is required when work orders start piling up. Because most factories work with a just-in-time (JIT) structure, workers often do not have stable jobs and are paid only when there is work to do. All these conditions are further exacerbated by the fact that these workers are refused basic labor rights, like the right to participate in organized labor unions in order to push for better conditions. Thus, migrant labor is vulnerable to, in McMichael's words (2008), "super exploitation".

The unheard voices of the "Orang Bangla" in Malaysia

No country's development is uniquely because of its own, but rather is contingent upon contributions from different sources. One of the sources is cheap foreign labor. Bangladeshi labor migrants, locally known as "Orang Bangla", albeit in a derogatory sense, continue to serve Malaysia to perpetuate its status as an "economic tiger" in Asia. There were around 350,000 Bangladeshi workers in Malaysia in 2006; today this number increases to a million including the illegal ones. Workers range from the unskilled working in manufacturing, construction and plantations, to highly skilled ones, including top engineers in constructing PETRONAS towers, an icon of Malaysia's miraculous development. Estimates show that workers spend around 80 percent of their income in Malaysia, and thereby contribute to, and keep revitalizing, the local economy (Islam et al., 2006).

Apart from Bangladeshi workers in different development sectors, there are more than 50,000 Bangladeshi students studying in Malaysia, a great education market for Malaysian universities. Reports also show that so far 1088 Bangladeshis, second place to the Chinese, applied for the "Malaysia My Second Home" (MM2H) program in 2006, and each candidate deposited 300,000 Malaysian ringgit (about US$82,000) to the Malaysian government (Islam et al 2006). Today, this number reaches more than 4000 Bangladeshis. On the top of this, the Malaysian government also expects to have more than 50,000 Bangladeshi travelers each year (Uddin, 2014). All these examples indicate how Bangladeshis are, apart from being accommodated to some extent, an integral part of Malaysia's development.

Different research shows, however, that migrant workers have contributed to the remarkable economic success but are hardly ever mentioned in analyses of this "miracle economy". Due to economic restructuring and the economic downturns, migrants are increasingly treated as scapegoats for all kinds of problems Malaysia is facing. Bangladeshi workers who came to Malaysia with hope for a brighter future are mostly from poor economic and educational backgrounds and not aware of employment procedures and conditions. As a result, they are prone to agent and employer exploitation. Based on our ethnographic field work (see also Islam et al., 2006), the following are some of the hurdles they confront:

(1) *The first shock in Malaysia.* Upon arriving in Malaysia, many Bangladeshi workers found a shocking difference between wages they were promised and what they actually received. Sometimes they had to sign a new agreement where salaries/wages were lower than the promised ones, and other benefits stated in the original contracts were not honored. Some cases were found in which recruitment agencies provided workers with work permits to work in companies that did not exist at all, and therefore they were deported by plane or sent to detention centers (camps). According to media reports, a majority of those who stayed for months in the camps were frail, weak, unnourished and stressed. Some even died.
(2) *Working hours and overtime.* Despite working for nine hours (basic is eight hours), many workers were not paid for the extra hour they work. The situation was even worse in many constructions sites and fast-food restaurants. According to the Malaysia Employment Act, "Every employee shall be entitled to a paid holiday at his ordinary rate of pay on ten gazetted public holidays in one calendar year". However, some employers do not allow their workers to enjoy the public holidays. Moreover, some companies do not pay them their due wages on time, and no payment slip is given to workers.
(3) *Extra benefits and living conditions.* Unlike domestic workers, foreign workers are, in many cases, deprived of many facilities and benefits, while both kinds of workers are supposed to be treated equally as Malaysian and International Labor Law prescribes. The Malaysian Charter on Human Rights (December 1994), article 8, mentioned, "Foreign workers should have access to all basic amenities, fair working conditions, a just and equal wage, a safe working environment and a channel to redress discriminations and exploitation". However, many of these are compromised in the case of Bangladeshi workers, especially when they are paid lower than their local counterparts.
(4) *Payment for work permits, levies and EPFs.* For work permits and levies, every Bangladeshi worker has to pay about 3000 Malaysian ringgit

(about US$820) a year. On the top of this, they must pay 11 percent of their wages to the Employment Provident Fund (EPF). Paying for these as well as for other living costs in Malaysia leaves them with very little or no savings. Workers can claim their EPF money after their work tenure; however, as they reported, harsh rules, bureaucratic complexity and long procedures make it almost uncertain they will get their money back.

(5) *Harassment by police and local thugs.* The fear of police and local thugs is very common among Bangladeshi workers. Despite having legal documents, some Bangladeshi workers complained that they faced harassment from police. Sometimes they were sent to detention camp without ability to contact their employers. In many instances, the police catch these legal workers and fine them 50, 30, or even 10 Malaysian ringgit without providing any receipt. There is a saying among the Bangladeshi workers that the thugs are coming for a "slap, threat and 50 Malaysian ringgit" (so give them 50 ringgit before getting the slap and threat). There are many incidents in which a number of Bangladeshi workers were punched, beaten up, robbed and even killed.

(6) *Compensation and treatment.* Some Bangladeshi workers were severely injured and lost valuable parts of their bodies while working, but no compensation was given to them. Mr. Foiz Ahmad, working in Trakuma Company in Shah Alam, lost two fingers while working but did not get any insurance or compensation. When he asked for insurance, he was deported to Bangladesh immediately. Another worker in the area of Meru lost one of his eyes while working in the timber industry. He was also denied any compensation. Many employers ignored this provision of insurance, and there was gross negligence of safety precautions in the workplace.

Despite undergoing dire exploitation, the so-called "Orang Bangla" do not have any forum to voice their concerns. They are not allowed to form any trade union for their collective interests. The Bangladesh High Commission in Malaysia is earning a huge revenue but is less responsive in addressing the problems Bangladeshi workers are facing.

Foreign domestic workers

Since the 1960s, transnational corporations (TNCs) started to outsource manufacturing jobs to Singapore due to a multitude of pull factors, including its subscription to neoliberal economic principles mediated by a strong state, which ensures free trade and capital flows. Export-oriented industrialization from the 1960s propelled Singapore to the status of a newly industrialized country. By the early 1970s, the financial and business sector had overtaken export manufacturing as the fastest-growing industry. The subsequent shift toward a knowledge-based economy further intensified the labor shortage in Singapore. The series of rapid industrialization and accelerated economic growth added pressure to the tight labor market (Lim, 1987). In a bid to encourage more Singaporean women to partake in the formal economy to make up for the labor shortage, the government introduced the Foreign Domestic Workers (FDWs) scheme in 1978 to allow Singaporean women to reenter the workforce, by outsourcing care and domestic work to full-time, live-in FDWs. This scheme grants a two-year working contract to FDWs that comes with strict terms and conditions such as a mandatory monthly levy and security bond paid by employers, mandatory medical examination to screen for pregnancy and sexually transmitted diseases every six months, and the prohibition of marriage to a Singaporean (Ueno, 2008). This underscores the differential treatment of FDWs who are perceived as low-skilled foreign workers from working professionals deemed "foreign talents" by the Singapore government.

Labor conditions

While there are many regulations to ensure the quality of FDWs in Singapore, such as minimum age and minimum years of formal education, the working conditions of these migrant women remain largely unregulated. FDWs are explicitly excluded from the Employment Act, signifying the lack of protection by legislation that would assure them of minimum wage, working hours, rest days and sick leave (Ueno, 2008). It is only since 2012 that the government mandated a weekly rest day or monetary compensation in lieu of a rest day for FDWs (Ministry of Manpower, 2012). However, other aspects of their working conditions are still unaddressed. The exploitative and poor working conditions of domestic helpers in Singapore are constantly under the spotlight. The Human Rights Watch has reported on the various ways in which the welfare and labor rights of FDWs in Singapore are undermined. These include forced confinement, inadequate living accommodation, restriction on religious freedom, deaths as a result of workplace accidents, exorbitant debts as opposed to wages that are way below minimum wage, etc. (Human Rights Watch, 2005). Food deprivation is also common among FDWs with 80 percent of domestic workers who seek help from the Humanitarian Organization for Migration Economics (HOME) claiming that they do not get sufficient food (Chang, 2014). Concerns over the mistreatment of maids have also prompted some governments to take action against Singapore. The Myanmar government, for instance, imposed a temporary ban on domestic helpers to Singapore recently amid allegations of verbal and physical abuse on maids (Ghosh and Baker, 2014).

The exploitation and abuse of female migrant workers can be attributed to the power relations between employers and FDWs, wherein employers wield overarching power over domestic helpers. The huge disparity in power can in turn be attributed to the lack of institutional support and legislations to protect the labor rights and welfare of FDWs in Singapore. As Singapore's Immigration Act stipulates that employers are responsible for the supervision of FDWs, employers could exercise discretionary power to the point of potentially abusing maids (Ueno, 2008). In order to prevent the loss of the $5000 security bond, some employers resorted to confiscating the passports and work permits of domestic helpers. FDWs are also subjected to surveillance by employers, as some domestic helpers are not allowed to use the phone or develop friendships with people other than the family members of employers (Human Rights Watch, 2005), thereby curtailing their freedom of movement and communication. These breaches in human and labor rights are further exacerbated by negative stereotypes toward FDWs, such as maids being perceived as untrustworthy and lazy (Ueno, 2008), thus justifying the excessive surveillance and control by employers. These prejudices are deeply dehumanizing, and they undermine the identities of domestic helpers as individuals worthy of respect.

As FDWs face restrictions in joining trade unions in Singapore, they do not enjoy collective bargaining power to negotiate their wages and working conditions. Furthermore, the employment contracts of FDWs are mediated by profit-driven maid agencies that prioritize their bottom line over the welfare of domestic workers. Agencies usually implement a free exchange plan, which allows employers to return FDWs to the agency within a time period with little or no penalty to the employers should the maid be found unsuitable. FDWs are often rendered helpless against the threats of employers due to fears of incurring additional debts when they are returned to the agency. Hence, it is evident that against the backdrop of the neoliberal economy, FDWs are treated as "expendable or refundable commodities" (Ueno, 2008: 153), bridging the care deficit in Singapore through their exploitative working conditions.

Contradictions and confrontations

There are at least two key contradictions with migrant women working as domestic helpers in Singapore: (1) displacement of maternal love from the Third World nations to the First World; and (2) differential treatment of domestic helpers in Singapore who are perceived as low-skilled foreign workers as opposed to working professionals deemed foreign talents. The displacement of love is evident in Singapore as care is commoditized through the use of FDWs in the provision of care to encourage Singaporean women to partake in the formal wage economy in order to solve the labor shortage in Singapore (Ueno, 2008). These FDWs are primarily from neighboring developing countries such as the Philippines, Indonesia and Sri Lanka (Yeoh, 1999), and Bangladesh. As these women migrate from their hometown to Singapore to work as maids, they leave behind their families and often their young children. Up to 30 percent of Filipino children have at least one parent who has migrated overseas for work. The consequences are obvious – these children fall ill more often, do not have strong parental influence over their lives, and as a result, are more likely to get into trouble in school (Hochschild, 2001). On the other hand, children in First World nations like Singapore receive genuine love and care from their maids, who are the mothers of these left-behind Filipino children.

As previously mentioned, Singaporean families employ maids to outsource domestic and care work because both parents are working. The contradiction lies in that while mothers from developing nations and Singapore go out to work, it is the children in developing countries that lose out from a motherly figure in their lives as their mothers migrate to Singapore to work as FDWs, pouring their love and concern on the Singaporean children. There is thus a displacement of love from the Third World nations to the First World; an inequality that stretches beyond just economic resources to that of the structure of the family and the love, care and concern received by children. As love and care are distributable resources (Hochschild, 2001) commoditized and transferred from the Third World to the First World, the displacement of love arguably alludes to the neoliberal paradox of "accumulation through dispossession" (Harvey, 2005; Islam, 2013), wherein the Singaporean middle and upper class can accumulate profits and capital by earning dual incomes due to two working parents, while dispossessing the children from developing nations of the basic love and care of their mothers.

Apart from the foreign domestic maids that migrate to Singapore to earn a living, there are a plethora of other foreign workers that also contribute to the Singapore economy. However, this group of foreigners are termed differently from their domestic helper counterparts. They are more commonly known as "foreign talent" even though in essence, they are also foreign workers who have migrated to Singapore in search of better job prospects. As Singapore intends to position itself as a cosmopolitan city-state with global interconnections, attracting top talent from all over the world remains its priority (Yeoh, 2004). Thus, the nation is constantly on the lookout for these foreign talents who can ensure the global competitiveness of this tiny city-state, and who can add the creativity and vibrancy to the arts scene. However, this cosmopolitanism is not all-inclusive – migrant workers such as the domestic helpers from various SEA countries are relegated to a low-status in society and are unrecognized in their backstage support in the family, which in turn aids Singaporean parents to contribute to the country's economic success. This can also be seen through their lack of autonomy to voice their frustrations or injustices experienced.

Scopes for social justice

There are some scopes for social justice and platforms on which domestic helpers can share their stories and have a voice. A Facebook group called "A Maid's Eye view of Singapore employers" was set up as a platform for domestic helpers to speak out against any injustices they may face. Social media has an advantage in that it can be instantaneously updated to raise public awareness of any injustice. However, the "About" section of the Facebook page warns the maids that their "likes" and activity on the page can be seen by everyone, including employers. It is a limitation of the platform in itself if maids are afraid of sharing their story of their abusive employer because the Facebook page warns maids not to participate if they do not have the "progressive and understanding type" of employers. This tells the sad truth of how even though the maids may have a platform to share their opinions, they cannot do so without first considering if they may get into trouble with their employers. In addition, online groups and social media are not very accessible for maids as they may not own smartphones enabled with data plans, and their use of computers may be limited to what their employers make availablc.

There are definitely efforts by NGOs in representing these maids and giving them a voice in society. In 2008, the National Committee for the United Nations Development Fund for Women Singapore (renamed Singapore Committee for UN Women), Transient Workers Count Too (TWC2) and the Humanitarian Organization for Migration Economics (HOME) launched a campaign calling for Singaporeans to give their maids at least one day off a month (UNW:SC, 2011). However, such coverage by the media is rare. Usually, when a foreign domestic helper makes the headlines, it portrays the maids as abusers or being problematic. The very representation of maids in the media tells of the biased and lack of social justice for them. Hence, while there are indeed platforms and community support groups that advocate greater recognition of the contributions and labor rights of domestic workers, they are helpful only to a limited extent.

Slave labor and global sex workers

Referring to the "Global Slavery Index" published by Australia-based Walk Free Foundation, Smith (2013) reveals an alarming picture:

> Almost 30 million people across the globe are living in modern-day slavery, [with] the African nation of Mauritania, Haiti, Pakistan, and India [having] the highest number of slaves in proportion to population. But taken in absolute terms, global powers such as China and Russia were near the top of the list of countries with the largest total of people living in slavery.

In the index, "slavery" is used to mean "a variety of conditions, such as forced labor, human trafficking, the sale and exploitation of children, and forced marriage". Smith (2013) added,

> As many as half of the estimated global total of 29.8 million slaves are living in India, the index said. With between 13.3 million and 14.7 million slaves – more than the population the U.S. state of Illinois – around 10 percent of India's population are facing these conditions. The second highest is China, with around 3 million people estimated to be living in slavery.

The index said the figure for China includes "the forced labor of men, women and children in many parts of the economy, including domestic servitude and forced begging, the sexual exploitation of women and children, and forced marriage". The index ranked 162 countries based on three factors: estimated prevalence of modern slavery by population, levels of child marriage and levels of human trafficking into and out of the country. The US came in at 134th – worse off than Barbados (135), South Korea (137), Hong Kong (141), Costa Rica (146) and Cuba (149). While deeming the US and Canada "very low risk", it said they were prime destinations for human trafficking because of "their demand for cheap labor and relatively porous land borders". The UK, Ireland and Iceland were given the best ratings and came in at joint 160th. "This does not mean these countries are slavery free", the report said. "On the contrary, it is estimated that there are between 4,200–4,600 people in modern slavery in the United Kingdom alone". A significant number of this slave labor can be found in the global sex industry.

Sex sells. This statement alone is enough to show the profitability of the sex trade as well as explain the rise of global sex industries (GSI). Available statistics from a 2004 European Parliamentary report estimated that the GSI is worth $5–7 trillion (Pritchard, 2010). Any businesses that deal with products and services related to sex are involved in the sex trade. As such, the sex industry comprises a wide variety of commercial activities that include sexual goods and services like strip clubs, sex shops, pornography and, more importantly, prostitution (Sloan, 2000). The global porn industry, for example, generated an estimated $97 billion in revenues in 2006 (Knufken, 2010). As an estimated $108 billion market, prostitution, which involves recruiting, providing and transporting individuals for sex in exchange for money, is an area of concern as it not only provides a window of opportunity for migrant labor to enter the sex industry but also consequently gives rise to global human trafficking and abuse.

The sex industry, like any other industry, works on the principle of supply and demand (Thompson, 2005). Evidently, the success of the global sex industry can be seen as largely attributed to globalization and its posse of methods and developments. The four prominent processes resulting from the globalization project, namely outsourcing, displacement, informalization and global relocation (McMichael, 2008), are integrated and go hand in hand in exacerbating participation in the global sex industry. The expansion and development of information and communication technologies (ICT) facilitated access and mobility, which aggravated the exploitation of the global sex industry. All these contribute to the creation of supply and demand factors that led to its booming success.

The globalization project not only facilitates the mobility of economic exchange, but also expedites the movement of ideas, values and lifestyle of the North to the South. This could be a possible explanation for the global relocation of people from the South to the North as McMichael (2008: 199) eloquently contends that "young people are at once seduced by, and excluded from, symbols of modernity associated with off-farm work". He then quotes Jacques Attali to conclude that people in the periphery look for a better future in the North as they are "enraged by the constant stimulation of wants that can't be satisfied" (ibid.: 203). Essentially, the migrant labor makes up the supply that meets the demand for prostitutes to service the growing sex industries (Hughes, 2004).

With the sex industry as such a profit-making trade, women and children who desire a better life are the most vulnerable social group since they can be easily tricked into prostitution, and thus become the main targets of traffickers in the sex industries (Brewer, 2011). Gullible and uneducated, they are taken advantage of by recruiters and agents in the human trafficking criminal chain who ruthlessly coerce them into the sex trade (Flamm, 2003). They are often enticed by false promises of employment or education and the possibility of money remittances for their families. Some families even sell their children in hope of a better future for the child and themselves (Ark of Hope for Children, 2013). With the potent combination of displacement, inferior working conditions and the prospects of a better life abroad, the stage is set for a steady supply of women and children for the global sex industry. As the state of technology in the South improved, Friedman (2005) highlights the phenomenon of "democratization of technology" to show that the South's access to technology, the Internet and hence information, enabled them to participate at the same level as the North. However, the South's increased access to ICTs do not come without a price, as the lack of regulation of online activities give rise to the "escalation of the global sexual exploitation of women and children through global advertising of prostitution tours and online marketing" (Hughes, 2000: 35). On the other side of the world, the Internet functions as a sex forum by increasing demand and facilitating access to the global sex industry. Increasing disposable income in developed countries allows for a growth in consumption of sex-related products and services, thus creating a demand in the sex industry not only in their home countries but also worldwide as sex tourism becomes a global phenomenon (Beeks and Amir, 2006). In essence, the income disparity between North and South and developments in ICTs made it easy for those either pursuing the "services" of, looking to participate in, or seeking to exploit the global sex industry.

Organized crime syndicates are the mastermind behind international sex trafficking where victims are deceived into prostitution. The Trafficking in Persons Report (2013) sees sex trafficking "in which a commercial sex act is induced by force, fraud, or coercion; or in which the person induced to perform such an act has not attained 18 years of age" (U.S. Department of State, 2013). Nevertheless, the law does not act as a barrier to traffickers who belong to organized crime groups because human trafficking involves minimal risks and yields the highest return for them (Simic, 2004). With improved accessibility due to globalization, syndicates are able to move people without much difficulty and even make it challenging for relevant authorities to identify the illicit activity. Hence, organized crimes can become transnational since these crimes are able to integrate into the global system and penetrate the global economy through extensive criminal economy networks and connections. Global sex industries consequently become lucrative businesses, which in turn drive the tourism industry as it becomes a diversified market to meet demands in the sex trade. Below are some case studies showing conditions, contradictions and confrontations experienced by sex workers in different countries.

Sex workers in Kenya

An exemplar of the working conditions can be discerned from a comprehensive ILO study, "Baseline Survey on Children in Commercial Sex in Kenya's Four Towns of Nairobi, Kisumu, Eldoret and Nyeri" (Ogola and Ochieng, 2008) in Kenya that shows the various conditions in which domestic sex workers face. The survey collected information from 360 respondents, out of which 66 were children sex workers. The respondents identified numerous hazards during their line of work. The greatest hazards during work saw 16.4 percent identifying nonpayment and rape as the greatest threat, followed by police harassment at 10.4 percent, and genital infections and gangster attacks at 6 percent and 3 percent, respectively.

Child sex workers showed that 28.8 percent of their clients were rude and with as high as 9.6 percent also physically abusive. Furthermore, if the clients refused to pay, 30.8 percent of the girls hardly reacted to the scenario, leaving them exploited and abused. Some clients were reported to turn violent, and it is seen from the survey that 19.2 percent of the girls took no action to protect themselves. Mature sex workers were also reporting hazards similar to the children's. However, in addition to the aforementioned problems, mature sex workers face additional violence from the client's spouses and girlfriends. The ILO survey also reports that on top of the health hazards that come with the trade, ability to seek help is also met with stigmatization. For example, 23.1 percent found public hospitals discriminatory. In addition, abortion in Kenya is considered illegal and hence, they will have to seek treatment from private clinics.

The reasons for the child sex labor serving local clientele shows a variety of factors that are rooted in poverty, such as:

- The need for quick money and economic gains from an alternative source of income
- The increasing demands for a better life

- Some were expelled from home as a result of pregnancy and therefore need to resort to commercial sex for income to support their children
- Due to the rampant HIV/AIDs in Kenya, many of these children are left orphaned without social support and need to survive
- Some were encouraged by relatives and immediate family as there was a need for income.

A simple comparison between the occupational hazards and the push factors toward the sex trade will illustrate that poverty and the lure of a better life are causal factors that lead these workers to become victims within the sex trade and thus further marginalized within society. The reasons for poverty can then be linked to the World Bank's agricultural reforms. Some of these Development Plans such as the 1994 report of the Economic Recovery, Sustainable Development Year 2000, 1994 National Food Policy and the 1996 Policy Framework Report, facilitated rural industrialization, liberalization of agricultural markets and the removal of price controls (Bigman, 2002). These contributed to poverty and limited options, which became a push factor for children and women to seek employment in the sex trade. Hence, the sex workers merely act in response to the structural problems imposed by the Bretton Woods system on the nation that trickles down to the plight of the rural poor.

Sex industry in Thailand

A contrasting study from Kenya is Thailand where its sex trade is oriented outwards toward the attraction of sex tourism. Prostitution was legal up until the 1960 Prostitution Suppression Act. However, due to the large US military presence, a 1966 Entertainment Places Act enabled military personnel to visit for rest and recreation in Thailand (Singh and Hart, 2007). It is estimated that the US military was spending as much as $20 million in the first four years of the Entertainment Places Act. As Vanaspong (2002) commented, the lure of the sex trade draws millions of dollars and has developed into part of the Thai national image. The Tourism Authority of Thailand (TAT) does not specifically refer to certain "entertainment" establishments that solicit commercial sex, but the TAT neither deters sex tourism in the country.

Rural-urban division and modernization are cited as the key factors leading to Thai sex work (Bishop and Robinson, 1998). Due to the income inequality between the rural and urban areas, displacement of the rural population toward the urban areas saw many falling into the traps of an urban life. These migrants from the rural areas are often confronted by extortion, exploitation and poverty. On the flip side, there is a demand stemming from the globalized economy that draws upon real or imagined notions of the exotic appeal of sex in Thailand (Singh and Hart, 2007). This exoticism is seen from the promises of youth and virginity of sex workers, where men are sold the child-like innocence of the prostitutes. Clients particularly demand services they find attractive in Thai women: simplicity, loyalty, affection and innocence. The women are also, in their eyes, small, without body hair and, most importantly of all, childish (Montgomery, 2008).

On a darker side of the sex trade, there is no doubt that children are also forced to work and suffer under the dictates of traffickers and pedophiles (Singh and Hart, 2007). These children were often taken away from their homes and forced into indentured labor to help pay off their family's debts. These sex workers will face the same societal pressures as those in Kenya where they will be stigmatized, losing self-respect in their community. They will also have to deal with the trade-associated risks of arrests and incarceration, abuses endured from the clients and spread of an assortment of sexual diseases.

Migrant sex workers in Batam

Batam, an Indonesian city, has been a popular tourist destination for the sex trade, attracting as many as 600 Singaporean men every Saturday (Othman and Alkhatib, 2012). Informalization is at its peak here, where there are as many as 7000 registered prostitutes in Batam, excluding the 14,000 unregistered sex workers, recorded in a documentary titled *Indonesia's Weekend Wives and Sex Tourists* (Yu, 2004). The sex trade in Batam is seen as a livelihood response for the lack of formal economic opportunities to cater to its increasing migrant population. The film documents that sex workers often come from all parts of Indonesia, such as Sumatra and West Java, outsourced by prostitution agencies that promise them a better life. These agencies attract young women from rural villages of Indonesia, promising work in local factories and restaurants, a pull factor for those who need to support their impoverished families back home.

However, this was not the case upon reaching Batam. Many of these women were forced into prostitution, with life-threatening consequences should they refute. Moreover, as commented by Elisa, a sex worker in the documentary, these working conditions were varying, in which during worst-case scenarios, they were beaten up or forced to engage in violent sexual acts with their clients.

Sex workers in Batam are often displaced workers, for prostitution is illegal in Batam. This poses multilayered risks for the sex workers, as they are not protected by the constitution. Sex workers often do not have fixed working hours, their wages are not fixed, but rather often subjected to the number of services they provide in a day, and they do not have labor rights due to the illegitimate nature of their work. Furthermore, they are often exposed to HIV or other sexually transmitted diseases, which are detrimental to their personal health and that of their clients. This is also a result of the reluctance of condom use by their clients when engaging in sexual intercourse.

The lack of one's quality of life back home has led to a huge influx of migrants from all parts of Indonesia in Batam. This relocation of migrants saw an increase of 3000 local dwellers to a population of 600,000, all in search of a falsely given sense of a better standard of living. The excess population in Batam led to even more poverty and more exploitation of sex workers in the area. Living conditions put forth by a local sex worker in a documentary called *B.A.T.A.M.* (Unifem, 2010) were depressing in Batam as compared to her village in Java. Hence, the sex trade in Batam questions the legitimacy of the globalization project and its universal goal of improving the human condition.

In these case studies, we can view both the supply and demand factors as more intricately linked to the orientation toward tourism. Secondly, we can discern that the push factors, which create the supply of sex workers, stem also from the rural-urban migration that results in their systematic exploitation. Despite having slightly different trajectories in the above three cases, the conditions for the sex workers are unnervingly similar. The structural forces that impose on the agency of the marginalized individuals and the informal economy show an inherent contradiction between the dominant notion of globalization and the actual realities for the forgotten.

Conclusion

In this chapter, we have analyzed different case studies on the conditions, contradictions and confrontations that migrant labors experience today in the age of globalization. Many continue to work in coercive and exploitative jobs because it is their only means of livelihood; they have few alternatives as they are already marginalized by the formal economy induced in and introduced by the globalization itself. While globalization has promised positive impacts on global development and welfare, we have witnessed new forms of inequality and "super-exploitation" in allowing transnational corporations to profit at the expense of the migrant workers. Thus, the common notions that globalization would bring the world together falls flat on its face in the case of migrant workers. Much of the revenues that corporations get from EPZs, remittances received by the countries through "new labor export", economic returns gained by host countries from foreign labor migrants, and love and care received from FWDs are largely based on the foundation of exploitation, denial, dehumanization and neglect.

8

Profit over Life: Industrial Disasters and Implications for Labor and Gender

with Md Saiful Islam

Introduction

The history of the industrial revolution in England in the late 18th century reveals the inhuman life of the working-class people. It is the nascent picture of class struggle between employer and workers from which a powerful group reaps benefit exploiting the powerless. A similar trend of exploitation is still rampant in today's context, although the nature, extent and severity may have changed. With the expansion of world markets, the participation of marginalized women in the production industry is overwhelming; however, at the same time, salaries have seen tremendous erosion, something which Moghadam refers to as the process of "female proletarianization" (Moghadam, 1999). Workers are deprived in all spheres of life. From dawn to dusk, they work hard for their survival but receive minimum returns for their toils and struggles. The most woeful situation of all is the workplace, which remains a hazardous and unsafe cesspool. Frequent industrial accidents cause innumerable deaths and physical disability. Survivors often face a difficult strain due to a lack of treatment, medicines and other familial needs (*Daily Amardesh,* 2014). Physical disability forces them to be dependent on others for their livelihood. Psychologically they become depressed and as a consequence, intolerable trauma and the inability of maintaining the costs of treatment ultimately forces some of them to even commit suicide. Family members face great hardship to meet their daily needs after losing their breadwinners. Orphans arising from such situations lose all their hopes and desires while struggling for survival after losing their parents. According to one report, 4000 workers were trapped inside and tens of thousands of their dependents trapped outside of the Rana Plaza (RISE, 2014). An in-depth survey of 1500 survivors from the Rana Plaza incident showed that the victims and their families required long-term support, including counseling and guidance to enable them to make their own occupational choices as many of them are carrying injuries and trauma (Ryder, 2014). Therefore, some crucial questions are still unresolved, such as: How are the survivors passing their days? How do they struggle in search of subsistence? What are the roles of the state and other corporate partners to protect these unfortunate workers? This chapter will specifically deal with these issues.

Workplace safety and workers' well-being

Workplace safety encompasses protection for a worker from all sorts of hazards that could potentially harm him or her in the form of death, injury and other concomitant diseases. All workers have the right to work in an environment that is safe and not detrimental to their health. To keep pace with technological and economic changes, a number of measures and strategies designed to prevent, control, reduce or eliminate occupational hazards and risks have been developed and applied continuously at the national and global level. In spite of these efforts, occupational hazards and industrial accidents occur on a regular basis, and the number of deaths and injuries are increasingly alarming. It is reported that the workplace claims more than 2.3 million deaths per year, out of which 350,000 are fatal accidents and close to 2 million are work-related diseases. In addition, 313 million accidents occur on the job annually, with many of these resulting in extended absences from work. The human cost of this daily adversity is vast and the economic burden of poor occupational safety and health practices is estimated at 4 percent of global gross domestic product (GDP) each year (ILO, 2014).

In light of this unforeseen form of human suffering, the constitution of ILO announced the principle of protecting workers from all sorts of sickness, disease and injury arising from their employment. ILO adopted a number of conventions and recommendations to protect the rights of workers (Box 8.1). These documents laid down the foundation of responsibility for different actors within the system and outlined the actions to be taken by governments and within enterprises to promote occupational safety and health and to improve working conditions (ILO, 1981). In addition to occupational safety and health, ILO is also concerned about the social safety and security of the workers. As part of this effort, Social Security Convention (No. 102) covers the wide range of social security systems, which include sickness, unemployment, maternity, medical and family benefits as well as survivors' benefits. The Employment Injury Benefits Convention (No. 121) states more detailed principles for the payment of compensation for damages sustained during employment in the workplace. It ensures the minimum standards of payments with 60 percent of wages in the case of temporary or permanent incapacity for work and 50 percent of wages in case of death of the breadwinner. Following the international law and ILO's guidelines, member states are supposed to take effective measures for protection of labor in the home country.

Regulatory means for improving workplace safety and security in Bangladesh

The Bangladesh government has yet to ratify either Convention 102 or 121. However, after the independence of Bangladesh, the industrial development of the country has been instructed by several industrial policies, among them being the Industrial Policy of 1973, the New Industrial Policy of 1982, the Revised Industrial Policy of 1986, Industrial Policy of 1999 and Industrial Policy of 2010. Following these policies, the Bangladesh government has adopted labor laws to protect the rights of the workers. Among the many rights, workplace safety and security is the prime focus. The Labor Law of 2006 clearly states that factory buildings must meet legal standards, electrical equipment should be properly maintained and managers, supervisors and workers should receive adequate training with regards to fire and safety procedures, the emergency exit route should be spacious so that sufficient numbers of workers can avail during an emergency, and the factory gates should be kept unlocked when workers are inside the building. However, as we found in our study, it is unfortunate that neither government nor private owners within the industry are much concerned with the enforcement of these provisions.

Every year deaths and property destruction take place within the industry due to industrial disasters. The number of deaths and property losses could be reduced significantly if a functioning inspection system was in place and owners took effective measures. Undoubtedly, the inspection system is very weak and ineffective due to a lack of personnel and transparency in the administration. Bangladesh Occupational Safety, Health and Environment Foundation (BOSHE) stated that in the year of 2008 there were only 80 personnel involved in inspection activities for the entire country, divided among four major cities with jurisdiction over 24,299 registered factories, roughly 3 million shops and establishments, and two major ports. Among these personnel, only 20 were responsible for occupational health and safety issues (BOSHE, 2013). ILO stated that the number of new workplaces has dramatically increased during recent decades, but the number of inspectors had increased by only 93 in the industry sector. The ILO Committee of Experts vehemently criticized the Bangladesh government for failing to provide for the security of workers in the garment sector. According to a report by Human Rights Watch (HRW), there were only 18 inspectors to monitor an estimated 100,000 factories in and around Dhaka until June 2012 (HRW, 2013). The Expert Committee Report of 2011 mentioned that the Bangladesh government is reluctant to recruit new inspectors into this sector of the industry while also claiming that the existing inspectors have no accountability and training.

Box 8.1 Major ILO instruments for occupational safety and health

From the inception of ILO in 1919 to 2007, roughly half of 188 conventions and 199 recommendations directly or indirectly address the issue of occupational health and safety. The general conditions are contained in the following documents:

- Protection of Worker's Health Recommendation (No. 97), 1953
- Occupational Safety and Health Convention (No. 155) and Recommendation (No. 164), 1981
- Occupational Health Services Convention (No. 161) and Recommendations (No. 171), 1985
- Prevention of Major Industrial Accidents Convention (No. 174) and Recommendation (No. 181), 1993
- List of Occupational Diseases Recommendation (No. 194), 2002
- Protocol of 2002 to the Occupational Safety and Health Convention (No. 155), 1981
- Promotional Framework for Occupational Safety and Health Convention (No. 187) and Recommendation (No. 197), 2006.

Industrial disasters and fate of RMG workers: gender and environment nexus

The most glaring feature that has persisted in the RMG industry of Bangladesh is the poor workplace and the lack of occupational safety. Deaths from fatal fires and collapses of factory buildings occur on a regular basis leading to, along with huge numbers of deaths, physical injuries and property losses. According to a sample investigation report by the Department of Fire Service and Civil Defense, 243 factories out of 797 are at high risk of industrial accidents. Most of the factories have no emergency exit and those that do, have spaces that are too narrow or doors that are kept locked with the prevention of theft cited as a reason. Stampedes triggered by a sense of anxiety and panic have also led to unrecoverable injuries and even death of many workers. As a result, these numbers are growing at an unprecedented rate. According to a report prepared by Research Initiative for Social Equity (RISE) in 2013, fires and factory building collapses have caused at least 1717 deaths from 1999 to 2013 (Table 8.1). A review study based on the reports published in the daily newspapers showed that there were 6271 garment workers who died and 11,783 who were injured in Bangladesh during the period

Table 8.1 Number of deaths and injured in major industrial accidents in the RMG (approx.)

Year	Type of incident	Name of factory	Deaths	Wounded
1990	Fire	Sareka Garments	27	Undocumented
1996	Fire	Lusaka Garments	2	Undocumented
1997	Fire	Tamanna Garments	27	Undocumented
	Fire	Rahman & Rahman Apparels	22	Undocumented
2000	Fire	Chowdhury Knitwear	53	150
2001	Fire	Maico Sweater	24	Undocumented
2002	Fire	Globe Knitting	12	Undocumented
2004	Fire	Misco Supermarket	9	Undocumented
2005	Building Collapse	Spectrum Factory	64	64
	Fire	Shan Knitting	23	Undocumented
2006	Fire	KTS Garments	83	150
	Fire	Jamuna Spinning Mill	6	6
	Fire	Phoenix Fabrics	21	50
	Fire	Sayem Fashion	6	50
2010	Fire	Garib and Garib Sweater	21	10
	Fire	Hameem Group	30	100
2011	Fire	EuroTex	2	62
2012	Fire	Tazreen Fashions	124[a]	300
2013	Fire	Smart Fashion	10	33
	Building Collapse	Rana Plaza	1150[a]	2000
	Fire	Tung Hai Sweater Factory	8	Undocumented

[a] This figure is only for the dead bodies recovered, but many were not found. According to official estimates a total of 332 workers were unidentified. Relatives of the missing workers authenticated documents such as pay slip, appointment letter, identity card (Moazzem, 2013). Over 1000 workers were wounded and permanently disabled. Many injured workers are struggling with their lives in hospitals and dying.

Source: Research Initiative for Social Equity (2015).

of 2005 to 2009, solely from industrial disasters (*Daily Star,* 2014). After the deadly incident of Rana Plaza, rescuers recovered the dead bodies of 1135 workers and 2438 workers with severe physical injuries, and over the next few months, many injured workers expired at hospitals while under treatment (*Odhikar,* 2013).

A study exploring the causes of industrial disasters in Bangladesh was not deemed to be attractive enough to the academics and researchers although it was crucial for the sustainability of the RMG industry. However, this issue received wider coverage and is now well documented by academics and researchers after the Rana Plaza incident. The literatures show that huge losses of properties and lives occurred mainly due to locked exits, the unavailability and inability of using the fire suppression tools and equipment, an insufficient ventilation system and a lack of knowledge about emergency exits during the disaster (Ahmed and Nathan, 2014; Wadud, Huda and Ahmed, 2014; Akhtar and Shimul, 2012). The authorities of the industries are painfully unaware of the possible risks to the workers caused from industrial disasters. Owners' negligence often causes the greatest damage of properties and lost lives. It is well documented by the researchers that the deaths and loss of properties many times over, resulting from industrial disasters, are due to the reluctant and irresponsible role of the employers. The losses could be reduced significantly if employers were conscious about their ethical roles to the workers. Employers are ambivalent to fire safety protocols and ignore building codes when constructing their factories.

Akther et al. (2010) discovered that most of the buildings of garment factories are situated in the center of the city and housed in old buildings that were neither built nor designed for industrial use. Generally, these buildings were built for residential purposes and many of the buildings were not approved by the *Rajdhani Unnayan Kartripakkha* (RAJUK) [the Capital Development Authority of the government of Bangladesh]. The motivating factors for renting these old buildings are often the abundant supply of cheap labor inside the city, shortages of industrial spaces and the comparatively cheap rent. As a result industrial accidents are more likely to occur in the RMG sector. The existing events of industrial accidents in Bangladesh reflect a blend of gender and environment. Most of these industrial accidents are directly associated with poor workplace environment affecting women disproportionately to men. The numbers of women victims are three or four times higher than men, approximately 80 percent of women workers (Slopova, 2013).[1]

Struggling for survival: views from the victims and their families

The resultant consequences of industrial disasters are unbelievable. The sufferings of a deceased worker end as soon as they lose their breath, but survivors carry it till their last breath. Based on in-depth interviews, the following sections mirror the untold miseries of the Rana Plaza survivors.

One of the fatal consequences of the Rana Plaza disaster is the physical disability of the workers. They have lost their hands and legs, and some have even lost their eyesight. After losing parts of their body, they have become fully dependent on their family members for their daily needs. Disabled people experience shame in requiring help from family members for the simplest of tasks such as having meals, using the bathroom and even just to stand up. Sheuly, one of the survivors who lost her hand, lamented:

> As I have lost my hand, I can't do any work. I am fully dependent on my husband for all household work including cooking, cleaning, washing even rearing up children. Although my parents along with my brothers and sisters live in the same house, they do not respond to me very well. When I seek help from my family members, they try to avoid and neglect me. I can't tolerate their negligence. Therefore, I feel that it would [be] better to die than to live.

Some survivors sustained severe head wounds and damange to other parts of the body, while others experienced unbearable trauma throughout the body, and the pain is gradually increasing as the days go by. It is also reported that some workers have already been affected by bone cancer. During the initial stages, workers were provided free medical care services through labor organizations and NGO-initiated medical camps and physiotherapy centers. These services are no longer available to them. Survivors have not continued their treatment for lack of medicine and other essential care services. Victims are counting down the days in the hospital beds while new names are being added to the death list.

The financial crisis of the victims heightens their vulnerability. Victims find themselves in a situation more desperate than they were before. Usually, workers come from rural poor families that are incapable of protecting their members financially. In many families, victims were often the main breadwinner. As a result, many families have lost all sources of income due to the death or injury of the breadwinner after the incident. Victims who suffered injuries, both physical and psychological, struggle to afford the cost of treatment before they find alternative employment. In addition, family members have become burdened by buying food, medicines, clothes and other necessities for the victims. The most unfortunate case is that many women workers who were injured in the Rana Plaza incident and can no longer earn a livelihood have been abandoned by their in-laws. They are also unable to secure help from their own parents and siblings. Psychological trauma is an indispensable part of the victims' daily lives. Many workers reported that they can't even go to sleep. As soon as they fall asleep, they recall the trauma they endured. Nilufa Begum, a 29-year-old woman whose right leg has been crippled, reported:

> After the incident, I could not sleep for a single day. The tragic incident would appear in my mind all the [time]. When I go to bed and close my eyes, I see the roof of the house is falling down [on] me and soon after I run away from my sleep. I have passed uncounted nights without having any sleep and still it is continuing.

The Rana Plaza disaster has created long-term consequences for workers' lives. They suffer from anxiety and have a decreased will to live. After the incidents, many survivors do not have the courage to go outside alone. Very often they are scared and puzzled to be in close proximity to a high-rise building or crowded places. One victim mentioned that she fears entering into a multistoried building. Any sudden noises make her pulse spike, imagining once more the events on that fateful day where debris rained upon her. The severity of pain is twofold among the survivors who have lost their loved ones. They are unable to overcome the loss of their beloved. This deadly incident has been the cause of widowhood for many young women. These young widows are physically and mentally harassed by their in-laws and local touts. Shopna, a young 20-year-old survivor who has not found her husband yet, shared her helplessness and harassment in the following way:

> We [me and husband] got married without the consent of our family and ran away from home leaving all of them. Last few years, we had no contact with our parents' home. As a result, I can't go back either to my parents' home or to my in-laws' house. I have nowhere to go. I can't forget my husband for a single minute. Although I feel severe pain in my head, I do not find any interest or urge to go to

> hospital. The family members of my in-laws' house ask me to give them money. On the contrary, some young boys frequently call me, taking advantage of my widowhood. Some people also wish to marry me, demanding huge amount of dowry. All people assume that I have received huge amount of money for my deceased husband, but truly I receive nothing as the dead body of my husband has not been found. My misfortune is that no one is sympathetic to me. No one think[s] how I am passing my days losing my husband. All are greedy for money, but none are ready to give me a shelter.

Survivors have lost their mental strength and courage. Many of the victims have been cheated by greedy people. Since victims have received some amount of compensation, greedy and cunning men have come forward in the guise of marriage and have robbed them of their money. Losing all forms of financial support, these women lost their will to live and a great number of them resorted to suicide. The resultant loss of parents is a crucial blow from industrial disasters. Many children have lost their father, mother or both. The bereavement of the innocent orphan can never truly end. The orphans are forced to grow up deprived of the love and affection of their parents, which can often lead to harsh effects on the psychological and emotional development of the child. Juli, a 5-year-old girl, lashes out by biting other children, and very often she becomes senseless as a result of the extreme shock of losing her parents. Juli's grandmother said:

> Juli was three years old when she lost her parents. She could not understand yet what happened and therefore believed that they will come back. She is still looking for them on the way through which they used to get back home every day after their work. [It] keeps her silent and [she] shows disinterest to talk with other children. She doesn't like to take shower and have meal on time but rather cries to be fed by her mother.

The interview data also shows the insufficiency and mismanagement of the compensation process. While many of the victims have not received any compensation, some fraudulent people have sought to benefit by making false claims,[2] which is rightly explained by Naomi Klein (2000) in the concept of "Disaster Capitalism". Confirming these malpractices, one of the workers, Selina (pseudonym) reported:

> From [the] Rana Plaza incident some people have become rich while some have become vagabond. Although I have lost my husband,

> become disabled, and am trapped in poverty, I cannot make a valid claim as I lost my identity card; while others, who were not employed in the factories housed in Rana Plaza, have received compensation. Many have made false claims showing their previous identity card. Unfortunately, these fraudulent claims remain unknown to mass people. If I could get a chance to talk with any television [news] channel, I would share my experience with the masses.

Industrial disasters, workers' compensation and corporate social responsibility

Industrial accidents are not new in Bangladesh, but what is more alarming is that factory fires and other tragic accidents are still occurring so frequently. Given the constant pressure to lower costs and the dearth of meaningful government oversight, businesses are continually tempted to reduce costs to the detriment of the workers' safety. All of the incidents documented in recent years could have been avoided if proper regulation and inspection systems took place. Faulty electrical wiring and old and badly maintained equipment and buildings have often been the cause of disasters. Death and serious injury tolls have been high due to the lack of training, procedures and equipment for use both by workers and managers and by the emergency services themselves. Locked, blocked and inadequate exit routes have also been a common factor.

Looking into the current failure in making a safer workplace, we question the role of the actors involved in the global production chain of the garments industry of Bangladesh. The answer to remedy labor injustice lies in holding accountable those responsible for providing and ensuring labor justice. Based on the parameters of power, privilege, interest and collective ability, Iris Young (2006) proposes for shared responsibility of the actors and accordingly sketches the kinds of issues the actors should address and the kinds of actions the actors should take. For her, all actors are not equally responsible due to the variation in power, privilege, interest and ability and therefore, agents must share responsibility with others who are differently situated but connected to bring effective change. According to her social connection model, it is the ethical and legal responsibility of the owners who acquire relative privilege. It is reported that the losses of lives could have been avoided if owners had played a responsible role in both the events of Rana Plaza and Tazreen Fashions (Kernaghan, 2012; Odhikar, 2013). Workers were forced to work unaware of such conditions. In a report, it is stated that most of the women workers were trapped inside the factory and burned alive. All of the workers heard the fire alarm and tried to escape, but the production manager instructed them to continue working and locked the exit gate (Kernaghan, 2012). The same thing happened for Rana Plaza. Workers had no choice but to enter a factory deemed unsafe by inspectors the day before due to intimidation and threats of losing their jobs and the withholding of payment (Sommer, 2014). Therefore, owners of the factory and building must be held accountable for their negligence to uphold adequate safety standards in the workplaces they own and run. Along with owners, the state cannot deny the holding of responsibility for protection of the workers as a citizen and drivers of the economy of the country. Factory and building owners were the main culprit at Tazreen Fashions and Rana Plaza, but no less culpable are the international brands with big orders and tight deadlines that exploit lax safety standards and labor rights. Moreover, the fair share of the profit goes to the corporations who exalt the upholding of labor standards and end up compensating the victims under their act of "corporate social responsibility" (CSR). In general CSR is taken to denote corporate activities, beyond profit making, which include protecting the environment, caring for employees and being ethical in trading and getting involved in the local community (Dusuki, 2008).

The recent fire at Tazreen Fashions and the collapse of Rana Plaza drew the world's attention to the RMG industry in Bangladesh. Global media outlets, international stakeholders, human rights organizations, and also workers' rights and human rights groups have increased the pressure and are demanding compensation and rehabilitation for the disaster victims. Prompt and just compensation needs to be paid, but the question is by whom? Industrial experts, human rights activists, scholars and all concerned people are in consensus that along with the state, corporate partners have an ethical responsibility to ensure a safe workplace and to rehabilitate and compensate the victims and their family members. Since production and services have expanded globally and the state's ability to protect the worker on the national level has been undermined, the main challenge is to find an appropriate institutional agent. The only solution, as explained by Guy Ryder, the Director General of ILO, is

> Prompt and just compensation needs to be paid. It has to be paid to those whose families have lost not only loved ones but a livelihood and future security. It needs to be paid to those who have survived with reduced prospects for future income. Compensation for loss and adversity is as much a right as a fair wage, and it needs to be paid by those who have benefited from such unsafe conditions. In a globalized world, this extends to the consumers, the ultimate

beneficiaries of those who have toiled in unsafe conditions. This is a global imperative and a shared responsibility. (ILO, 2014)

Immediately after the Rana Plaza disaster, victims and their families received emergency allowances from the government, NGOs and a few brand companies. To meet the immediate cost for treatment and other basic needs of the survivors and their families, "Rana Plaza Donors Trust Fund" was formed under the scheme of "Rana Plaza Arrangement" who received the voluntary donations from global brands and private donors, thanks to the initiative by ILO. Global Unions and international NGOs continue to put pressure on multinational brands especially, who were the clients of the factories housed in the building, to donate to the voluntary fund. According to the compensation process, 3600 eligible victims were identified and 80 percent of the victims have received the amount of BDT 96,000 [about US$1200] on average (FIDH, 2014). The amount received by the survivors and their families just after the disaster was wholly insufficient, taking into account the fact that they had just lost their sources of income, while also accruing the burden of rising income costs. One victim said:

> I received BDT 96,000 after the event. However, all amount had to be spent for my treatment purposes. After the incident, my husband who used to work as a day laborer can't go to his workplace due to his engagement to bring me here and there for treatment purpose. Having no income, we are unable even to pay the house rent. I am unable to send my 6-year-old son to school for lack of money. On the other hand, the condition of my leg is becoming worse day by day. Now I am completely unable to move myself due to severe pain. My physician advises me to cut off the leg, but I have no ability to bear the cost for operation. I find no hope to be alive. I want to end my life but can't do it for the affection of my son. If I die, he will be orphan, and then who will take care of him?

In addition, BDT 1,000,000 was given as a fixed deposit to each physically disabled worker who had become disabled at Rana Plaza so that they could find a source of income to maintain their needs.[3] This amount is insufficient to maintain the essential needs of the workers. Sheuly, a beneficiary of the security fund, said:

> My husband can't go to his workplace for household responsibility. At the moment, we don't have any income except the bank interest

> against the fixed deposit that I received as donation from the Prime Minister. I am unable to meet our daily needs including medicines, educational expenses of my elder girl and baby food for 7-month-old girl. Previously, we earned 20,000 taka together in a month, but now we are receiving only 10,000 taka. Therefore, we are passing our days in hardship. It seems that we have to die without having food.

It is unfortunate that all victims have not received their compensation despite two years having already passed. Only 30 disabled workers from the Rana Plaza incident have received their compensation, but family members of the deceased victims have yet to receive any amount. This can be attributed to the lack of proper attention by the multinationals. Although there were about 25 brands and buyers involved with Tazreen Fashions, only Li & Fung and C&A came forward to help the victims and their families.[4] So far Li & Fung has distributed approximately BDT 100,000 (US$1285) payments each to 89 injured workers and the families of 99 deceased workers. C&A has also paid a lump sum of BDT 100,000 to each deceased through the BGMEA and is providing monthly payments of US$15 to the same families (Fozvog et al., 2013). In addition, US$35 is being paid into a savings account for children who lost a parent in the fire. However, the compensation packages are not based on international standards or established best practices and as such are insufficient in fully compensating the losses incurred by victims as a result of the fire. Moreover, many victims have not been covered by this scheme.

A similar situation is observed in the case of Rana Plaza. There were 29 retailers who were linked with the factories in Rana Plaza, but only 13 have committed to compensating the victims (Nelson, 2014). Some multinational corporations were quick to provide one-off payments to victims while others have not yet contributed to the compensation fund.[5] It is an unfortunate reality that two years on since the Rana Plaza incident, many corporations have yet to distribute the initial sum and are unwilling to compensate in full. The Rana Plaza Coordination Committee (RPCC) estimated a revised budget close to US$30 million to fund all authorized payments and medical costs, which includes income replacement payments, and medical and allied care costs, and the available funds are close to US$21 million with a shortfall of US$9 million.[6] The association of the factory owners has not taken any fruitful initiative except initiating the payments three months after the incident. Many of the survivors expressed their dissatisfaction at being mistreated by members of BGMEA. One of the survivors expressed her experiences in the following way:

> After the disaster, my employer has been locked in the jail and all other management staffs are out of contact. Therefore, I am not able to contact my employer. Sometimes, I tried to contact with an elected member of BGMEA seeking help for my treatment. At the initial stage, he gave me hope of helping me but finally made me despair by not receiving my call.

Another initiative was undertaken by a joint collaboration with the German Institute for Cooperation Development (GIZ), Centre for Rehabilitation of the Paralysed (CRP) and BGMEA through the signing of a memorandum of understanding (MoU). This MoU is aimed at helping people to cope with their handicap and return to their work in which CRP provides medical care, counseling, vocational training, rehabilitation and other forms of support to people with disabilities, particularly the Rana Plaza survivors (Textile Today, 2013). Some voluntary and nongovernment organizations particularly NITOR, BILS, Suhrawardy Hospital, BIRDEM General Hospital, Japan-Bangladesh Friendship Hospital, Enam Medical College and Hospital, Dhaka Ahsania Mission, Super Clinic and Diagnostic Centre, and Afnan Hospital and Diagnostic Centre, offered special medical services for the treatment of Rana Plaza victims. These agencies also offered advocacy and counseling services to the traumatized workers. While various efforts are underway, both the government and other stakeholders, including Western retailers, need to do more to make Bangladesh factories safer.

Two years after the collapse of Rana Plaza (April 24, 2013) killed more than 1000 people, garment workers in Bangladesh are still facing "poor working conditions and anti-union tactics by employers including assaults on union organizers", said by Phil Robertson, Asia deputy director, HRW (April 22, 2015). Quoted in Human Rights Watch 2015, said:

> If Bangladesh wants to avoid another Rana Plaza disaster, it needs to effectively enforce its labor law and ensure that garment workers enjoy the right to voice their concerns about safety and working conditions without fear of retaliation or dismissal. If Bangladesh does not hold factory managers accountable who attack workers and deny the right to form unions, the government will perpetuate practices that have cost the lives of thousands of workers.

The 78-page report, "'Whoever Raises Their Head, Suffers the Most': Workers' Rights in Bangladesh's Garment Factories", is based on interviews with more than 160 workers from 44 factories, most of them making garments for retail companies in North America, Europe and Australia.

> Workers report violations including physical assault, verbal abuse – sometimes of a sexual nature – forced overtime, denial of paid maternity leave, and failure to pay wages and bonuses on time or in full. Despite recent labor law reforms, many workers who try to form unions to address such abuses face threats, intimidation, dismissal, and sometimes physical assault at the hands of factory management or hired third parties. (HRW, 2015)

Human Rights Watch called on the Bangladesh government, factory owners and Western retailers "to ensure respect for workers' rights and end the unlawful targeting of labor leaders by factory owners and supervisors".

Transparency International Bangladesh (TIB), in its report, pointed out lack of transparency and dillydallies in the disbursement of the fund for victims of the Rana Plaza collapse, the world's largest workplace disaster. The report said around US$19 million has been deposited to the Rana Plaza Donors' Trust Fund while around US$2.48 million was also added to this from the Prime Minister's fund to help the Rana Plaza victims. However, the list of people who have been compensated for the Rana Plaza tragedy and the amount of the compensation are yet to be made public, the report said. A lion's share of this money is missing; perhaps embezzled by the ruling kleptocracy (*Daily Star*, April 23, 2015). During a presentation of the report, TIB Chairman of the Board of Trustees Sultana Kamal said the accused of the Rana Plaza and Tazreen Fashions tragedies have not been made accountable yet, resulting in such types of accidents frequently. Dr. Iftekharuzzaman, Executive Director of the TIB, said the minimum wage of the RMG workers has been increased after the Rana Plaza tragedy, but it was irrational with their expenditure. The RMG workers are even being deprived of receiving their wages in a timely fashion, he added. Laws have been enacted to prevent accidents in the RMG sector, but it is being misused, he alleged. "A separate ministry should be introduced to ensure good governance in the RMG sector", he observed.

Rana Plaza disaster: a wakeup call for change

The Rana Plaza incident is not the first but has been the world's deadliest catastrophe in the history of industrial accidents. It serves as a grim warning for Bangladesh to the dangers of industrial disasters and to take effective measures to avoid any further incidents. Investors and the state should not wait for future disasters before they act to make the world's factories safe and a decent place to work at. Scholars want to see Rana Plaza and Tazreen Fashions as a turning point in making the apparel industry in Bangladesh safe and secure. The respective persons and institutions will take effective measures to avoid such an accident from happening in the future by taking lessons from these events just as the US did after the Triangle Shirtwaist Factory event. On March 25, 1911, a fire at Triangle Shirtwaist Company in New York caused the death of 146 workers, mostly Jewish immigrant female teenagers. Incredibly, the Triangle factory owners were acquitted of any wrongdoing and made US$60,000 from their insurance payout. Eventually public outcry led to legislation that achieved vast improvements in workers' conditions and factory safety (Yanklowitz, 2013). The US workplace has seen incredible improvement after that event. Similarly, it is expected that this event will be a teachable moment for Bangladesh and other such developing nations who should not be allowed to forget such a tragedy before essential safety measures are put in place. In a quick response, a tripartite statement signed by the government of Bangladesh, employers and workers stipulating the need for structural assessments of RMG factories was made. Subsequently, an integrated National Tripartite Plan of Action on Fire Safety and Structural Integrity in the RMG sector (NTPA) was signed by the government, employers' federations, BGMEA, BKMEA, National Coordination Committee for Workers Education (NCCWE) and the Industrial Bangladesh Council (IBC) representing nine unions. Being pressured by consumers, many retailers conducting business in Bangladesh have started to talk with the owners in order to find ways to improve safety at the factories. Others moved away from Bangladesh and set up their business elsewhere.

Consequently, two important initiatives took effect after the Rana Plaza disaster for fire and building safety: the formation of *Accord* (a platform of 150 retailers and brands mainly from Europe) and *Alliance* (a platform of 27 US-based apparel retailers and brands). These two agreements were signed with the goal of inspecting and setting safety standards in garments factories by the signatories over a five-year period (Greenhouse, 2013; ILO, 2014). Based on the study on the implementation status of initiatives and projects undertaken by various stakeholders, Transparency International of Bangladesh (TIB) noted that the *Accord* has so far carried out inspections of 80 out of 1626 factories and *Alliance* inspected 247 out of 626 factories. Meanwhile, Bangladesh University of Engineering and Technology (BUET) has completed the inspection at 247 out of approximately 2000 factories (TIB, 2014). It is clear that inspection and recovery initiatives will not be successful until inspection departments and fire service stations are equipped and rebuilt. As a result, the government of Bangladesh has made major commitments on the capacity building of the Department of Inspection of Factories and Establishments (DIFE) and Fire Service and Civil Defense (FSCD). By February 2015, 178 new inspectors had been appointed, bringing the total to 270 at DIFE and 210 staff at FSCD, bringing its total to 265 (ILO, 2015). Recruitment of new staff cannot necessarily upgrade the condition of occupational health and safety until employers, supervisors, managers or workers are trained properly. Therefore, an initiative launched under the ILO's RMG program supports the training of 100 master trainers from the BGMEA, BKMEA and BEF as well as the private sector. In a research report based on the experiences at "Next Collection" by Institute of Global Labor and Human Rights (IGLHR), it has been shown that the Bangladesh apparel industry has experienced unprecedented changes in working conditions through the strong monitoring and inspections after the Rana Plaza disaster (Kernaghan, 2014). Some labor advocates called the effort divisive and a sham. They argue that multinational corporations are more concerned with increasing workplace safety so that they can avoid future disasters, but nothing is seen from them in the form of compensation and rehabilitation of the victims. On the other hand, inspection of the factories will not make any significant improvement without renovating the old buildings and equipment, which requires huge investment. Workers' Rights Consortium Executive Director Scott Nova said, "The new effort contains no real obligation on the part of brands and retailers to pay for the building renovations necessary to convert death traps in Bangladesh into safe factories" (cited in Greenhouse, 2013).

Conclusion

Industrial disaster in the RMG sector is a frequent occurrence that causes innumerable deaths and property losses. The loss from the disaster is not compensable at all. It forces workers into a more vulnerable situation than they were in before the employment. In retrospect, industrial disaster often leads workers from poverty to destitution. In spite of all legal protection, the compensation process and initiatives for fire safety and work environment remain far below the legal minimum. It is the prime responsibility of the state to take effective measures so that employers cannot escape making improvements to the work environment. The government could potentially force the owners within the industry to comply with safety standards and enforce the law that prohibits the use of multistoried buildings as sites of industrial use and ensure that the industry has essential equipment for safety of the workers with due respect to local and international labor laws and regulations. The factory inspection system should be strengthened and be rid of any unfair practices. The state should ensure that the right to form associations and collective bargaining is not being obstructed. Along with the state, global corporations should be more aware of working conditions in the factory and equally liable to compensate and rehabilitate disabled workers and their dependent family members. Counseling and advocacy services are an emergent need for the mentally disrupted and traumatized workers. Occupational social work practice could be an effective alternative to help the workers adapt, releasing workplace stress and trauma in the process.

9
The Global Treadmill of Production and the Environment

Introduction

The intent of this chapter is to illustrate how the global "treadmill of production" (see the section below) arguably leads to the global "treadmill of destruction". Drawing upon the theory developed by Allan Schnaiberg (1980), the treadmill of production (ToP) focuses on production as the key process in explaining the increasing environmental problems in today's globalization of production, especially in developing countries whereby environmental degradation occurs as a direct result of production demand from advanced developed countries. Therefore, with the interaction of state, capital and the environment, ecological resources are increasingly converted into profits via transnational organization of production and market exchange. Consequently, with an intensification of production processes driven by competition and drive to increase profits in the capitalist world economy, there has been a rising amount of both resource withdrawals from and toxic additions to the environment (Islam, 2013; Schnaiberg, 1980). The endless production thus results in a continual process of environmental degradation that impacts ecosystems and human well-being.

Due to globalization of production, the organization of economic production has also become increasingly globalized whereby profit-oriented transnational corporations (TNCs) began to outsource their production plants and operations to developing countries in a bid to maximize profit by reducing production costs and increasing operational flexibility (McMichael, 2008). Under pressure to become more competitive and develop their economies, developing nations also contribute to the endless cycle of production by providing financial incentives, weak environmental regulations and low-wage labor to attract these corporations from developed countries. Consequently, there is a relocation of deskilled tasks from developed nations alongside the supply of cheap labor from the developing nations, which gave rise to the New International Division of Labor (NIDL). As mentioned in earlier chapters, the NIDL then led to the creation of a "world factory" with a proliferation of export platforms in developing nations such as export processing zones (EPZs) or other special economic zones (McMichael, 2008). As a consequence, environmental destruction became more prevalent in developing nations from the additions of toxic by-products from production processes into their local environment. Thus, with economic globalization, extensive trading in goods and services drives the endless cycle of production processes, which ultimately leads to the global "treadmill of destruction", whereby environmental destruction and its related problems are generated through these production processes (Islam, 2013).

Clearly then, the central tenets of the treadmill of production theory can be further understood within the broader framework of world systems theory in understanding how the dynamics of political-economic interactions between developed core countries and semi-peripheral/peripheral developing countries lead to an unequal distribution of environmental vulnerabilities (Rice, 2009). Driven to achieve economic growth and development, demands on increased production from the affluent developed nations inevitably led to increased additions of waste and environmental pollution in the semi-periphery/periphery nations where production takes place (Islam, 2013). Such "unequal ecological exchange" is also further perpetuated under the globalization project when financial markets are highly integrated through free trade and economic arrangements such as free-trade agreements. Therefore, an unequal relationship has been forged between the developed nations who dominate the core of the system and other developing countries that are dependent upon them for trade and business, allowing their environments and cheap labor to be exploited. Hence, following the treadmill of production and world systems theories, this chapter further covers analysis of case studies, such as the Chinese world factory, export processing zones (EPZs) in Bangladesh, and *maquiladoras* in Mexico, to illustrate how the treadmill of production leads to increased environmental vulnerabilities faced by these countries in their pursuit of development and economic agendas. Lastly, the environmental laws and regulations implemented in each of the case studies in light of the ecological problems faced will also be reviewed.

What is the "treadmill of production" theory?

Allan Schnaiberg (1980) coined the "treadmill of production" framework in an attempt to delineate the anthropogenic causes and consequences of environmental problems. This theory, a strand of neo-Marxist understanding of capitalism's relationship with the environment, argues that the continuous race of production, through a continuous enhancement of productive forces (biotechnology, for instance), and the need for its continued consumption –galvanized by, for example, the corporate-framed ideology of modernization, competitiveness, free trade, and social institutions such as education, family, labor union, and media – creates a critical interchange of "withdrawals" (extraction of resources from the environment) and "additions" (what is returned to the environment in the form of pollution and garbage) that can disorganize the biospheric system. As new technologies are more energy- and chemical-intensive, the industry takes more from the environment and returns more toxic elements. The theory proposes that under the capitalistic mode of production today, the world has embroiled itself in a vicious cycle culminating in global environmental destruction.

The treadmill of production theory proposes that the most fundamental characteristic of our capitalist mode of production is a never-ending "cycle of production" (Schneiberg, 1980; Islam, 2013). In the pursuit of global unending demands, withdrawals are made from the environment in the form of liberal resource extraction. These withdrawals are made in direct opposition to the addition that ensues. Additions are made in the form of toxic wastes and chemicals, much to the detriment of the environment. The economic growth that is achieved from the creative and skillful manipulation of withdrawn resources encourages a pursuit for further growth. Under the capitalistic mode of production, this is only achieved through intensified and accelerated rates of withdrawals and hence additions. As Islam (2013) explains, no consideration or attempt for a change in consumer lifestyle is encouraged: the pursuit of economic growth under this model simply encourages sourcing new areas for withdrawals after the resources in an area are exhausted to their limit.

The impacts of the treadmill of production, however, are realized and experienced differently in the global North and the global South. To capture this dynamic, we can refer to a recently developed "double-risk society" model that argues that compared with the global North, the global South is "doubly vulnerable" because of its preexisting vulnerable social system (characterized by, among other things, lack of democratic practices, pervasive social inequality and corruption, and poor record of rule of law) as well as external pressures (coming from, for example, global climate change, debt repayment schedule, etc.) (Islam, 2013; Islam and Lim, 2015). We will examine these impacts in the following sections.

Global debt regime

The debt regime played a pivotal rule in paving the way for a global treadmill of production when debt management came under the dictatorship of global managers including the World Bank (WB) and International Monetary Fund (IMF). McMichael (2008) argues that under this regime, WB's prerogative became providing policy loans in order to encourage market-oriented economic growth strategies in Third World states. However, these loans were a guise meant to coerce Southern economies into allowing resource extraction by transnational corporations (TNCs) in the name of development (McMichael, 2008; Islam, 2013, 2014). This debt regime that came under an obvious dictatorship had a dual consequence. First, loan conditions were constructed such that abiding countries were rewarded while non-abiding countries were penalized. Second, the managerial role of multinational corporations (MNCs) burgeoned to the extent that the WB could legally evaluate the governance of debtor countries without any consent from its constituent citizens. These forces played a central role in allowing TNCs and MNCs to engage in excessive withdrawals of raw materials from the environment for large-scale production and a resultant addition to it in the form of wastes.

For instance, in Chile, the restructuring of debt in the 1980s was facilitated by a massive decrease in social spending while a simultaneously occurring export boom helped rid the country of its debts. While Chile was lauded as a model for other countries by President Bush, little attention was paid to how the pursuit of global efficiency had weakened the domestic fabric of social security, local production and environmental sustainability (McMichael, 2008). This unprecedented growth by large-scale production was facilitated by resource and labor extraction in Chile. However, the consequence was a worrying trend of deepening social polarization. For example, by 1990, 40 percent population of Chile was living in impoverished slum conditions. At this instance, it becomes evident that the institutionalization of the debt regime played a critical role in devising the necessary climate for never-ending production through repeated withdrawals of labor and resources. That is, what was added to the society and environment was social insecurity in the form of starvation and impoverishment for local producers, and the irreversible and continued destruction of the environment.

The Chinese world factory

For the past 30 years till now, China has heralded the status of "world factory" and has been the magnet for global manufacturing companies. Since the open-door policy in 1978, China has been successful in attracting foreign investments. In the 1980s, the Chinese government encouraged and attracted foreign investments into its nation by establishing special economic zones (SEZs) in a bid to boost its economy (McMichael, 2008). With preferential tax and tariff treatment, the SEZs have been successful in gaining the attention of foreign investors and have become the preferred site for these investors (Liu and Diamond, 2005). Moreover as recorded in 1995, the nation provides a large pool of cheap labor with the ratio of factory wages in China to its neighboring countries such as South Korea/Taiwan and Japan to be approximately 1:30:80. Besides, it is common for the Chinese workers, who are largely from the poorer hinterlands to take on 12-hour shifts and seven-day work weeks. Therefore, apart from tax and tariff benefits of the SEZs, the cheap Chinese labor force further propels investors to relocate their manufacturing base and labor-intensive plants to China as they are able to reduce their production costs in order to be more competitive globally. Within the period of 1980 to 2001, a total of 380,000 foreign-owned exporting plants were set up in China, causing the Chinese proportion of world exports to increase sharply from 1 percent to nearly 50 percent (McMichael, 2008). Today, China produces 70 percent of the world's toys, 60 percent of its bicycles, 50 percent of its shoes and 33 percent of its luggage (Zhang, 2006). Thus, it is not surprising for China to be synonymous with the "world factory" and to find an item with the label "Made in China" in various parts of the world.

Taking on the status of "world factory", the huge influx of foreign trade and investments have fueled the Chinese economy, bringing about tremendous economic growth. Following the treadmill of production, it is unfortunately evident that China's economic growth is happening at the expense of its environment and human well-being. According to the *New York Times* (2007), many Chinese-owned manufacturing plants, which produce and export cheap products to consumer markets of developed areas such as the United States and Europe, were subcontracted by foreign companies who were the ones mainly responsible for leaving behind harmful pollutants. This includes discharging industrial wastes into rivers and pumping toxic smoke into the atmosphere. In addition, most of the foreign investors in China consume natural resources and leave pollutants behind, bringing adverse impacts to the environment. Furthermore, as of 1995, almost 30 percent of these foreign investment projects, such as chemical, petrochemical and dyeing, were located in pollution-intensive industries (PIIs), of which 13 percent were highly pollution-intensive industries (OECD, 2002). Often, these PIIs transfer pollution-intensive products and technologies that are outdated and illegal in their home country to China, causing severe and irreversible environmental damages (Liu and Diamond, 2005).

A considerable amount of news reports and literatures on the environmental woes in China have been published over the years. The environmental situation in China is negative and continuously deteriorating. A report by the Ministry of Environment Protection (MEP) reflected that 57.3 percent of the groundwater quality in 198 cities in 2012 measured as very poor, whereas 30 percent of the river basins were polluted by industrial wastes (Duggan, 2013; Hu, 2013). This threatens human well-being, as over half of the Chinese population relies on groundwater as a source of drinking water (Hu, 2013). As such, this pollution poses huge problems to the Chinese population as they face scarcity in clean drinking water, with one in every three people from the rural areas lacking access to safe drinking water (MacBean, 2007). Furthermore, the air quality in Northern China hit its peak low when thick smog blanketed more than 1 million square kilometers of area largely due to the burning of coal for energy, affecting hundreds of millions of people. It was reported that only 27 out of 113 key cities in China have reached air quality standards in 2012 (Duggan, 2013). With increased usage of energy from the proliferation of industrial and manufacturing plants, more coal will be burned, and this intensifies the entire air pollution problem in the nation. In addition, the rise in industrial and manufacturing plants also resulted in an increasing output of industrial waste gases into the atmosphere (Liu and Diamond, 2005). With that, the Chinese nation is confronted with increasing health-related problems from air pollution such as lung cancer and respiratory diseases among its people. Also, the bad air quality in China resulted in 1.2 million premature deaths as of 2010 (Wagstaff, 2013).

The central Chinese authorities have shown increasing awareness for the varied environmental problems with the introduction of more than 100 policies, laws and regulations to mitigate and control environmental degradation. However, the impressive body of environmental laws and regulations exists only on paper and lacks effective enforcement and implementation at the local levels as economic development supersedes environmental concern in the eyes of local governments (Liu and Diamond, 2005). In addition, financial penalties for the breach of these environmental regulations are usually low and, at times, refunded by the local governments via reduced taxes (MacBean, 2007). With that, the lax environmental control propels foreign investments into the nation with industrial plants discharging toxic wastes and untreated sewage into the environment in a bid for profit maximization by saving on the costs for treating these industrial wastes or investments on better, environmentally friendly technologies (OECD, 2002). Thus, this exacerbates the environmental problems in China and explains the mounting water and air pollution as mentioned above.

Both host governments and foreign manufacturers tend to only quantify economic costs and profits, while completely disregarding and neglecting the debilitating consequences of such extensive production on the environment. Ecological pollution and degradation are seldom given high consideration, resulting in unsustainable manufacturing practices that negatively impact the quality of life of individuals living in the surrounding areas of the EPZs. In China, numerous laws and regulations have been introduced in order to impose corporate social responsibility toward the protection of the environment. In 2007, administrative measures toward the control of electronic pollution were implemented to ensure safe recycling and disposal of wastes. However, the institutionalization of environmental laws is not necessarily complemented with regular enforcement by government officials (Fu and Gao, 2007). As such, there is little motivation on the part of employers to engage in special efforts and invest extra costs to ensure that they comply with environmental regulations.

Thus, manufacturing wastes are rarely treated properly or relocated to appropriate disposal sites. Instead, they are dumped into the surrounding areas, contaminating the water supply of the residents in the area (Fu and Gao, 2007). Poor water quality results in greater incidences of contracting diseases and risk of hepatitis A. Wildlife, flora and fauna found in the territory may be poisoned by the deteriorating quality of toxic air, water and soil due to pollution from the manufacturing sites (Madani, 1999). Furthermore, individuals who tend to be affected by such environmental degradation are mostly poor and ill-educated, and hence, have no power to contest such unfair and hazardous conditions. As such, while the creation of EPZs have enabled Third World nations to attain lower rates of unemployment and an increase in foreign investment, they have also encouraged the super-exploitation of workers, enhanced a gender-separated, unequal system and resulted in an ecological crisis with severe detrimental consequences on the Third World population and its environment. All in all, the influx of foreign trade and investments boosted the Chinese economy, but they have also led to even greater and irreversible ecological and environmental problems. This reflects how the treadmill of production in China ironically created endless destruction to the environment and its people.

Export processing zones – Bangladesh

As discussed earlier, even though the objectives of setting up EPZs are to facilitate economic growth and industrialization of developing nations, in reality many of these EPZs were generating the "race to the bottom" phenomenon due to the lack of social and environmental regulations. The EPZs in Dhaka, the capital city of Bangladesh, illustrated how more often than not, EPZs are generating the treadmill of destruction through the endless treadmill of production, where development proved to be a myth and these EPZs instead led to detrimental and perhaps irreversible damages in the environmental aspects of developing countries.

EPZs were established in Bangladesh during the formation of the Bangladesh Export Processing Zones Authority (BEPZA) in 1980. Similar to other Third World nations, the Bangladesh government allowed EPZs to be set up, with the aim of achieving economic growth. Even though EPZs were an important instrument for Bangladesh to attain economic development and create employment, research has shown that the drawbacks of EPZs greatly outweighed the economic benefits (Fakir, Miah and Hossain, 2013). Ever since the creation of EPZs and the move toward industrialization, Bangladesh was plagued with ecological and social problems it lacked the resources to cope with, specifically for Dhaka. The extreme level of environmental degradation faced by Dhaka can be primarily traced to the creation of EPZs within and around the city. EPZs led to the phenomenon of rapid urbanization and industrialization, which resulted in serious environmental problems such as pollution and health-related diseases suffered by the people dwelling in Dhaka (Rahman, 2011).

Some of the critical environmental issues caused by the EPZs are industrial pollution – bad air and water quality in the city. The emission of toxic gases from various industries in Dhaka had exceeded the safety level due to poor control and management over these industries (Rahman, 2011). Industrial pollution played a huge role in destroying Dhaka's environment. The major rivers surrounding Dhaka were heavily polluted by the discharge of unprocessed chemical and microbial substances from industries near the banks of these rivers. Not only did the industrial pollution result in degradation of air and water bodies in Dhaka, but it also caused widespread health-related problems, which will be elaborated later. This endless production by the industries in the city also made Dhaka a region with the poorest air and water quality, which posed a huge problem. The discharge of industrial wastes into the major rivers of Dhaka has also polluted the branches of water connected to these rivers, affecting almost every water body in the city. Furthermore, the authorities did not have the resources to handle this situation when the inhabitants in Dhaka required more than 2000 liters of clean water daily; but its Water Supply Authority (WASA) could only supply approximately 1300–1500 liters of water per person per day (Rahman, 2011).

Another serious issue faced is health problems due to high environmental pollution and degradation. Due to poor air quality in Dhaka, approximately 120,000 children died of respiratory problems, and the majority of such problems were caused by a form of air pollutant and suspended particulate matter (SPM). Additionally, water pollution also resulted in the spread of diseases such as diarrhea, skin problems and so forth. Bangladesh as a country has the highest rate of respiratory infections and diarrheal disease, caused by environmental degradation, compared to other southeast countries. In short, Bangladesh was an example of how EPZs have resulted in endless destruction in the city, ranging from environmental impacts to its related health problems. Thus, these EPZs have brought about more detrimental consequences than benefits to Bangladesh. The EPZ industries were the main culprits of the devastating level of air and water pollution in Dhaka. These problems were compounded by the lack of resources in Bangladesh to respond to and mitigate these challenging issues.

Nonetheless, these environmental problems also garnered responses from two main bodies, namely the government of Bangladesh and nongovernmental organizations (NGOs). In the past, the Bangladesh government had only set up a Department of Environment and Pollution Control (DEPC) under the Ministry of Local Affairs, which had limited power and control in protecting the environment. This was improved upon through the setup of an official branch of the Ministry for Environment and Forests (MoEF) to formulate policies that protect the environment. The Department of Environment (DoE) became responsible for implementing these policies. The NGOs also played a prominent role in mitigating these environmental issues. There are mainly two types of NGOs, one of which focuses solely on environmental protection while the other involves the cooperation of other NGOs to incorporate the environmental component into their projects. It is known as the Coalition of Environmental NGOs (CEN) . There was also cooperation between NGOs and the government in tackling these problems via the creation of the National Environment Management Action Plan (NEMAP) and other environmental projects such as the Sustainable Environment Management Project (SEMP) (Islam, 1999). But despite the efforts by the government of Bangladesh and NGOs, the environment continues to deteriorate, which shows the need for more adequate and effective policies to curb these issues in Bangladesh. Therefore, as discussed, the EPZs in Dhaka failed to alleviate poverty as promised and have intensified its environmental and social problems, lubricating the treadmill of destruction.

Mexico's *maquiladoras*

With growing international competition in the world capitalist economy, US corporations and other non-Mexican corporations began to offshore their factories and production operations to the nearby low-cost U.S.-Mexico border region, primarily to take advantage of lower production costs due made available through cheap labor and reduced transportation costs (Reblin, 1995). Accordingly, in response to such new forms of international production relationships as offshore assembly and international subcontracting, Mexico introduced the *maquiladora* program in 1965 to promote industrialization, with the aim of developing its economy, generating employment and attracting new technology (Williams, 1995). Financial incentives are also provided to foreign-owned manufacturers to enjoy duty-free entry of raw materials and production components into Mexico and the ease of access into primary consumer markets.

With that, the Mexican border became heavily dotted with a plethora of industries ranging from apparel, electrical and electronic, furniture and other manufacturing plants known as *maquiladoras*, with over a million workers employed in these assembly-for-export plants to assemble products that are exported to the United States for sale (Corpwatch, 1999). Subsequently, with globalization, the *maquiladora* program gained even greater impetus under the North American Free Trade Agreement (NAFTA) – a regional trade agreement forged by Canada, the United States and Mexico in 1994 to establish free trade privileges (e.g., no taxes are imposed on imported and exported goods) in the region to spur economic growth and create prosperity for the three countries (NAFTANOW.ORG, 2012).

Nonetheless, the economic advantages of international production sharing and the promised prosperity amplified by NAFTA were not equally shared by all partaking countries – Mexico in particular. Despite the creation of new income and job opportunities for the local population, many problems were also experienced by Mexicans when periods of rapid industrial growth and expansion in production contribute to environmental degradation and related health problems (Reblin, 1995).

As a dimension of the transnational organization of production designed to accelerate the treadmill of production, Mexico's *maquiladoras* are characterized by minimal restrictions on transnational movement of goods and investment capital and generally few environmental regulations (Rice, 2009). Raw and semi-processed materials flow from the United States and other developed countries into Mexico for subsequent assembly into finished products. Thus, the *maquiladoras* became one mechanism underlying the transferring of social and ecological costs of industrial production from the industrialized core to periphery or semi-periphery regions like the Mexican border (Rice, 2009).

Ecological additions to local environment via illegal dumping and trans-boundary movement of hazardous waste results in environmental degradation and affects human well-being. As the assembly plants practice unsafe and illegal disposal practices, raw sewage and toxic metals are indiscriminately added into the local environment, increasing the threat of environmental pollutions such as soil contamination and groundwater pollution. With the growth of electronics, chemical and furniture industries, the threat of environmental degradation has also correspondingly increased because the electronics industry poses enormous threats to surface water and groundwater due to the use of large amounts of industrial solvents in the production process (Williams, 1995). Furthermore, to avoid complying with the costly environmental laws and regulations in the United States, there have also been an increasing number of multinational corporations such as California's furniture industry moving their operations to the borderlands to benefit from Mexico's lax enforcement of environmental laws (Reblin, 1995). Consequently, hazardous waste from the United States is increasingly exported and dumped in the borderlands by US-owned *maquiladoras* due to Mexico's geographic proximity to the US and its desire to attract foreign investment. Such illegal trans-boundary movement and dumping of hazardous waste was further intensified with the introduction of NAFTA, which contributes to increased trade and cross-border traffic as well as industrial relocation (Eaton, 1995).

With illegal disposal of waste material continuing to threaten the borderlands environment with devastating degradation such as soil contamination and groundwater pollution, there is a concomitant increase in threat to the general well-being of Mexicans in the region. Being a poor country, Mexico faces severe limitations in financial resources to provide adequate and proper treatment, storage and disposal (TSD) facilities for the toxic by-products of manufacturing processes (Eaton, 1995). In addition, it also fails to satisfy the population's needs for sewage systems, potable water and proper housing facilities (Williams, 1995). Consequently, its people suffer serious health problems due to widespread environmental degradation. For example, between 1986 and 1991, there was reportedly an outbreak of 90 cases of deadly birth defects, known as anencephaly, which threatened the lives of unborn children in the borderlands with neural tube defects (Reblin, 1995). Although the cause of these birth defects has not been officially determined, researchers and residents along the Mexican border have largely attributed them to the discharge of toxic compounds into rivers caused by the *maquiladora* industries' poor environmental practices and insufficient sewage facilities. In response to environmental degradation in the borderlands, there have been various initiatives inspired by both the US and Mexican governments as well as environmental and social groups. Nevertheless, given the importance of the *maquiladora* industry to the NAFTA signatories in terms of economic returns, the governments' position on regulating and enforcing stringent environmental laws and regulations has been ineffective. Moreover, as NAFTA does not compel tri-national standardization of environmental regulations, governments are therefore generally less rigorous in enforcing strict environmental standards (Williams, 1995).

However, as the *maquiladora* industry and its related environmental dangers receive increased attention from environmentalists and social groups, growing focus on environmental issues has spawned. For example, an environmental side agreement to NAFTA, known as the North American Agreement on Environmental Cooperation (NAAEC) (Reblin, 1995) was negotiated to specifically address environmental protection. Over time, there is also a growth of bi-national environmental organizations such as the Border Environmental Cooperation Commission (BECC) that play a role in correcting undesirable practices that have caused environmental damage in the local environment (Williams, 1995). To counter the environmental degradation perpetrated by the *maquiladoras*, environmentalists also engage in activities such as collecting data and monitoring air and water standards as well as lobbying locally and transnationally to generate funds for initiatives directly related to the environmental issues posed by the region's *maquiladora* industry (Williams, 1995). Like the previous cases, the *maquiladora* program has generated disastrous environmental and health problems, mirroring the treadmill of destruction.

Military industrial complex

The military industrial complex (MIC) appears to have become the prerogative of powerful states in efforts to fend for themselves. This prerogative is another instance of a global treadmill of production and an eventual global treadmill of destruction. President Eisenhower first introduced the MIC in delineating the monetarily driven relationship among legislators, the national armed forces and the arms industry. This relationship is characterized by political donations of great proportions by defense corporations and approval for military expenditure by officials elected by defense corporations (Gould, 2007). Under this "iron triangle", a greater proportion of citizens' taxes are redistributed to military expenditures. For instance, Gould (2007) posits that 50 cents on every tax dollar since the 1940s has been dedicated to military expenditures. That is, priorities are immediately shifted from more important areas of concern like education, health and the environment. Furthermore, the MIC does not take into consideration its effects on the environment in attempting to establish "national security". The irony that it undermines the very environment it seeks to protect under the military industrial system is not recognized. On the contrary, military activities and productions are exempted from any environmental protection legislation (Gould, 2007). For example, a report by Weigley (2013) published that the 100 largest contractors sold $410 billion in arms and military services in 2011. This is an extremely telling piece of statistic on how lucrative the military industry is and the extent to which the industry has developed. However, this ever-increasing production is not without ecological consequences.

For instance, the film *Beyond Treason* (Lewis and Riley, 2005) paints a clear picture on the withdrawals and additions perpetuated by the military industrial complex in the United States. For the most part, mental patients, prostitutes and the general public were used as guinea pigs for military experiments and research, without their consent or knowledge. A consequence of this is the destruction suffered by the environment and human population during the Gulf War. In the infamously known Gulf War illness or "mystery disease", the use of illegal depleted uranium resulted in irreparable damage socially and environmentally. Despite making illegal depleted uranium, the US continued not only producing it in large quantities but also selling it to 17 other countries. According to Dr. Doug Rokke, 350 tons of depleted uranium was produced, and as a consequence, radioactive waste was thrown elsewhere even though there were memorandums stating the serious health threats these posed. This unending production in the guise of defense inadvertently resulted in generating environmental and social hazards. For instance, the estimated 300 million tons of depleted uranium used in the first Gulf War made food and water unusable, caused neurological complications for army personnel and affected Iraqi children, who began experiencing higher rates of birth defects, leukemia and immunity problems (Lewis and Riley, 2005). Despite the known fact that one pound of depleted uranium takes 9 billion years to be completely removed from the environment, the use was not administered and social and environmental risks were totally neglected.

Sustainable treadmill of production?

It is perhaps too simplistic a view to discount the treadmill of production theory as always inevitably resulting in environmental destruction. For example, there are paradigms that champion the capitalist mode of production claiming that perpetual production can occur in concordance with ecological considerations. In doing so, sustainable development is fostered and environmental damage is significantly reduced. One such paradigm is ecological modernization. Under this paradigm, the advent of super-industrialization and modernization under capitalism will establish green consumerism, environmentally friendly technologies and green policies. That is, the current conflict between the ecology and economy will be bridged and "harmonized" (Revell, 2002; Islam, 2013).

Proponents of ecological modernization believe that the issue of ecocide could and can be better handled if governments and legal institutions were to push for more stringent laws with harsher sanctions and penalties in place if firms and companies refuse to comply. While this may be difficult to execute, it is not impossible. For instance, as a response to the devastation in Matamoros, the United States and Mexican environmental agencies have started to communicate with each other in an attempt to alleviate the problem. Additionally, with regards to this issue, many felt that problems such as illegal dumping of toxic waste would perpetually burgeon if there is no strong new agreement or treaty on broader environmental issues (Kelly, 1993). Thus, this highlights the need for cooperation from the governments if environmentally sustainable production is to be realized.

Conclusion

The global treadmill of destruction is a serious phenomenon under the global treadmill of production in the capitalist system. Some of the processes that facilitate this phenomenon highlighted in this chapter are a testament to how ever-increasing additions and withdrawals have largely led to irreparable environmental and social destructions. This is evident in how many environments and communities continue to be blatantly exploited under relentless production by corporations. The disconnections inherent in economic-centric businesses and nature display little regard for the preservation of the environment. In considering "humans above nature" under the conditions of neoliberal globalization, there is limited or no effort made toward ecological protection by capitalist corporations. Until this human exceptionalist paradigm is annihilated and replaced with more sustainable development, the earth is headed down a path of destruction. Thus, there needs to be not only a reconsideration of current production and consumption patterns, but also a move toward more sustainable development. In that, the ecology-economy divide has to be bridged through sustainable development by engaging responsible governments, nongovernmental organizations (NGOs), unions, corporations, consumers and social justice movements.

10
Conclusion: Social Justice in the Globalization of Production

Globalization of production and the triangular nexus

Ever since its inception, capitalism has taken several forms to sustain its position as a dominant form of economic system. The basic form of capitalism was found in agrarian societies where commodity surpluses were sold for profit. During the Industrial Revolution, as society progressed into industrial capitalism, Henry Ford's remarkable invention of the assembly line that facilitated speedier production of cars was replicated in various industries throughout the global economy. This marked the beginning of the Fordist regime, where industries began to see unprecedented production of goods in the emergence of machineries. While this has brought about standardization and an increase in quality of commodities produced, workers were also subjected under strict and rigid control systems with no room for creativity to flourish as difference was seen as a compromise on standards. In addition, people began to work in factories and produce not for themselves but consumers whom they might never have met. Profit was also consolidated in the hands of the owners of those with means of production, while workers were reduced to getting wages for their labor. During the Fordist regime, males were traditional breadwinners and were predominant in the workforce. The majority of the women took on roles of the traditional homemaker, and few participated in the industrial economy. Also in the Fordist regime, increased demand and the advancement of technology enabled, expedited and intensified extraction of raw materials and resources, creating huge amounts of land wastes that were not disposed of properly. However, the issue was put on the back burner due to pressing issues such as unemployment and economic crises.

The fall of Fordism led to a shift to the post-Fordist regime whereby capitalism was spread across the world through the "development project" which impelled Second and Third World countries to successfully participate in the world market (McMichael, 2008; Islam, 2013). The emergence of global managers headed by First World economies and their leaders constructed various structural policies that compelled Third World countries to free up their markets. Subjected under their heavy debt regimes, Third World countries had few alternatives but to give up their governing sovereignty to private corporations. During this period, many state enterprises were acquired by profit-driven private corporations, resulting in huge amounts of state budget withdrawn from Third World citizens. These private corporations continue to exploit cheap labor costs in Third World countries that have no bargaining power. Under the new policy of deregulation, the concentricity of jobs in capital-intensive countries led to displacement of many while those with no access to knowledge were left with low-skilled labor in Third World countries. However, low-skilled labor is unattractive and characterized by instability due to subcontracting, suppressed wages, deprivation of rights and access to health care. Many of these workers work in export processing zones (EPZs), normally cut off from the outside world. The majority of the workers in the EPZs are females, stereotyped for being suited to the jobs because of their "dexterity and patience" but are, in effect, subjected to gender inequality in a patriarchal market system (Islam, 2008). Last but not least, the post-Fordist regime also saw the emergence of various counter-globalization movements with respect to the environment. While environmental degradation was put on the backburner before, signs of climate change have given environmentalists the urgency of the hour to raise awareness with regard to industrial practices that are harmful to the environment. Therefore, the critical triangular nexus among labor, gender and the environment in the globalization of production is profound.

Contemporary globalization of production is made up of networks of "commodity chains", or sequences of production stages, located in a number of countries at sites that provide inputs of labor and materials contributing to the fabrication of a final product. This concept helps us illuminate the global social and environmental linkages in the products we consume. It links people, processes and places from different origins, coming together to form a product, an experience. The primary focus of global commodity chain is the international trading system and the increasing economic integration of international production and marketing chains. For many countries and companies, this involves searching for the lowest possible costs, which are then done through and often result in, for example, outsourcing, displacement, informalization and recolonization (McMichael, 2008). In the earlier chapters we have seen these outcomes.

Outsourcing, the relocation of goods and services production as a cost-reduction strategy and a means to increase flexibility for an organization, largely relies on the development of information and communication technologies in order to ensure smooth processing and cost efficiency. Outsourcing trends, generally characterized by movement from the North to the South, tend to move to Third World countries and exploit their cheap labor and the environment. When states privatize, they outsource public sectors as well. Outsourcing has also spawned several other phenomena, such as the increase in ecological footprints, ghost acres and ecological overshooting (McMichael, 2008). *Displacement*, which in our case is the spread of loss of jobs, is caused by structural unemployment. This trajectory is the result of casualization, automation of processes, and outsourcing, causing unemployment for local people. Other causes of displacement in different parts of the world include forced resettlement by infrastructure projects, civil wars, food revolutions and the destabilization of rural communities by market forces. People can be displaced not only by but also for development. In 2000, over one billion workers were unemployed or underemployed, giving rise to, among other things, *informalization*. As we have seen earlier, neoliberal globalization generated different kinds of informalized sectors such as: informal self-employed (street vendors, garbage pickers), informal labor of the formal sector (contracted and migrant workers), and in-fact informal labor – formal workers in an informalizing formal economy (workers who have little power in terms of legal rights, workers in developing countries). The "informal self-employed" category is more prevalent in poorer developing countries, the "informal labor of the formal sector" category in relatively more developed countries, and the "in-fact informal labor" exists in both developed and less developed countries. The redundant labor forces, structurally unemployed and marginalized live in shanty towns, slums and ghettos. Starting with EPZs, labor has been progressively disorganized through weakening and dismantling of labor laws and regulations, in cycles of competition, which includes first-generation labor forces as de-peasantization has progressed. The last major trajectory in the globalization of production is that of re-colonization, where globalization occurs by means of accumulation, dispossession and neglect. In short, along with some local dynamics, neoliberal globalization of production has reshaped and reconstituted precarious labor patterns for its continued accumulation, exploited and reinforced gendered ideology in place, and generated a treadmill of environmental destruction. Is there any way out or a viable alternative?

Toward a social justice

The neoliberal globalization of production and skewed distribution of resources creates resource gaps but stimulates a desire to enhance social justice. As suggested in Chapter 2, application of a capability-based social justice can serve as a viable approach in unpacking and addressing the triangular nexus among labor, gender and the environment. This approach provides an important tool to analyze individual situations, trajectories and potentialities; to examine the efficiency and fairness of social structures and collective arrangements (Bonvin, 2012); and to study environmental impacts and relationships. The operationalization of this normative framework in the world of labor and gender relies on two key concepts: capability for work and capability for voice. "Capability for work" refers to job quality – the valuable work not only in terms of cash wages but also conditions of work and benefits received. "Capability for voice", on the other hand, designates the extent to which people are allowed to express their wishes, expectations and concerns in the collective decision-making process. To demonstrate this "capability", we have, throughout this book, brought historical transformation of capitalism, central intellectual debates on labor and gender issues, and diverse case studies. We have also discussed the treadmill of production theory to substantiate the inherent environmental nexus in the globalization of production.

In our in-depth study of the readymade garment (RMG) industry of Bangladesh, we found that the regulation of labor has undergone various transformations in recent years as a result of, for example, price competition in the global market. To remain globally competitive, producers tend to follow the deregulation process of labor, leading to both feminization and flexibility. We found a paradox: despite having an opportunity to participate in the labor market and thus enhance their social status, the female workforce has been, and continues to be, severely exploited. Abundant supply of cheap labor, prevalent traditional beliefs concerning gender norms, and the few and unsuitable alternatives for employment limit women's collective voice and resistance. They are expected to accept detrimental working conditions that have persisted over time. A gradual change in labor regulations to bring labor, gender and environmental justice has been witnessed, although reinforcement is very lax. Along with the traditional actors involved in the industrial relations system (employers, workers and the state), the global actors (lead firms, retailers, environmental and social justice groups, and even consumers) are actively taking part in labor regulation and contributing to improving labor rights in the workplace. The role of these actors creates a "new industrial relations system". Our key findings are as follows.

Women workers' rights: systematic denial of local and international standards

The first research outcome concerning the current state of labor practices and the contributing factors that shapes the terrain of gender and employment relations consists of contested views among its key participants. The study demonstrates the gross violation of labor rights in the RMG industry of Bangladesh and elsewhere in terms of well-being and agency freedom of the workers set by the local and international bodies. Violations of local and international laws were noticed, such as, absence of job contracts and appointment letters, insufficient wages for subsistence, long working hours with minimum compensation, lack of occupational safety and unhealthy working conditions, little access to maternity and childcare benefits, arbitrary punishment (job loss, salary cuts) and workplace harassment (physical, verbal and sexual), presence of forced and compulsory labor, persisting workplace discrimination, and absence of unions and collective bargaining. Gendered norms, local vulnerabilities, and capitalists' pursuit of maximizing profit form a synergy that propagates the exploitation of women workers. It is the women who suffer more than men – not in the sense that women constitute a larger share of the workforce, but because the issues that are mostly neglected in the workplace relate to women. The gendered norms are arbitrarily set and practiced (women are sincere and docile, can accept low wages, are less likely to join a trade union and challenge management) to justify unfair labor practices and exploitation. Women workers urgently need jobs in this sector as it is often a means for survival for many of them, and employers take advantage of this vulnerability by giving them low wages and benefits. So, our findings suggest that workers' basic rights, in terms of both well-being and freedom, are violated in the global manufacturing industry.

Differences of labor rights among factories: size and economic zone matter

We found that export processing zones (EPZs) were a new phenomenon brought about by the shift from development to globalization project, which saw to the push for free markets and export-oriented industrialization. EPZs became a tool for the economic development policies of many developing nations to attract foreign investments and technology transfers and to stimulate economic growth. EPZs, also commonly referred to as free trade zones (FTZs), are areas that specialize in manufacturing exports, set up by local government to attract firms that are offshoring their production of goods and services to low-cost regions. Incentives such as exemption from national taxes, weak labor and environmental regulations as well as minimal customs control would be implemented by governments in these zones to attract firms that seek cheap labor and low production costs to set up their industries. The EPZs are often built like enclaves, separated from the rest of the country through the fencing up of territory by barbed fences, gates and tight security (McMichael, 2008).

We found differences of labor rights among the factories in two contexts: differences between EPZ and non-EPZ factories, and differences between large and small factories within the same zone (either EPZs or non-EPZs). The EPZ factories and larger factories of non-EPZ areas are under close and more frequent surveillance of buyers' monitoring and inspection of "codes of conduct" because they are directly connected with the foreign buyers. The small factories in non-EPZ areas are mostly run by subcontractors employed by larger factories or mid-level buying houses, and thus have little connection with the buyers. Thus, buyers' monitoring and inspection are almost completely absent. High-skilled management and financial stability of the factories are positively associated with better labor practices, and larger factories are, to some extent, credited with having this characteristic. Corporate social responsibility of the owners of EPZs and large factories (non-EPZ) is also notable in this respect. Since smaller factories are financially weak and are run on the principle of subcontracting, they are pressed for time and squeezed for profits, which adversely affect workers' rights. The old and dilapidated houses in congested areas that desperately need renovation are where most of the small factories are located and as a result are more susceptible to poor working conditions and industrial accidents. We also found that the labor practices in the non-EPZ factories are often worse than those of EPZ factories.

Traditional industrial relations actors: unequal power relations

We found that the scope of collective negotiation through sound industrial relations among the actors is the most effective way that offers a win-win situation for all the parties involved. However, the traditional tripartite industrial relations system is not working effectively due to, among other reasons, the unequal power relations among the actors. Here we have discerned some of these dynamics.

Employers' association and management: hold dominant power. Management ideologies as well as power and behavior are key factors for a weak industrial relations system in the RMG factories. Employers (or associations) hold dominant power. They unilaterally set the rules of regulating labor; facilitate hostile and intimidating relationships with workers and never welcome workers' participation in decision-making processes. Employers and management hardly consider workers as their colleagues and are rarely willing to sit together for collective negotiation. A rigid social stratification is maintained inside and outside the factory; workers belong to a different social class, namely the "working class" that holds lower social status and power.

Workers union: stay in the bottom rung. The main barrier to confronting labor injustice is the lack of women's agency, socially responsible collective voices to achieve desired outcomes. In the absence of collective bargaining association, women workers are unable to shape an environment that would favor the workers. Women workers do not hold sufficient power that can force the employers to sit down for any negotiation. Due to the absence of workers' unions at the factory and the staunch anti-union role of employers, workers are not able to raise their voice against workplace injustice and exploitation. However, it is not the case that workers are absolutely loyal to the authority. Actually, aggrieved workers try to raise their concerns outside the factory premises, either through road blockades or street protest rallies. Inadvertently these protests can sometimes turn into violent mobs that stretch beyond the control of union leaders as well as law enforcement agencies, which often results in huge losses in terms of destruction of properties as agitated workers ransack vehicles or the factories.

State: limited control. The state's role is usually to negotiate between the two competing groups – workers and employers – but the state has been so very ineffectual. We found that the government's labor regulatory institutions do not act independently. The Inspection Department of Factories and Establishments, a state-owned institution responsible for monitoring and inspection, never carries the expected role as it is often being influenced by employers or their own vested interest. Industrialists, who are directly involved with garment manufacturing and are part of the government as members of parliament, influence the government to protect their interests while formulating new labor-regulating policies and influencing their execution. Sometimes inspectors are forced to issue a compliance certificate without visiting the factory due to connections between employers at factories and the ruling political elite. Due to a poor economic base, welfare measures are continually insufficient to protect workers during recession, or other socioeconomic changes.

So, as we found, traditional actors are not taking proactive roles for establishing sound industrial relationships and protecting labor rights. The roles of external actors can therefore be important push factors for ensuring social justice.

Nontraditional industrial relations actors: growing and promising

Despite precarious labor conditions, exploitative gender relations, and alarming environmental impacts in Bangladesh and elsewhere in the absence of a sound industrial relations system, we found that labor rights and environmental sustainability are increasingly influenced by the role of local and transnational actors, such as follows.

Multinational corporations: ambiguous and paradoxical. In the demise of the tripartite industrial relations system due to unequal power relations, buyers' pressure on the producers to comply with codes of conduct has been granted as the best alternative for ensuring labor, gender and environmental justice. Our interview data confirmed that the labor standards in RMG factories are gradually improving and the MNCs are credited with the changes that have taken place so far. The labor standards are comparatively better in those factories where the MNCs have direct contact with the producers and monitoring and inspection systems are strengthened although it is still far beyond the expected role of the MNCs in ensuring labor justice. A strong commitment to corporate social responsibility is lacking: corporations make profit their top priority and pay almost no attention whatsoever to labor rights. They are reluctant to share the cost for improving labor standards, while solely monitoring and inspecting will not produce any effective results without an equitable share of the burden. Buyers' pressure without sharing the cost adversely affects labor rights protection in the factory. Being pressured by buyers, employers or producers exerts extreme pressure on workers to increase production by setting higher production targets and/or relying on more flexible workers.

NGOs and human rights organization: insufficient but growing. International and local NGOs can play an important role in improving the labor rights situation through organizing workers and networking with corporate buyers and human rights organizations. For instance, the Bangladesh Independent Garment Workers Union Federation (BIGUF) supported by American Centre for Workers Solidarity and *Karmajibi*

Nari (KN) (organizing workers), Change Associate (health awareness), *Ain O Salish Kendra* (legal aid) and Bangladesh Legal Aid and Services Trust (legal aid), *Odhikar* (documentation, fact finding, training and advocacy) and *Nari Uddog Kendra* (low-cost accommodation) are all working to improve labor justice. One structural barrier in enhancing labor justice is the laborers themselves: RMG workers are mostly rural poor women who are mostly illiterate and unaware of their rights. "Capabilities to function" (Sen, 2009) is therefore a vital element in ensuring broader labor justice that includes, for example, creating awareness among the workers, employers and civil society through individual contact, organizing workers' conventions, seminars and even mass processions. Deployment of the "code of conduct" may not work well unless there is awareness and structural arrangements at the grassroots levels.

Consumers and citizens movement: hope for unfortunate workers. Consumers, on the other hand, can also play a pivotal role in enhancing social justice. All union leaders, labor experts and labor welfare officers in the factory interviewed for this study think that consumer pressure upon MNCs through boycott and movements against unjust labor practices and environmental destruction can have a significant contribution to the improvement of labor rights, gender equity and better environmental performance in the local supply chains; although it may also exacerbate the labor conditions in the event that the global buyers stop buying commodities. After the case of the factory building collapse in Bangladesh, agitated consumers chanted slogans in front of retail shops carrying placards reading "No clothes with blood". As a result, US retailers such as GAP, JCPenney, Sears, Target and Walmart announced a "new plan" for safety in their outsourcing garment factories (Wohl, 2013). So, overall, nontraditional actors are not playing enough responsible roles as they are supposed to do; however, this is gradually increasing and proves promising.

Migrant labor and traces of slavery

In our study of migrant labor, which is now a "new export" from the developing nations impoverished by the "double-risk society" (Islam, 2013), we found precarious conditions, apparent contradictions and unfortunate confrontations. Slavery in the 1926 Slavery Convention is defined as "the status or condition of a person over whom any or all of the powers attaching to the right of ownership are exercised". In addition, the Universal Declaration of Human Rights states that "no person is to be held in such slavery or servitude". Hence, when we contrast the official stance of human rights against that of the definition of slavery, it should not take anyone too long to draw the links to the "modern forms of slavery", which are sex trafficking and forced prostitution. Globalization and the complex networks of organized vice rings have been efficient in establishing trafficking networks. Based on today's borderless world, organized crimes related to trafficking can operate beyond the local arena. Likewise, in China, sex trafficking is considerably rampant with over 600,000 workers who migrate annually overseas, recruited based on false promises and then forced into undesirable employments such as prostitution. Recruitment fees can run as high as US$70,000 wherein these unsuspecting victims will be bounded by debt bondage (human-trafficking.org, 2012). Based on the case studies presented earlier, we can glean the situations in which the victims fall prey to the lure of a better life, which then cause them to become indebted and grossly exploited. Paradoxically, despite the numerous and extensive prevention measures with supranational agencies working to prevent human trafficking and migrant sex labor, the International Organization for Migration (IOM) reports that international trafficking accounts for 64 percent of the cases and internal (within national borders) trafficking is at a distant 31 percent (International Organization for Migration, 2012). The nature of trafficking is therefore overwhelmingly anchored by globalization wherein crime syndicates operate across borders, illustrating how the North-South exploitative relations are also prevalent in the informal economy.

To recapitulate, we have identified factors associated with globalization that bolster the global sex industry. The global sex industry ranks high as one of the most profitable commerce mechanisms along with the drugs and weapons trade; it generates an enormously large revenue every year. However, the profits received by sex workers are disproportionately small as they do not gain equal returns for their "labor". This point of contention, along with other contradictions related to labor in global sex industries, justifies the need for intervention. In fact, there have already been confrontations about the issue with the presence of movements against sex trafficking and campaigning for the rights of sex workers. With the case studies of sex labor in Kenya, Thailand and Indonesia, the trials and tribulations of sex workers are brought to light. Sadly, these difficulties and challenges are also faced by sex workers worldwide who simply wish for a better life.

While there are some who do not consider themselves victims, measures still need to be taken to provide help for those who require it. As such, there is a need for mitigation of the problems the labor workers in global sex industries face so as to ensure social justice. Policymakers need to understand that the sex industry is essentially economic in nature with many powerful vested interests. Thus, effective policies are those inclusive of sex workers as well as the profit-making activities associated with them. Complete eradication of child prostitution should be the top priority of policymakers and with its elimination, many problems of adult prostitution would consequently be solved. Although the global sex trade may seem like a complex problem that is too large to tackle, a creation of networks incorporating the state, corporations, nongovernmental organizations, families and individuals should be able to render assistance through an interweaving of knowledge and resources. After all, every successful social justice movement starts from just a single action.

Industrial disasters: globalization of production in its worst form

The globalizing national economy is accompanied by disregard for workers' safety and labor rights. The major industrial disasters highlighted the minimum standards of workers protection and long-term negative consequences on the well-being of their families. States and corporations pay little attention to environmental protection practices such as disaster response and level of preparedness. Current laws and regulations are either weak or not strictly enforced. The safety, health and welfare of workers was neglected in the pursuit of increasing productivity to attract foreign investments. We are thus able to see the ongoing crisis of workplace safety as a sociopolitical consequence of the globalization of production. In recent years, there has been increasing awareness among consumers about the improper practices involved in making their products. As such, counter-movements such as the Anti-Globalization Movement are calling for a review of the mechanisms of capitalism and to eradicate exploitation. However, the success of these movements remains uncertain. Profits of corporations continue to be on the rise as the culture of consumerism continues to stay ingrained within people, leading to a global treadmill of production.

Six months after the Savar tragedy, only one brand involved provided direct compensation to the victims. That brand, Primark, has provided workers three months' worth of salary amounting to US$190 per victim – a paltry compensation, considering the magnitude of the tragedy. Other companies are still deciding the extent to which they should be liable for the workers, since they were subcontracted anyway (Ogrodnik, 2013). Compensation is always a tricky issue due to the prevalence of subcontracting in global commodity chains. Legally, companies are not responsible for subcontracted workers, even if they bear most of the risks associated with production. Some companies such as Japan's Fast Retailing, which operates brands such as Uniqlo, have said that they will not sign a legally binding pact to improve worker safety at factories in Bangladesh, even in light of the Savar tragedy. Instead, they merely mention that they will be looking into improving disaster vigilance on their own. This is the same stance taken by US-based Walmart (Mathew, 2013).

Some transnational companies are rethinking their investments in Bangladesh following the high incidence of industrial disasters there. The Walt Disney Company, for instance, has since ordered an end to the production of branded merchandise in Bangladesh and sent a letter to thousands of licensees and vendors setting out new rules for overseas production. Although this move was widely lauded, it should be noted that less that 1 percent of the factories used by Disney's contractors are in Bangladesh, implying that the company will not be suffering massive operational losses (Greenhouse, 2013a). Bangladesh's sole Nobel Peace Prize winner, Muhammad Yunus, suggests for Bangladesh not to throw the baby out with the bathwater, since it needs foreign investors to generate employment – especially for women, who were previously left out of the formal employment sphere (Yunus, 2013b). He echoes other economists, like Paul Kruger (1997: 3), who agree that exploitation is an inevitable part of pursuing profit, but finds that it is better to exploit rather than exclude countries from development. His stance might be the most pragmatic one to take considering how difficult it is to convince consumers to not support unethical consumption, given that the system, on the surface, rewards them the most. Furthermore, it would be unwise to completely uproot Bangladesh from the economic network when so many depend on it to survive.

There are two main solutions Bangladesh can consider in order to put its workers in a more equitable position. Firstly, political groups and civil society in Bangladesh must be prepared to implement a zero-tolerance policy on corruption. Only then can labor regulations be effective and workers' rights be better protected. Women-friendly regulations, such as maternity leave, should also be considered. Secondly, workers should be allowed to unionize even in EPZs, where labor regulations are notoriously lax. Other developing countries sharing the same experience as Bangladesh in terms of labor exploitation should implement this as well if they fear losing out to one another, since there is strength in numbers and solidarity. Past movements involving Third World countries have had reasonable success in ensuring that they are treated more fairly by developed nations. One such movement is the Non-Alignment Movement (NAM), which had succeeded in turning the World Bank's attention to the economic needs of Third World nations, such that a new subsidiary, the International Development Association (IDA), was created by the World Bank in 1960 to pander to such needs (McMichael, 2008).

As much as developed nations are complicit in the exploitation of developing nations, there are signs that they are more aware of the impact of their actions and are working toward creating a more equitable global economic environment. Transnational labor rights protection already exists in the form of organizations such as the International Labor Organization and the Clean Clothes Campaign, the first of which has actually refused to let Bangladesh join a textile monitoring program until the country improved its labor laws, following the Savar disaster (Schneider, 2013). US President Obama has also suspended trade privileges with Bangladesh after learning about the collapse, removing tariff breaks and increasing the price of Bangladeshi products in the United States (Greenhouse, 2013b). Ironically, the removal of tariff breaks does seem to reinforce and reward the practice of cutting cost to deliver inexpensive products to consumers. While this shows the limits to which one can transform the discourse of profit in capitalism, it does not mean that change is impossible. If Bangladesh is able to unify its political parties, eradicate corruption and seek allies amongst developing countries in taking a stand against blatant exploitation, labor would be better protected – especially women, who are doubly exploited because of their subservient position to men in many societies.

From the treadmill of destruction to sustainability

The treadmill of production, the endless cycle of production processes inherent in our current capitalistic mode of production in modern industrial society, generates large quantities of oft-toxic waste, which is usually dumped back into the environment. We found this pattern in our study of two great food revolutions – green and blue. Labor patterns and gender relations, too, in the food-processing factories, are similar to what we found in other global factories. In our analysis, we found that the world factory, export processing zones and Mexico's *maquiladoras* have illustrated how the global treadmill of production is in fact generating a global treadmill of destruction. As shown, the resultant degradation from these export platforms in developing nations impacts upon natural ecosystems and human well-being. In light of these case studies, environmental regulations and policies that were implemented in a bid to mitigate these problems were faced with limited success. This can be attributed to countries and corporations placing environment as a lower priority in decision making as they pursue economic growth and profit-making objectives. In the globalization of production, the environment is not regarded as an inherent part of our existence, but rather treated as an "externality" that would be addressed later. Therefore, the treadmill of production portrays a bleak future for the environment within the capitalistic mode of system. If the global treadmill of production is really leading to the treadmill of destruction, as argued, the world must focus on mitigating these challenges with environmental regulations and certification issues. This, however, could be a far more difficult task as it requires the buy-in of not only those countries concerned, but the global population in order to truly make a difference.

To evade the treadmill of destruction, the world needs a comprehensive agenda that includes an individual worldview that is reflexive – environmentally, socially and economically; a political system that secures effective citizen participation in decision making; an economic system that is able to generate surpluses and technical knowledge on a self-reliant and sustained basis; a social system that provides for solutions for tensions arising from disharmonious development; a production system that respects the obligation to preserve the ecological base for development; a technological system that can search continuously for new solutions; an international system that fosters sustainable patterns of trade and finance; and an administrative system that is flexible and has capacity for self-correction. For this comprehensive agenda, we need to promote at least three sets of ideas that: cohabitation with nature is necessary, there are limits to the scope of human activity, and the benefits of human activity need to be widely shared (Kates, 1994: 118). More specifically, we need to stabilize human populations, reduce excess material consumption and change damaging technologies into environmentally more benign ones (Harper, 2008: 307).

Policy implication and notes for further research

Our study clearly indicates that improvements of the labor rights situation, gender relations and environmental conditions in the globalization of production are of paramount need, not only for workers, employers and the state, but also for transnational actors such as buyers, retailers and consumers. First, it is important for the workers because the poor working conditions and lack of or no benefits have detrimental effects on their lives and families. Due to insufficient wages, workers are struggling with poverty and malnutrition, little access to healthcare facilities, are unable to send their children to school, and live in suffocating shelters that reduce the employers' chance of getting a healthy and prospective workforce. Workers have a shortened economic life as a result of these poor conditions. The average duration of employment is about five years. Along with super-exploitation in the factories leading to deterioration of physical strengths, other social factors such as marriage, childbirth, and finding alternative and additional ways of survival are assumed to be a major reason for their early retirement. Most workers are unable to continue their job after a few years as they lose their strength and stamina due to long working hours and high physical pressure. Hunger and malnutrition often exacerbate this condition. Workers' suffering increases many-fold after quitting their jobs due to illness and ailments, as they are unable to afford food, medicines or other basic needs. On top of that, frequent industrial accidents (e.g., factory fire, building collapse) result in death for some and the most tragic consequences to the survivors who lose parts of their body. Dependents on these sole breadwinners suffer perhaps the worst. Unable to bear the prolonged pain and hunger, many even resort to suicide. These are clear violations of rights as human beings stated in the Universal Declaration of Human Rights.

Second, improvement in labor conditions also benefits the employers. A sick and unhealthy workforce is a possible threat to the sustainability of the RMG and other industries because workers' productivity decreases. Moreover, poor safety measures and violations of labor rights create dissatisfaction among the workers that contributes to workers' unrest, which have dual threats on the industry: workers' violent protests cause huge losses of properties during unrest, and products lose out on the global market. For instance, after the deadly incident of factory building collapse, at least dozens of factories had been vandalized by the aggrieved workers during the unrest, which cost over US$150 million in losses (IndustryWeek, May 13, 2013), and at the same time, many global buyers decided not to buy products from Bangladesh. The grimmest message to employers is the cancelation of GSP (Generalized System of Preferences, which allows duty-free entry of over 5000 goods to the US market from least-developed countries) by the United States, the largest of importing countries of Bangladeshi garments, due to the failure of maintaining labor standards in the factory. Third, the sustainability of the economy of Bangladesh and other developing nations largely depends on the RMG and other export-oriented industries. For Bangladesh, the RMG sector contributes to about 78 percent of total export earnings. Losing the demand from the global markets will force employers to shut down their factories, which in turn drastically reduces the export earnings of the country, leaving millions of workers (mainly women) jobless. Bangladesh simply cannot afford to face this challenge. So, boycotting products from Bangladesh or canceling GSP privilege can be a wakeup call for the producers temporarily but are not a long-term solution to the problem. The solution lies in improving labor conditions, ensuring gender equity and warranting long-term environmental sustainability.

The pressing question is how to improve the labor rights situation in an interdependent world where employers and the state have little control on the market prices. The study suggests that tripartite industrial relations should be strengthened where all of the actors (workers, employers and state) would play responsible roles. However, in a trajectory where employers hold strong power and state institutions are corrupt and undemocratic, workers' agency will almost certainly not be established. In the demise of the tripartite industrial relations system due to unequal power relations, the buyers' pressure on producers in complying with codes of conduct is now considered the best way for ensuring labor justice. The multinational corporations have the power and are equally responsible, too, because the maximum share of profit from global business goes to their hand. Unfortunately, the economic rationality of maximizing profits often entices them not to address workers' rights properly. Consumers and citizens' movements supported by NGOs and human rights organizations (both local and international) are essential to oblige the MNCs into taking the responsibility of labor justice. We suggest that the industrial relations system needs to be revived and elevated through the involvement of all actors including workers, employers, state, corporations, NGOs, environmental and consumer movements, and social justice groups. This plural engagement needs to be guided and steered by the "capability approach" propounded by Amartya Sen in order to establish social partnership of different actors. These require further investigation.

Notes

2 Labor, Gender and the Environment: Analytic Framework

1. The term "gender" is not synonymous with "sex". Sex is biologically based, whereas gender is defined by social rules and practices that deploy differential roles and expectations for men and women in a given society. These gender-differentiated norms are created by and embedded in social institutions.
2. Rawlsian principles of justice have followed some changes in language and orderings from the first formulation in 1971 to the later development in 2001.
3. The term entitlements refers to capacities or abilities to meet basic necessities that are essential for survival while the term capabilities refers to a wide range of capacities and opportunities required for human well-being as a whole (Alexander, 2008).

4 Women in Employment: Local Dynamics, Global Pressures

1. The dictionary meaning of *Purdah* is veil or curtail, but it functions as a system of social control that excludes women from the world outside of home. This system draws a demarcation between private and public spheres and women's world is in the private sphere, away from the outside (*baire*) world of men.
2. About 80 percent people are directly or indirectly dependent on agricultural production.
3. Readymade garment in Bangladesh is a subsector of textiles and clothing, comprised by two independent industries (e.g., woven and knitwear). It consists of a range of manufacturing activities and processes integrated by backward and forward linkages, which includes textiles, handlooms, processing and printing, dying, woven and knitwear, embroidery, and spinning and pressing of cotton, etc.
4. For example, *Dheki* husking was one of the main sources of women employment in the rural economy. With the introduction of rice milling, many women lost the traditional way of employment, which led them to explore strategies of income diversification.
5. These families may live is *Pukka* (brick) houses and have land, but they are cash poor. They never become aristocrats but wish to maintain a social distance from poor peasants.
6. Bangladeshi women are traditionally experts in sewing work. Almost every woman learns to sew early in life and gets involved in sewing work for other members of the family.

7. The estimated value for living wages in Bangladesh is about US$104per month. This value is calculated based on the current market price of the necessary goods and services by BILS in 2013.
8. Scholars have argued that the first shift starts with regular work hours in the morning, overtime work is the second shift and the third shift starts after returning home from the workplace for household responsibility.
9. Bangladesh did not sign the convention No. 138 on the minimum age to enter into employment. The reason for not signing this convention is that it may force many of the children into more vulnerable situations. Many children are surviving with their own employment.
10. RMG is the largest and fastest-growing manufacturing industry in Bangladesh, employing about 4 million workers.
11. It is claimed that this law is not fair and just toward workers' rights because it has given more power to the employers, and some articles directly violate the human rights of workers in terms of work hours, accident compensation, strikes in new establishments, preserving service books, pay for fired workers, punishment for molestation, non-implementation of maternity benefits by the employer, and so on.
12. The cabinet approved the proposed amendment to the Bangladesh Labor Law of 2006. In place of profit sharing, a new provision for creating a welfare fund with 5 percent profit for the workers has been incorporated. Some other new provisions are including allowing trade unions at the RMG unit, workers' safety and their welfare ("Cabinet Approves Labor Law Management" in *Financial Express*, April 23, 2013).

5 Third World Industrialization: Women Workers between Exploitation and Survival

1. Union registration process requires a list of workers who pay union fees to be filed with the application (Section 178 of Labor Law 2006). Workers are hesitant in identifying themselves through giving full details. It is because very often this list is handed over to employers who then retaliate against the workers through harsh discipline or dismissal.
2. During our interview, employers expressed that workers' leaders are not well educated and lack training as to how to deal and negotiate with the employers

6 Globalizing Food and a Tale of Two Revolutions: Labor, Gender and the Environment

1. Agenda 21 is a comprehensive plan of action to be taken globally, nationally and locally by the United Nations' System of Organizations, governments and major groups in every area in which humans impact the environment.

8 Profit over Life: Industrial Disasters and Implications for Labor and Gender

1. There is no accurate figure about death and injuries based on sex. Moreover, many were missing and unidentifiable. The number is estimated based on the proportion of women workers engaged in the industry.
2. Rescuing of Reshma after 17 days of the incident without any injury is one of the examples that support such kind of fraudulent case. During interviews of the workers, the authors asked many of them whether they knew Reshma before. None of the workers had certified Reshma as their colleague, but they strongly opposed this claim though she was guaranteed by Prime Minister's compensation and got income security by the management of Hotel Raddison.
3. This amount is distributed from the Prime Minister Relief and Welfare Fund to injured survivors and families of those killed at Rana Plaza. Cash payments paid directly to beneficiaries by the joint scheme at $2,480,857, where donation from Bangladesh Garments Manufacturer and Exporters Association is included.
4. Other brands associated with Tazreen Fashions are Delta Apparel (USA), Dickies (USA), Edinburgh Woollen Mill (UK), El Corte Ingles (Spain), Enyce (USA), KiK (Germany), Piazza Italia (Italy), Sears (USA), Teddy Smith (France), Walmart (USA) and Disney (USA) refused to compensate for the victims and their family.
5. The total amount for about 600 beneficiaries from the New Wave Bottoms factory to be paid directly by Primark is expected at US$6,300,000 or the amount needed to cover income replacement and future medical care needs.
6. The amount of awards is calculated on RPCC's 17th meeting on December 4, 2014, based on the provisions of ILO Convention No. 121.

References

ABC News. 2012. *Apple Chinese Factory Foxconn Nightline*. Retrieved November 1, 2014 (https://www.youtube.com/watch?v=h1_XAuJ8qCc).

Absar, S. S. 2000. "Conditions, Concerns and Needs of Garment Workers in Bangladesh." *Development Bulletin* 51: 82–85.

Absar, S. S. 2001. "Problems Surrounding Wages: The Readymade Garments Sector in Bangladesh." *Labour and Management in Development* 2(7): 1–17.

Absar, M. M. N. 2012. "Industrial Relations in Bangladesh: A Comparative Scenario between Public and Private Sectors." *Indian Journal of Industrial Relations* 18(1): 19–27.

Acker, J. 2004. "Gender, Capitalism and Globalization." *Critical Sociology* 30: 17–41.

Afsar, R. 2001. "Sociological implications of female labour migration in Bangladesh." Pp. 91–166 in *Globalization and Gender: Changing Patterns of Women Employment in Bangladesh*, edited by R. Sobhan and N. Khundker. Dhaka: Centre for Policy Dialogue and University Press Limited.

Agarwal, B. 1996. "From Mexico 1975 to Beijing 1995." *Indian Journal of Gender Studies* 3(1): 21–35.

Ahmed, F. E. 2004. "The Rise of Bangladesh Garment Industry: Globalization, Women Workers and Voice." *Feminist Formations* 16(2): 34–45.

Ahmed, N. 2006. *Bangladesh Apparel Industry and Its Workers in a Changing World Economy* (PhD Thesis). University of Wagenengen, The Netherlands.

Ahmed, N. 2009. "Sustaining Ready-made Garment Exports from Bangladesh." *Journal of Contemporary Asia* 39(4): 597–618.

Ahmed, N. and Nazneen, D. 2014. "Improving Wages and Working Conditions in the Bangladeshi Garment Sector: The Role of Horizontal and Vertical Relations." *Working Paper 40*. United Kingdom: Capturing the Gains.

Akhter, S. and Asheek, M. S. 2012. "Working Hazards as Indicators of Occupational Stress of Industrial Workers of Bangladesh." *Asian Business Review* 1(1): 140–44.

Akhter, S., Salahuddin, A., Iqbal, M., Malek, A., and Jahan, N. 2010. "Health and Occupational Safety for Female Workforce of Garment Industries in Bangladesh." *Journal of Mechanical Engineering* 41(1): 65–70.

Alam, K. and Blanch, L. 2011. *Stitched Up. Women Workers in the Bangladeshi Garment Sector*. United Kingdom: War on Want.

Ali, S. 2013. "The Tale of Two Ponds: Rana Plaza and the Spectrum Sweater Factory." *The Daily Star*, May 17. Retrieved November 4, 2013 (http://www.thedailystar.net/beta2/news/rana-plaza-and-spectrum-sweater-factory/).

Al-Mahmood, S. Z. and Harding, L. 2013. "Bangladeshi Garment Factory Death Toll Rises as Owner Arrested on Border." *The Guardian*, April 28. Retrieved November 4, 2013 (http://www.theguardian.com/world/2013/apr/28/bangladesh-garment-factory-collapse-owner-held).

Amengual, M. and Milberg, W. 2008. *Economic Development and Working Conditions in Export Processing Zones: A Survey of Trends*. Geneva: International Labor Office.

Amin, S., Diamond, I., Naved, R. T., and Newby, M. 1998. "Transition to Adulthood of Female Factory Workers." *Studies in Family Planning* 29(2): 185–200.

Anner, M. 2012. "Corporate Social Responsibility and Freedom of Association Rights: The Precarious Quest for Legitimacy and Control in Global Supply Chains." *Politics and Society* 40(4): 609–44.

Antrobus, P. 2004. *The Global Women's Movement: Origins, Issues and Strategies*. London and New York: Zed Books.

Apodaca, C. 2001. "Global Economic Patterns and Personal Integrity Rights after the Cold War." *International Studies Quarterly* 45(4): 587–602.

Appadurai, A. 2001. *Globalization*. Durham and London: Duke University Press.

Appadurai, A. 2004. "Capacity to Aspire: Culture and the Term of Recognition." Pp. 59–84 in *Culture and Public Action*, edited V. Rao and M. Walton. Stanford, CA: Stanford University Press.

Appendini, K. 2009. *Economic Liberalization, Changing Livelihoods and Gender Dimensions in Rural Mexico, Gaps, Trends and Current Research in Gender Dimensions of Agricultural and Rural Employment: Differentiated Pathways Out of Poverty*. Rome: FAO-IFAD-ILO.

Arizpe, L. and Josefina, A. 1981. "The Comparative Advantages of Women's Disadvantages: Women Workers in the Strawberry Export Agribusiness in Mexico." *Signs* 7(2): 453–73.

Ark of Hope for Children. 2013. "Child Trafficking Statistics." August 10. Retrieved November 13, 2013 (http://www.arkofhopeforchildren.org/issues/child-trafficking-statistics#.UohDauJbg0t).

Armstrong, P. and Connelly, M. P. 1999. "Feminism, Political Economy and the State." Pp. 1–21 in *Feminism, Political Economy and the State: Contested Terrain*, edited by P. Armstrong and M. P. Connelly. Torronto: Canadian Scholars Press.

Arnold, D. and Bongiovi, J. R. 2013. "Precarious, Informalizing and Flexible Work: Transcending Concepts and Understandings." *American Behavioral Scientist* 57(3): 289–308.

Asia Watch and The Women's Rights Project. 1993. *A Modern Form of Slavery: Trafficking of Burmese Women and Girls into Brothels in Thailand*. New York, Washington : Human Rights Watch.

Banerjee, M. M. 2011. "Social Work Scholars' Representation of Rawls: A Critique." *Journal of Social Work Education* 47(2): 189–221.

Banerjee, M. M. and Canda, E. R. 2012. "Comparing Rawlsian Justice and the Capabilities Approach to Justice from a Spiritually Sensitive Social Work Perspective." *Journal of Religion & Spirituality in Social Work: Social Thought* 31(1–2): 9–31.

Bangladesh Bureau of Statistics (BBS). 2010. *Bangladesh Labour Force Survey*. People's Republic of Bangladesh. Retrieved March 18, 2015 (http://203.112.218.66/WebTestApplication/userfiles/Image/Latest%20Statistics%20Release/LFS%20Report%202010.pdf).

Bangladesh Bureau of Statistics (BBS). 2011. *Population and Housing Census Report*. People's Republic of Bangladesh. Retrieved March 18, 2015 (http://203.112.218.66/WebTestApplication/userfiles/Image/BBS/Socio_Economic.pdf).

Bangladesh Export Promotion Bureau (BEPB). 2013. *Ministry of Trade*. Dhaka: People's Republic of Bangladesh. Retrieved March 19, 2015 (http://www.epb.gov.bd/index.php/home/afterindex).

Bangladesh Garment Manufacturers and Exporters Association (BGMEA). 2013. Retrieved March 19, 2015 (http://bgmea.com.bd/home/pages/aboutus).

Bangladesh Occupational Safety, Health and Environment Foundation (BOSHE). 2008. Retrieved March 19, 2015 (http://www.oshebd.org/).

Banuri, T. and Schor, J. B. 1992. *Financial Openness and National Autonomy: Opportunities and Constraints*. Oxford: Oxford University Press.

Barker, R. L. 2003. *The Social Work Dictionary (5th edn)*. Washington, DC: National Association of Social Workers Press.

Barraclough, S. and Finger-Stich, F. 1996. *Some Ecological and Social Implications of Commercial Shrimp Farming in Asia*. United Nations Research Institute for Social Development. Geneva: UNRISD. Retrieved March 19, 2015 (http://www.unrisd.org/80256B3C005BCCF9/%28httpAuxPages%29/A90A3147DD72ACC480256B67005B6935/$file/dp74.pdf).

Barrientos, S. 2003. "A Gendered Value Chain Approach to Codes of Conduct in African Horticulture." *World Development* 31(9): 1511–26.

Barrientos, S., Kabeer, N., and Hossain, N. 2004. "The Gender Dimension of the Globalization of Production." *Working Paper No. 17*, ILO: Geneva. Retrieved March 20, 2015 (http://www.ilo.int/wcmsp5/groups/public/---dgreports/---integration/documents/publication/wcms_079121.pdf).

Basu, R. 2011. "Sex, Lies & Trafficking: Of Human Bondage and Paid Sex." *The Straits Times*, June 11, p. 1. Retrieved November 15, 2011 (http://www.straitstimes.com/The-Big-Story/The-Big-Story-3/Story/STIStory_809119.html).

Bauman, Z. 1990. "Modernity and Ambivalence." *Theory, Culture & Society* 7(2): 143–69.

Beck, U., Bonss, W., and Lau, C. 2003. "The Theory of Reflexive Modernization: Problematic, Hypotheses and Research Programme." *Theory, Culture & Society* 20(2): 1–33.

Beeks, K. and Amir, D. 2006. *Trafficking and the Global Sex Industry*. Lanham, MD: Lexington Books.

Bellemare, G. 2000. "End Users: Actors in the Industrial Relations System?" *British Journal of Industrial Relations* 38(3): 383–405.

Beneria, L. 2001. "Shifting the Risk: New Employment Patterns, Informalization, and Women's Work." *International Journal of Politics Culture and Society* 15(1): 27–53.

Beneria, L. 2003. *Gender, Development and Globalization*. New York: Routledge.

Bergeron, S. 2001. "Political Economy Discourses of Globalization and Feminist Politics." *Signs* 26(4): 983–1006.

Bernal, A. M. 2011. "Power, Powerlessness and Petroleum: Indigenous Environmental Claims and the Limits of Transnational Law". *New Political Science* 33(2): 143–67.

Beverly, D. P. and McSweeney, E. A. 1987. *Social Welfare and Social Justice*. Englewood Cliffs, NJ: Prentice-Hall.

Bigman, D. 2002. *Globalization and the Developing Countries: Emerging Strategies for Rural Development and Poverty Alleviation*. Wallingford Oxon, UK: CABI Publishing.

Bonvin, J.-M. 2012. "Individual Working Lives and Collective Action: An Introduction to Capability for Work and Capability for Voice." *Transfer* 18(1): 9–18.

Boserup, E. 1970. *Women's Role in Economic Development*. London: George Allen and Unwin LTD.

Brenner, J. 2003. "Transnational Feminism and Struggle for Global Justice." *New Politics* 9(2): 78–100.

Brewer, D. 2009. "Globalization and Human Trafficking." *Topical Research Digest: Human Rights and Human Trafficking*. Retrieved March 16, 2015 (https://www.du.edu/korbel/hrhw/researchdigest/trafficking/Globalization.pdf).

Browne, J., Deakin, S., and Wilkinson, F. 2002. "Capabilities, Social Justice and European Market Integration." *Working Paper No. 253*. ESRC Centre for Business Research, University of Cambridge.

Bulut, T. and Lane, C. 2011. "The Private Regulation of Labour: Standards and Rights in the Global Clothing Industry: An Evaluation of Its Effectiveness in Two Developing Countries." *New Political Economy* 16(1): 41–71.

Butler, C. L. and Garcia, D. K. 2004. *The Future of Food*. North America: Lily Films.

Cadman, T. 2011. *Quality and Legitimacy of Global Governance: Case Lessons from Forestry*. London: Palgrave Macmillan.

Cagatay, N., Elson, D., and Grown, C. 1995. "Introduction." *World Development* 23(11): 1827–36.

Cain, M. T. 1977. "The Economic Activities of Children in a Village in Bangladesh." *Population and Development Review* 3(3): 201–27.

Caraway, T. L. 2005. "The Political Economy of Feminization: From Cheap Labor to Gendered Discourses of Work." *Politics & Gender* 3: 399–429.

Caraway, T. L. 2007. *Assembling Women: The Feminization of Global Manufacturing*. Ithaka, NY and London: Cornell University Press.

Carr, M. and Chen, M. 2004. "Globalization, Social Exclusion and Gender." *International Labour Review* 143(1–2): 129–60.

Castells, M. 1996. *Rise of the Network Society*. Cornwall: Blackwell.

Chan, A. and Wang, H. 2005. "The Impact of the State on Workers' Conditions – Comparing Taiwanese Factories in China and Vietnam." *Pacific Affairs* 77(4): 629–46.

Chang, D.-O. 2009. "Informalising Labour in Asia's Global Factory." *Journal of Contemporary Asia* 39(2): 161–79.

Chang, M. C. 2014. "More Foreign Domestic Workers Say They Do Not Get Enough to Eat." *The Straits Times*, October 25. Retrieved November 10, 2014 (http://www.straitstimes.com/news/singapore/more-singapore-stories/story/more-foreign-domestic-workers-say-they-do-not-get-enough).

Chew, S. C. 2001. *World Ecological Degradation: Accumulation, Urbanization, and Deforestation 3000 B.C.–A.D. 2000, Vol 1*. Lanham, MD: AltaMira Press.

Clarke, S. and Pringle, T. 2009. "Can Party Led Trade Unions Represent Their Members?" *Post-Communist Economics* 21(1): 85–101.

Clean Clothes Campaign (CCC). 2005. *Made By Women*. Gender, Global Garment Industry and The Movement for Women Workers' Rights. Netherlands.

Clean Clothes Campaign (CCC). 2009. *Cashing In*. Giant Retailers, Purchasing Practices and Working Condition in the Garment Industry. Netherlands.

Clean Clothes Campaign (CCC). 2012. *Hazardous Workplaces: Making the Bangladesh Garment Industry Safe*. Retrieved March 18, 2015 (http://www.cleanclothes.org/news/new-resources-clean-clothes-newsletter-nr24/115).

CNN. 2013. "Death Toll Rises from Bangladesh Building Collapse." May 13. Retrieved November 4, 2013 (http://www.cnn.com.sg/2013/05/12/world/asia/bangladesh-building-collapse/index.html).

Cohen, M. G. 2001. "From Public Good to Private Exploitation: GAT and Restructuring of Canadian Electrical Utilities." *Canadian-American Public Policy* 48: 1–79.

Cohen, M. G. 2004. "Globalization's challenge to feminist political economy and the law." Pp. 33–49 in *New Socialism: Futures beyond Globalization*, edited by R. Albriltton, S. Bell, J. R. Bell and R. Westra. London and New York: Routledge.

Collier, P. 1994. "Gender aspects of labour allocation during structural adjustment." Pp. 277–346 in *Labour Market in an Era of Adjustment*, edited by S. Horton, R. Kanbur and D. Mazumder. Washington, DC: World Bank.

Collins, J. L. 2003. *Threads: Gender Labour and Power in the Global Apparel Industry*. Chicago and London: Chicago University Press

Corpwatch. 1999. "Corpwatch: Maquiladoras at a Glance. San Francisco." *Corpwatch*. USA. Retrieved November 13, 2013 (http://www.corpwatch.org/article.php?id=1528).

Custers, P. 2012. *Women, Labour and Capital Accumulation in Asia (2nd edn)*. New York: Monthly Review Press.

Dahan, Y., Lerner, H. and Milman-Sivan, F. 2011. "Global Justice, Labour Standards and Responsibility." *Theoretical Inquiries in Law* 12(2): 117–42.

Daily Amardesh. 2014. "Compensation before Ramadan: Agitation and Human Chain in front of Rana Plaza." *Daily Amardesh*, June 7. Retrieved March 17, 2015 (http://www.amardeshonline.com/pages/details/2014/06/07/246069#.VUYEEvmqqko).

Daily Star. 2010a. "Law to Protect EPZ Workers Rights Demanded." *The Daily Star*, May 24. Retrieved May 29, 2014 (http://archive.thedailystar.net/newDesign/news-details.php?nid=139762).

Daily Star. 2010b. "Industrial Police Launched." *The Daily Star*, October 4. Retrieved October 25, 2015 (http://archive.thedailystar.net/newDesign/news-details.php?nid=157098).

Daily Star. 2015. "Rana Plaza: Tk 108cr PMO fund unused, says TIB." *The Daily Star*, April 22. Retrieved April 30, 2015 (http://www.thedailystar.net/online/rana-plaza-tk-108cr-pmo-fund-unused-says-tib-78478).

Dannecker, P. 2002. *Between Conformity and Resistance: Women Garment Workers in Bangladesh*. Dhaka: University Press Limited.

Delgado, C. L., Wada, N., Rosegrant, M. W., Meijer, S., and Ahmed, M. 2003. *Fish to 2020: Supply and Demand in Changing Global Markets*. Penang, Malaysia: IIFORI and WorldFish Center.

Deneulin, S. and McGregor, J. A. 2010. "The Capability Approach and the Politics of a Social Conception of Well-being." *European Journal of Social Theory* 13(4): 501–19.

Diamond, J. 1997. *Guns, Germs and Steel*. New York: Norton.

Diamond, J. 2005. *Collapse: How Societies Choose to Fail or Succeed*. New York: Penguin.

Diller, J. 1999. "A Social Conscience in the Global Marketplace? Labour Dimensions of Codes of Conduct, Social Labeling and Investor Initiatives." *International Labour Review* 138(2): 99–129.

Dolan, C. and Humphrey, J. 2000. "Governance and Trade in Fresh Vegetables: The Impact of UK Supermarkets on the African Horticulture Industry." *Journal of Development Studies* 37(2): 147–76.

Donnelly, J. 2003. *Universal Human Rights in Theory and Practice* (2nd edn). Ithaca: Cornell University Press.

Doumbia-Henry, C. and Gravel, E. 2006. "Free Trade Agreements and Labour Rights: Recent Development." *International Labour Review* 145(3): 185–206.

Duggan, J. 2013. "China's Environmental Problems are Grim, Admits Ministry Report". *The Guardian*, June 7. Retrieved November 11, 2013 (http://www.theguardian.com/environment/chinas-choice/2013/jun/07/chinas-environmental-problems-grim-ministry-report).

Dusuki, A. W. 2008. "What Does Islam Say about Corporate Social Responsibility?" *Review of Islamic Economics* 12(1): 5–28.

Eaton, D. W. 1995. "NAFTA and the Environment: A Proposal for Free Trade in Hazardous Waste between the United States and Mexico." *St. Mary's Law Journal* 27(4): 715–65.

Economic and Social Council (ECOSOC). 2000. *Committee on Economic Social and Cultural Rights. Report on the 22nd, 23rd and 24th Sessions.* New York & Geneva: United Nations.

Eichengreen, B. 1997. "The Tyrany of the Financial Markets." *Current History* 96: 377–82.

Elliot, K. A. and Freeman, R. B. 2003. *Can Labour Standards Improve under Globalization?* Washington, DC: Institute for International Economics.

Elson, D. 1999. "Labor Markets as Gendered Institutions: Equality, Efficiency and Empowerment Issues." *World Development* 27(3): 611–27.

Elson, D. 2005. "Unpaid Work, the Millennium Development Goals, and Capital Accumulation." Conference, October 1–3, 2005, on Unpaid Work and the Economy: Gender, Poverty and Millennium Development Goals. United Nations Development Program and Levy Economics Institute of Bard College.

Elson, D. and Pearson, R. 1981. "Nimble Fingers Make Cheap Workers: An Analysis of Women's Employment in Third World Export Manufacturing." *Feminist Review* 7: 87–107.

Elson, D. and Pearson, R. 1997. "The subordination of women and the internationalization of factory production." Pp. 191–203 in *The Women Gender and Development Reader*, edited by N. Visvanathan, L. Duggan, L. Nisonoff and N. Wiegersma. London: Zed Books.

Engman, M., Onodera, O. and Pinali, E. 2007. "Export Processing Zones: Past and Future Role in Trade and Development." Organisation for Economic Co-operation and Development. Trade Committee.

EPZ Workers Association and Industrial Relation Act, 2004. (Act No. 36 of 2004). Ministry of Law, Justice and Parliament, Peoples Republic of Bangladesh.

Esbenshade, J. 2004. *Monitoring Sweatshops: Workers, Consumers and the Global Apparel Industry*. Philadelphia, PA: Temple University Press.

Escobar, A. 1995. *Encountering Development: The Making and Unmaking of the Third World*. New Jersey: Princeton University Press.

Esping-Anderson, G. 1990. *Three Worlds of Welfare Capitalism*. Princeton: Princeton University Press.

Fadli. 2005. "Prostitutes Face Harder Life in Batam." *The Jakarta Post*, January 28. Retrieved November 10, 2013 (http://www.thejakartapost.com/news/2005/01/28/prostitutes-face-harder-life-batam.html).

Fairiss, D. 2007. "The Effects of Living Wages on Workers and Firms: Evidence from the Los Angeles Ordinance." *Policy Matters* 1(3): 1–11.

Fakir, A., Miah, M. S., and Hossain, M. S. 2013. "Export Diversification and Role of Export Processing Zones (EPZ) in Bangladesh." *ASA University Review* 7(1): 89–105.

FAO. 2008. *The State of Food and Agriculture in Asia and the Pacific Region 2008.* Food and Agriculture Organization of the United Nations. Bangkok: Regional Office for Asia and the Pacific.

FAO. 2011. *Selected Indicators of Food and Agriculture Development in the Asia-Pacific Region 2000–2010.* Food and Agriculture Organization of the United Nations. Bangkok: Regional Office for Asia and the Pacific.

Faruque, A. 2009. *Current Status and Evolution of Industrial Relation System in Bangladesh.* Geneva: ILO.

Feldman, S. 1993. "Contradictions of gender inequality: urban class formation in contemporary Bangladesh." Pp. 215–45 in *Gender and Political Economy: Explorations of South Asian Systems,* edited by Alice W. Clark. Delhi: Oxford University Press.

Feldman, S. 2001. "Exploring Theories of Patriarchy: A Perspective from Contemporary Bangladesh." *Signs* 26(4): 1097–1127.

Feldman, S. 2009. "Historicizing Garment Manufacturing in Bangladesh: Gender Generation and New Regulatory Regimes." *Journal of International Women's Studies* 11(1): 68–88.

Flamm, M. 2003. "Trafficking of Women and Children in South-East Asia." *UN Chronicle* 40(2): 34. Retrieved March 22, 2015 (http://scholar.googleusercontent.com/scholar?q=cache:GvSNkziDbqoJ:scholar.google.com/+causes+of+prostitution+in+asia&hl=en&as_sdt=0,5).

Flynn, J. P. 1995. "Social justice in social agencies." Pp. 2173–79 in *Encyclopaedia of Social Work,* edited by R. L. Edwards. Washington, DC: NASW Press.

Food and Agriculture Organization of the United Nations (FAO). 2003. *The Role of Agriculture in Improving Food Security and Nutrition.* Committee on World Food Security. Retrieved January 23, 2012 (http://www.fao.org/DOCREP/MEETING/006/Y8871e.HTM).

Food and Agriculture Organization of the United Nations (FAO). 2010. *The State of Food Insecurity in the World: Addressing Food Security in Protracted Crises.* FAO.

Foxvog, L., Gearhart, J., Maher, S., Parker, L., Vanpeperstraete, B., and Zeldenrust, I. 2013. *Still Waiting: Six Months after History's Deadliest Apparel Industry Disaster, Workers Continue to Fight for Compensation.* Amsterdam and New York: Clean Cloths Campaign and International Labour Rights Forum.

Frank, R., Hoare, J. E., Kollner, P., Pares, S., and Epstein, S. 2012. *Korea 2012: Politics, Economy and Society.* Leiden: Brill Academic Pub.

Friedman, T. 2005. *The World Is Flat: A Brief History of the Twenty-First Century.* New York: Farrar, Straus & Giroux.

Fu, X. and Gao, Y. 2007. *Export Processing Zones in China: A Survey.* International Labour Organization. Retrieved March 20, 2015 (http://www.ilo.org/public/french/dialogue/download/epzchineenglish.pdf).

Fudge, J. 2007. "The New Discourse of Labour Rights: From Social to Fundamental Rights?" *Comparative Labour Law and Policy Journal* 29(1): 29–66.

Gereffi, G. 1994. "The organization of buyer-driven global commodity chain: how US retailers shape overseas production networks." Pp. 95–122 in *Commodity Chain and Global Capitalism,* edited by G. Gereffi and M. Korzeniewicz. Westport, CT & London: Praeger.

Gereffi, G. and Korzeniewicz, M. 1994. *Commodity Chain and Global Capitalism*. Westport, CT & London: Praeger.
Ghosh, N. and Baker, A. J. 2014. "Myanmar Imposes Temporary Ban on Maids to Singapore." *The Straits Times*, September 13. Retrieved November 10, 2014 (http://www.straitstimes.com/the-big-story/asia-report/myanmar/story/myanmar-imposes-temporary-ban-maids-singapore-20140913).
Giddens, A. 1991. *Modernity and Self-identity: Self and Society in the Late Modern Age*. Stanford, California: Stanford University Press.
Gills, S. D.-S. 2002. "Globalization of Production and Women in Asia." *The ANNALS of the American Academy of Political and Social Science* 581: 106–20.
Gills, S. D.-S. and Piper, N. 2002. *Women and Work in Globalizing Asia*. London: Routledge.
Gould, K. A. 2007. "The Ecological Costs of Militarization." *Peace Review* 19(3): 331–34.
Gould, K. and Lewis, T. 2009. *Twenty Lessons in Environmental Sociology*. New York: Oxford University Press.
Greenhouse, S. 2013a. "Some Retailers Rethink Role in Bangladesh." *New York Times*, May 1. Retrieved November 4, 2013 (http://www.nytimes.com/2013/05/02/business/some-retailers-rethink-their-role-in-bangladesh.html).
Greenhouse, S. 2013b. "US retailers announce new factory safety plan." *New York Times*, May 30. Retrieved March 14, 2015 (http://www.nytimes.com/2013/05/31/business/american-retailers-announce-new-effort-for-factory-safety-in-bangladesh.html?_r=0).
Greenhouse, S. 2013c. "Obama to Suspend Trade Privileges in Bangladesh." *New York Times*, June 27. Retrieved November 7, 2013 (http://www.nytimes.com/2013/06/28/business/us-to-suspend-trade-privileges-with-bangladesh-officials-say.html).
Grewal, I. and Kaplan, C. 1994. *Scattered Hegemonies: Postmodernity and Transnational Feminist Practices*. Minneapolis: University of Minnesota Press.
Grown, C, Elson, D., and Cagatay, N. 2000. Introduction. *World Development* 28(7): 1145–56.
Guerrero, R. D. 1994. "Tilapia Farming in the Philippines: A Success Story." Asia-Pacific Association of Agricultural Research Institutions. Bangkok: APAARI.
Guha, R. 2000. *Environmentalism: A Global History*. New York: Longman.
Gulati, A., Minot, N., Delgado, C., and Bora, S. 2005. "Growth in High-Value Agriculture in Asia and the Emergence of Vertical Links with Farmers." *Linking Small-Scale Producers to Markets: Old and New Challenges*. The World Bank.
Harper, C. L. 2010. *Environment and Society: Human Perspectives on Environmental Issues*. New Jersey: Pearson.
Hart, J.P. and Hart, S. A. 2007. "Sex Workers and Cultural Policy: Mapping the Issues and Actors in Thailand." *Review of Policy Research* 24(2): 155–73.
Harvey, D. 1991. *The Condition of Postmodernity*. Oxford: Blackwell.
Harvey, D. 2005. *A Brief History of Neoliberalism*. Oxford: Oxford University Press.
Harvey, D. 2010. *The Enigma of Capital and the Crises of Capitalism*. London: Profile.
Hirschman, A. O. 1970. *Exit, Voice and Loyalty: Responses to Decline in Firms, Organizations and States*. Cambridge and London: Harvard University Press.

Hirst, P. and Thompson, G. 1996. *Globalization in Question: The International Economy and Possibilities of Governance.* Cambridge: Polity Press.

Hochschild, A. H. 2003. "Love and gold." Pp. 15–30 in *Global Woman: Nannies, Maids, Sex Workers in the New Economy,* edited by B. Ehrenreich and A. H. Hochschild. London: Granta Books.

Hopkins, T. K. and Wallerstein, I. 1986. "Commodity Chains in the World-Economy Prior to 1800." *Review* 10(1): 157–70.

Hossain, N. 2011. "Export, Equity and Employment: The Effects of Readymade Garments Manufacturing Employment on Gender Equality in Bangladesh." Washington DC: The World Bank, *Background Paper for the World Development Report 2012: Gender Equality and Development.* Retrieved March 17, 2015 (http://siteresources.worldbank.org/INTWDR2012/Resources/7778105-1299699968583/7786210-1322671773271/Hossain-Export-Equity-employment.pdf).

Hossain, F. 2013. "Bangladesh Factory Inspectors Suspended, Accused of Negligence." *Huffington Post,* July 11. Retrieved March 19, 2015 (http://www.huffingtonpost.com/2013/06/10/bangladesh-factory-inspectors_n_3414426.html).

Hossain, I., Al-Amin, and Alam, J. 2012. "NGO Interventions and Women Development in Bangladesh: Do Feminist Theories Work?" *Hong Kong Journal of Social Work* 46(1–2): 13–29.

Hossain, I., Mathbor, G. M., and Semenza, R. 2013. "Feminization and Labour Vulnerability in Global Manufacturing Industries: Does Gendered Discourse Matter?" *Asian Social Work and Policy Review* 7(3): 197–212.

Hu, Q. 2013. "57% of Groundwater Poor: MEP." *Global Times,* June 4. Retrieved November 10, 2013 (http://www.globaltimes.cn/content/786760.shtml#.UoTQaPlmiSp).

Huang, S. and Yeoh, B. S. 2003. "The Difference Gender Makes: State Policy and Contract Migrant Workers in Singapore." *Asian and Pacific Migration Journal* 12(1–2): 75–98.

Hughes, D. M. 2000. "The Internet and Sex Industries: Partners in Global Sexual Exploitation." *Technology and Society Magazine, IEEE* 19(1): 35–42.

Hughes, D. M. 2004. "Prostitution: Causes and Solutions." Presentation at Female Prostitution: Prostitution and Intervention held in Santiago de Compostela, Spain. Retrieved November 13, 2013 (http://www.uri.edu/artsci/wms/hughes/prostitution_spain_july04.pdf).

Human Rights Watch (HRW). 2013. "Bangladesh: Tragedy Shows Urgency of Worker Protections." Human Rights Watch, April 25. Retrieved March 19, 2015 (http://www.hrw.org/news/2013/04/25/bangladesh-tragedy-shows-urgency-worker-protections).

Human Rights Watch (HRW). 2015. "Bangladesh: 2 Years after Rana Plaza, Workers Denied Rights." Human Rights Watch, April 22. Retrieved April 30, 2015 (http://www.hrw.org/news/2015/04/22/bangladesh-2-years-after-rana-plaza-workers-denied-rights).

Human Trafficking. 2012. "China: China National Plan of Action on Combating Trafficking in Women and Children (2008–2012)." *Human Trafficking.* Retrieved November 15, 2013 (www.humantrafficking.org/countries/china).

Hutter, B. M. 2006. "The Role of Non-State Actors in Regulation." *Discussion Paper No. 37.* Economic and Social Research Council, London School of Economics and Political Science.

IFPRI. 2002. "Green Revolution: Curse or Blessing?" *International Food Policy Research Institute*. Retrieved March 14, 2015 (http://www.ifpri.org/sites/default/files/publications/ib11.pdf).

ILO. 2014. "Post Rana Plaza: a vision for the future, a statement made by Director general of ILO to the high level meeting on garment and textile production in Bangladesh." Copenhagen: ILO.

Industry Week. 2013. "Hundreds of Bangladesh textile plants shut indefinitely." *Industry Week*, May 13. Retrieved May 26, 2013 (http://www.industryweek.com/safety/hundreds-bangladesh-textile-plants-shut-indefinitely).

International Federation for Human Rights (FIDH). 2014. "One Year after the Rana Plaza Catastrophe: Slow Progress and Insufficient Compensation." *FIDH*. Retrieved March 23, 2015 (https://www.fidh.org/International-Federation-for-Human-Rights/globalisation-human-rights/15179-one-year-after-the-rana-plaza-catastrophe-slow-progress-and-insufficient).

International Labor Office. 2003. *Employment and Social Policy in Respect of Export Processing Zones*. International Labor Organization: Committee on Employment and Social Policy. Geneva: International Labor Organization.

International Labour Organization (ILO). 1944. *ILO Declaration of Philadelphia*. Philadelphia: ILO.

International Labour Organization (ILO). 2000. *Maternity Protection Convention (No. 183)*. Geneva: ILO.

International Labour Organization (ILO). 2008. *Declaration on Social Justice for a Fair Globalization*. Geneva: ILO.

International Labour Organization (ILO). 2010a. *Global Employment Trends*. Geneva: ILO Retrieved June 24, 2011 (http://www.ilo.org/wcmsp5/groups/public/---ed_Emp/---emp_Elm/---trends/documents/publication/wcms_120471.pdf).

International Labour Organization (ILO). 2010b. *Women in Labour Markets: Measuring Progress and Identifying Challenges*. Geneva: ILO. Retrieved June 24, 2011 (http://www.ilo.org/wcmsp5/groups/public/---ed_Emp/---emp_Elm/---trends/documents/publication/wcms_123835.pdf).

International Labor Organization (ILO). 2015. *Improving Working Conditions in the Readymade Garment Industry: Progress and Achievements*. Retrieved April 29, 2015 (http://www.ilo.org/dhaka/Informationresources/Publicinformation/Pressreleases/WCMS_240343/lang--en/index.htm).

International Organization for Migration. 2012. *IOM 2011 Case Data on Human Trafficking: Global Figures and Trends*. Case Data. International Organization for Migration (IOM). United States.

Inter Pares. 2004. "Towards a Feminist Political Economy." *Occasional Paper No. 5*. Retrieved March 22, 2015 (http://www.interpares.ca/en/publications/pdf/feminist_political_Economy.pdf).

Islam, N. 2000. *Protecting Bangladesh's Environment*. Atlanta: Emory University.

Islam, S. 2008a. "From Sea to Shrimp Processing Factories in Bangladesh: Gender and Employment at the Bottom of a Global Commodity Chain." *Journal of South Asian Development* 3(2): 211–36.

Islam, S. 2008b. "From Pond to Plate: Towards a Twin-driven Commodity Chain in Bangladesh Shrimp Aquaculture." *Food Policy* 33(3): 209–23.

Islam, S. 2009. "From 'development project' to globalization: understanding Third World politics, class relations and development choices." Pp. 107–24 in

Globalization: Understanding, Management, and Effects, edited by H. V. Baines and J. R. Ursah. Hauppauge, NY: Nova Science Publishers, Inc.

Islam, S. 2010. "Regimes of Environmental Regulations and Governance: Opportunities and Challenges for Shrimp Aquaculture in Bangladesh." *Journal of Bangladesh Studies* 12(1): 44–61.

Islam, S. 2013. *Development, Power and the Environment: Neoliberal Paradox in the Age of Vulnerability.* New York: Routledge.

Islam, S. 2014. *Confronting the Blue Revolution: Industrial Aquaculture and Sustainability in the Global South.* Toronto: University of Toronto Press.

Islam, S.S., Hoque, M., Hossain, D., and Kabir, K. S. 2006. "The Unheard Voices of the Orang Bangla." *Countercurrents.org,* October 20. Retrieved March 22, 2015 (http://www.countercurrents.org/hr-islam201006.htm).

Islam, S. and Lim, S. H. 2015. "When 'Nature' Strikes: A Sociology of Climate Change and Disaster Vulnerabilities in Asia." *Nature and Culture* 10(1): 57–80.

Jaggar, A. M. 2001. "Is Globalization Good for Women?" *Comparative Literature* 53(4): 298–314.

Kabeer, N. 1991. *Gender Production and Wellbeing: Rethinking the Household Economy.* Brighton, UK: Institute of Development Studies.

Kabeer, N. 2000. *The Power to Choose: Bangladeshi Women and Labour Market Decisions in London and Dhaka.* London: Verso.

Kabeer, N. 2004. "Globalization, Labour Standards and Women's Rights: Dilemmas of Collective (In)action in an Interdependent World." *Feminist Economics* 10(1): 3–35.

Kabeer, N. 2008. "Paid Work, Women's Empowerment and Gender Justice: Critical Pathways of Social Change." *Pathways Working Paper 3.* Brighton: IDS.

Kabeer, N. and Mahmud, S. 2004a. "Globalization Gender and Poverty: Bangladeshi Women Workers in Export and Local Markets." *Journal of international Development* 16: 93–109.

Kabeer, N. and Mahmud, S. 2004b. "Rag riches and women workers: export oriented garment manufacturing in Bangladesh." Pp. 133–64 in *Chains of Fortune: Linking Women Producers and Workers with Global Markets,* edited by M. Carr. London, UK: Commonwealth Secretariat.

Kahn, J. and Yardley, J. 2006. "As China Roars, Pollution Reaches Deadly Extremes." Beijing, China: *New York Times,* August 26. Retrieved November 5, 2013 (http://www.nytimes.com/2007/08/26/world/asia/26china.html?pagewanted=all&_r=0).

Kalleberg, A. L. 2009. "Precarious Work, Insecure Workers: Employment Relations in Transition." *American Sociological Review* 74(1): 1–22.

Kates, R. 1994. "Sustaining Life on Earth." *Scientific American* 271(4): 114–22.

Kaufmann, A., Tiantubtim, E., Pussayapibul, N., and Davids, P. 2004. "Implementing Voluntary Codes of Conduct in the Thai Garment Industry." *Journal of Corporate Citizenship* 13: 91–99.

Kayatekin, S. and Ruccio, D. 1998. "Global Fragments: Subjectivity and Class Politics in Discourse of Globalization." *Economy and Society* 27(1): 74–96.

Kelly, M. E. 1993. "Free Trade: The Politics of Toxic Waste." *Multinational Monitor.* Retrieved November 6, 2014 (http://www.multinationalmonitor.org/hyper/issues/1993/10/mm1093_03.html).

Kendall, D. 2006. *Sociology in Our Times: The Essentials.* Belmont, CA: Thomson Higher Education.

Kernaghan, C. 2012. *Criminal Negligence Leads to Tragedy at the Tazreen Fashions Factory in Bangladesh*. Institute of Global Labour and Human Rights. Pittsburgh: Institute of Global Labour and Human Rights (IGLHR). Retrieved March 28, 2015 (http://www.globallabourrights.org/documents/121127-Tazreen-factory-fire-in-Bangladesh.pdf).

Kernaghan, C. 2014. *Unprecedented Changes*. USA: Institute of Global Labour and Human Rights.

Khan, S. I. 2004. "Gender issues and the ready-made garment industry of Bangladesh: The trade union context." Pp. 167–218 in *Globalisation and Gender: Changing Patterns of Women's Employment in Bangladesh*, edited by R. Sobhan and N. Khundker. Dhaka: University Press Ltd.

Khandker, S. R., Faruqee, R., and Samad, H. A. 2013. "Are Microcredit Borrowers in Bangladesh Over-Indebted?" *World Bank Policy Research Working Paper No. 6574*. World Bank Development Research Group, Washington.

Khatun, F., Rahman, M., Bhattacharya, D., and Moazzem, K. G. 2008. "Gender and Trade Liberalisation in Bangladesh: The Case of the Readymade Garments." *Research Monograph 2*. Dhaka: Centre for Policy Dialogue.

Khosla, N. 2009. "The Ready-made Garment Industry in Bangladesh: A Means to Reducing Gender-based Social Exclusion of Women?" *Journal of International Women's Studies* 11(1): 289–303.

Kibria, N. 1995. "Culture, Social Class and Income Control in the Lives of Women Garments Workers in Bangladesh." *Gender and Society* 9(3): 289–309.

Kidder, T. and Raworth, K. 2004. "Good Jobs and Hidden Costs: Women Workers Documenting the Price of Precarious Employment." *Gender and Development* 12(2): 12–21.

Klein, N. 2000. *No Logo*. London: Harper Perennial.

Klein, N. 2009. *No Logo*. Picador.

Knufken, D. 2010. "The World's Most Lucrative Business Markets." *Business Pundit*, May 26. Retrieved November 15, 2013 (http://www.businesspundit.com/the-worlds-most-lucrative-business-markets/).

Kruger, P. 1997. "In Praise of Cheap Labour." *Slate-The Dismal Science*, March 20. Retrieved November 4, 2013 (http://web.mit.edu/krugman/www/smokey.html).

Labour Law 2006. Ministry of Law, Justice and Parliament. Peoples Republic of Bangladesh.

Lewis, W. and Riley, J. 2005. *Beyond Treason*. DVD. USA: Indieflix.

Lim, Y. C. L. 1987. "The State and Private Capital in Singapore's Economic Development." *Political Economy: Studies in the Surplus Approach* 3(2): 201–22.

Lim, Y. C. L. 1997. "Capitalism imperialism and patriarchy: the dilemma of third-world women workers in multinational factories." Pp. 216–29 in *The Women Gender and Development Reader*, edited by N. Visvanathan, L. Duggan, L. Nisonoff and N. Wiegersma. London: Zed Books.

Lim, L. L. 1998. *The Sex Sector: The Economic and Social Bases of Prostitution in Southeast Asia*. Geneva: International Labor Organization.

Lindquist, J. 2010. B.A.T.A.M. DVD. Documentary Educational Films.

Liu, J. G. and Diamond, J. 2005. "China's Environment in a Globalizing World." *Nature* 435: 1179–86.

Lober, J. 1994. *Paradoxes of Gender*. Yale: University Press.

Locke, R., Kochan, T., Romis, M. and Qin, F. 2007. "Beyond Corporate Codes of Conduct: Work Organization and Labour Standards at Nike's Suppliers." *International Labour Review* 146(1–2): 21–40.

Lyons, L. 2007. "Dignity Overdue: Women's Rights Activism in Support of Foreign Domestic Workers in Singapore." *Women's Studies Quarterly* 35(3–4): 106–22.

MacBean, A. 2007. "China's Environment: Problems and Policies." *World Economy* 30(2): 292–307.

MacNaughton, G. and Frey, D. F. 2011. "Decent Work for All: A Holistic Human Rights Approach." *American University International Labour Review* 26(2): 441–83.

Madani, D. 1999. *A Review of the Role and Impact of Export Processing Zones*. World Bank.

Mahmud, W. U. 2008. "Social Development in Bangladesh: Pathways, Surprises and Challenges." *Indian Journal of Human Development* 2(1): 79–92.

Mamic, I. 2004. *Implementing Codes of Conduct: How Business Manage Social Performance in Global Supply Chains*. ILO. Geneva: ILO.

Maneschi, A. 1998. *Comparative Advantage in International Trade: A Historical Perspective*. Cheltenham, UK: Edward Elgar Publishing.

Manik, J. A. and Bajaj, V. 2012. "Killing of Bangladeshi labour organizer signals an escalation in violence." *New York Times*, April 9. Retrieved March 27, 2015 (http://www.nytimes.com/2012/04/10/world/asia/bangladeshi-labor-organizer-is-found-killed.html?_r=0).

Marks, S. P. 2005. "The human rights framework for development: seven approaches." Pp. 23–60 in *Reflections on the Right to Development*, edited by A. Sengupta., A. Negi and M. Basu. Cambridge: Thousands Oaks, India: Sage Publication Ltd.

Marotta, V. 2002. "Zygmunt Bauman: Order, Strangerhood and Freedom." *Thesis Eleven* 70(1): 36–54.

Marshall, T. H. 2009. "Citizenship and social class." Pp. 148–154 in *Inequality and Society*, edited by J. Manza and M. Sauder. New York: W. W. Norton and Co.

Marymount University Center for Ethical Concerns. 1999. The Consumers and Sweatshops. Arlington, VA: Marymount University Center for Ethical Concerns. Retrieved November 29, 1999 (http://www.marymount.edu/news/garmentstudy/overview.html).

Mathbor, G. M. 2007. "Enhancement of Community Preparedness for Natural Disasters: The Role of Social Work in Building Capital for Sustainable Disaster Relief and Management." *International Social Work* 50(3): 357–69.

Mathbor, G. M. 2008. *Effective Community Participation in Coastal Development*. Chicago: Lyceum Books, Inc.

Mathew, J. 2013. "Rana Plaza Disaster: Uniqlo Won't Sign Safety Pact for Bangladesh Factories." *International Business Times*, May 28. Retrieved November 20, 2013 (http://www.ibtimes.co.uk/articles/471799/20130528/rana-plaza-disaster-fast-retailing-uniqlo.htm).

McCallum, J. K. 2011. *Export Processing Zones: Comparative Data from China, Honduras, Nicaragua and South Africa*. ILO. Geneva: International Labor Organization .

McMichael, P. 2008. *Development and Social Change: A Global Perspective*. Thousand Oaks, CA: Pine Forge Press.

Mendez, J. B. 2005. *From the Revolution to the Maquiladoras: Gender, Labor and Globalization in Nicaragua*. Durham, NC: Duke University Press.

Mill, J. S. 1863. *Utilitarianism*. London: Parker, Son and Bourn.

Ministry of Manpower (MOM). 2012. "Weekly Rest Days for Foreign Domestic Workers." *Ministry of Manpower*, March 5. Retrieved November 10, 2014 (http://www.mom.gov.sg/newsroom/Pages/PressReleasesDetail.aspx?listid=411).

Ministry of Manpower (MOM). 2013. *Labour Relations*. Retrieved November 13, 2013 (http://www.mom.gov.sg/legislation/Pages/labor-relations.aspx).

Moazzem, K. G. 2013. *100 Days of Rana Plaza Tragedy: A Report on Commitment and Deliveries*. Dhaka: Centre for Policy Dialogue (CPD). Retrieved March 19, 2015 (http://cpd.org.bd/wp-content/uploads/2013/08/100-Days-of-Rana-Plaza-Tragedy-A-Report-on-Commitments-and-Delivery.pdf).

Moghadam, V. 1999. "Gender and Globalization: Female Labour and Women's Mobilization." *Journal of World System Research* 2: 367–88.

Moghadam, V. 2005. *Globalizing Women: Transnational Feminist Networks*. Baltimore and London: Johns Hopkins University.

Momen, M. 2006. "Empowering Whom? Garments Worker in Bangladesh." *Empowerment: A Journal of Women for Women* 13: 23–38.

Montgomery, H. 2008. "Buying Innocence: Child-Sex Tourists in Thailand." *Third World Quarterly* 29(5): 903–17.

Muhammad, A. 2011. "Wealth and Deprivation: Readymade Garments Industry in Bangladesh." *Economic & Political Weekly, XLVI* (34): 23–27.

Munck, R. 2002. *Globalisation and Labour: The New Great Transformation*. London: Zed Books.

Murayama, M. and Nobuko, Y. 2009. "Revisiting Labor and Gender Issues in Export Processing Zones: The Cases of South Korea, Bangladesh and India." *Economic and Political Weekly* 44(20): 73–83.

NAFTA. 1993. "Safe Haven for Polluters." *NAFTA Fact Check*. Retrieved November 6, 2014 (http://www.multinationalmonitor.org/hyper/issues/1993/10/mm1093_03.html).

NAFTANOW.ORG. 2012. *NAFTA. USA, Canada, Mexico*. Retrieved November 15, 2013 (http://www.naftanow.org/).

Nash, J. and Fernandez-Kelly, M. P. 1983. *Women, Men and the International Division of Labor*. Albany: SUNY Press.

National Institute of Population Research and Training (NIPORT). 2011. *Bangladesh Demographic and Health Survey*. Dhaka: National Institute of Population Research and Training (NIPORT).

Naved, R. T., Newby, M. and Amin, S. 2001. "The Effects of Migration and Work on Marriage of Female Garment Workers in Bangladesh." *International Journal of Population Geography* 7(2): 91–104.

Naylor, R. 2012. "Marine Finfish Aquaculture: A solution of problem for wild fishes?" Woods Institute for the Environment Stanford University. Retrieved January 30, 2012 (http://woods.stanford.edu/docs/fifth-anniversary/Rosamond-Naylor-Woods-Institute-Symposium.pdf).

Nelson, D. 2014. "Bangladesh's Rana Plaza tragedy lives on for the child workers who survived." *The Telegraph*, April 24. Retrieved March 29, 2015 (http://www.telegraph.co.uk/news/worldnews/asia/bangladesh/10783733/Bangladeshs-Rana-Plaza-tragedy-lives-on-for-the-child-workers-who-survived.html).

Ngai, P. 2005. *Made in China: Women Factory Workers in a Global Workplace.* Durham and London: Duke University Press.

Nickel, J. W. 2008. "Rethinking Indivisibility: Towards a Theory of Supporting Relations between Human Rights." *Human Rights Quarterly* 30(4): 984–1000.

Nozick, R. 1974. *Anarchy State and Utopia.* New York: Saint Martin's Press.

Nussbaum, M. 2000a. "The Gender Impacts of Growth of Export-oriented Manufacturing in Bangladesh: A Case Study on Ready-made Garment Industry of Bangladesh." A background paper prepared by the Bangladesh Institute of Development Studies (BIDS) for the World Bank. Dhaka: World Bank.

Nussbaum, M. 2000b. "Women's Capabilities and Social Justice." *Journal of Human Development* 1(2): 219–47.

Nussbaum, M. 2002. "Capabilities and Social Justice." *International Studies Review* 4(2): 123–35.

Nussbaum, M. 2003. "Capabilities as Fundamental Entitlements: Sen and Social Justice." *Feminist Economics* 9(2–3): 33–59.

Nussbaum, M. 2006. *Engendering Garment Industry: The Bangladesh Context.* Dhaka: University Press Ltd.

O'Brien, R. 2004. "Continuing Incivility: Labour Rights in a Global Economy." *Journal of Human Rights* 3(2): 203–14.

Odhikar. 2013. "Human Rights Monitoring Report 2013." Odhikar. Retrieved March 26, 2015 (http://odhikar.org/wp-content/uploads/2013/06/human-rights-monitoring-monthly-report-may-2013-eng.pdf).

Ofreneo, R. E. 2010. "Labour Law Reforms in Globalizing East Asia." Paper presented at the Manila *Biennial Conference of the Asian Society of Labour Law*, held at the UP College of Law, November 20–21.Bangkok: ILO.

Ogola, S. O. and Ochieng, P. J. 2008. "Baseline Survey on Children in Commercial Sex in Kenya's Four Towns of Nairobi, Kisumu, Eldoret and Nyeri." *ILO.* Retrieved March 22, 2015 (www.ilo.org/ipecinfo/product/download.do?type=document&id=16155).

Ogrodnik, I. 2013. "6 Months Later: What Has Changed Since the Rana Plaza Factory Disaster?" *Global News*, October 24. Retrieved November 4, 2013 (http://globalnews.ca/news/922926/6-months-later-what-has-changed-since-the-rana-plaza-factory-disaster/).

Organisation for Economic Co-operation and Development (OECD). 2002. "Environmental Priorities for China's Sustainable Development." Pp. 581–622 in *China in the World Economy: The Domestic Policy Challenges.* OECD Publishing.

Othman, Z. and Alkhatib, S. 2012 . "Batam Losing Its Sex Appeal." *AsiaOne News*, October 3. Retrieved November 10, 2013 (http://news.asiaone.com/News/Latest+News/Singapore/Story/A1Story20121001-374845.html).

Oya, C. 2010. "Rural Inequality, Wage Employment and Labor Market Formation in Africa: Historical and Micro-Level Evidence." *Working Paper No. 97.* Policy Integration Department. Geneva: ILO.

Paul-Majunder, P. and Begum, A. 1997. "Upward Occupational Mobility among Female Workers in Garment Industry of Bangladesh." *Working Paper 153.* Dhaka: BIDS.

Piore, M. J. and Sabel, C. F. 1984. *The Second Industrial Divide: Possibilities for Prosperity.* New York: Basic Books.

Polanyi, K. [1944] 1968. *The Great Transformation: The Political and Economic Origins of Our Time.* Boston, MA: Beacon Press.

Polaski, S. 2006. "Combining Global and Local Forces: The Case of Labour Rights in Cambodia." *World Development* 34(5): 919–32.

Prasad, M., Kimeldorf, H., Meyer, R. and Robinson, I. 2004. "Consumers of the World Unite: A Market-Based Response to Sweatshop." *Labor Studies Journal* 29(3): 57–80.

Pritchard, J. 2010. "The Sex Work Debate." *International Socialism* 125: 81–102.

Psacharopoulos, G. and Tzannatos, Z. 1989. "Female Labour Force Participation: An International Perspective." *World Bank Research Observer* 4(2): 187–201.

Rahman, R. I. 2005. "The Dynamics of Labour Market and Employment in Bangladesh: A Focus on Gender Dimension." *Employment Strategy Papers.* Employment and Policy Unit. Geneva: ILO.

Rahman, M. 2011. *Rapid Urbanization and Environmental Degradation – The Case of Mega City Dhaka.* Lund University: Centre for East and Southeast Asian Studies.

Rahman, M., Khondaker, G. M., and Syed, S. H. 2009. "Impact of the Global Economic Crisis on the Employment and Labour Market of Bangladesh: A Preliminary Assessment." *Paper 80.* Dhaka: Centre for Policy Dialogue.

Rahman, M., Uttam, K. D., Fahmida, K. and Khondaker, G. M. 2008. "Current WTO Negotiations under Doha Round: Insights from CPD's Geneva Tracking Mission." *CPD Working Paper 66.* Dhaka: Centre for Policy Dialogue (CPD).

Rai, S. 2002. *Gender and Political Economy of Development.* Cambridge: Polity Press.

Rand, A. 1961. "Man's rights." Pp. 88–95 in *The Virtue of Selfishness*, edited by A. Rand. New York: The New American Library Inc.

Rashid, M. A. 2006. "Rise of readymade garment industry in Bangladesh: Entrepreneurial ingenuity or Public Policy." Paper presented at the workshop on Governance and Development, World Bank and Bangladesh Institute of Development Studies. November 11–12, 2006. Dhaka: World Bank.

Rasmussen, D. B. 1974. "A Critique of Rawls' Theory of Justice." *The Personalist* 55(3): 303–18.

Rawls, J. 1971. *A Theory of Justice. Cambridge.* Cambridge, MA: Belknap Press

Rawls, J. 1999. *A Theory of Justice (Revised edition).* Cambridge, MA: Belknap Press.

Rawls, J. 2001. *Justice as Fairness: A Restatement.* Cambridge, MA: Belknap Press.

Raworth, K. 2004. *Trading Away Our Rights. Women Working in Global Supply Chains.* Parkstone, UK: Oxfam International.

Razavi, S. 2001. "Globalization, employment and women's empowerment." Paper presented at expert group meeting of United Nations Division for the Advancement of Women (DAP) on Empowerment of Women throughout the Life Cycle as a Transformative Strategy for Poverty Eradication, November 26–29, 2001. New Delhi, India: UNDAP.

Reblin, K. L. 1995. "NAFTA and the Environment: Dealing with Abnormally High Birth Defect Rates among Children of Texas-Mexico Border Towns." *St. Mary's Law Journal* 27: 929–65.

Reich, R. 1991. *The Work of Nations: Preparing Ourselves for 21st Century Capitalism.* New York: Knopf.

Research Initiative for Social Equity (RISE). 2014. *Bangladesh Fails to Regain GSP – Improvements Not Enough.* Research Initiative for Social Equity. Retrieved March 22, 2015 (http://risebd.com/2015/01/19/gsp-ustr-bangladesh-2015/).

Revell, A. 2002. "Ecological Modernisation of Small Firms in Japan." *Environmental Economics & Policy Studies* 5(4): 291–317.

Rice, J. 2009. "The Transnational Organization of Production and Uneven Environmental Degradation and Change in the World Economy." *International Journal of Comparative Sociology* 50(3–4): 215–36.

Richards, D. L. and Gelleny, R. G. 2007. "Women's Status and Economic Globalization." *International Studies Quarterly* 51(4): 855–76.

Richards, D. L, Gelleney, R. G., and Sacko, D. H. 2001. "Money with a Mean Streak? Foreign Economic Penetration and Government Respect for Human Rights in Developing Countries." *International Studies Quarterly* 45(2): 219–39.

Richerson, P. J., Mulder, M. B., and Vila, B. J. 1991. *Principles of Human Ecology.* USA: University of California Davis & University of Wyoming.

Riley, M. O. P. 2008. *A Feminist Political Economic Framework*. Center of Concern. Retrieved March 22, 2015 (https://www.coc.org/files/Riley%20-%20FPE_0.pdf).

Robeyns, I. 2003. "Sen's Capability Approach and Gender Inequality: Selecting Relevant Capabilities." *Feminist Economics* 9(2–3): 61–92.

Robeyns, I. 2005. "The Capability Approach: A Theoretical Survey." *Journal of Human Development* 6(1): 93–113.

Rodriguez-Garavito, C. A. 2005. "Global Governance and Labour Rights: Codes of Conduct and Anti-Sweatshop Struggles in Global Apparel Factories in Mexico and Guatemala." *Politics and Society* 33(2): 203–33.

Rodrik, D. 1998. "Has Globalization Gone Too Far?" *Challenge* 41(2): 81–94.

Rossi, A. 2011. "Economic and social upgrading in global production networks: The case of the garment industry in Morocco." *PhD Dissertation*. Brighton: Institute of Development Studies, University of Sussex.

Rudra, N. 2002. "Globalization and the Decline of Welfare State in Less Developed Countries." *International Organization* 56(2): 411–45.

Ryder, G. 2014. "Rana Plaza Legacy Must Be Improved Working Conditions Globally." *ILO*, April 3. Retrieved March 23, 2015 (http://www.ilo.org/global/about-the-ilo/newsroom/news/WCMS_240371/lang--en/index.htm).

Salzinger, L. 2003. *Genders in Production: Making Workers in Mexico's Global Factories.* Berkeley, Los Angeles and London: California University Press.

Santoro, M. A. 2003. "Defending Labour: On the Barricades and in the Boardrooms." *Brown Journal of World Affairs* 9(2): 303–19.

Scherer, A. G. and Palazzo, G. 2011. "The New Political Role of Business in a Globalized World – a Review of a New Perspective on CSR and Its Implications for the Firms, Governance and Democracy." *Journal of Management Studies* 48(4): 899–931.

Schnaiberg, A. 1994. "The Political Economy of Environmental Problems and Policies: Consciousness, Conflict, and Control Capacity." *Advances in Human Ecology* 3: 23–64.

Schnaiberg, A. 1980. *The Environment: From Surplus to Scarcity*. New York: Oxford University Press.

Schrage, E. J. 2004. "Promoting International Worker Rights through Private Voluntary Initiatives: Public Relation or Public Policy?" *A Global Workspace Research Initiative*. University of Iowa Center for Human Rights.

Scott, C. 1999. "Reaching Beyond (without Abandoning) the Category of Economic, Social and Cultural Rights." *Human Rights Quarterly* 21(3): 633–60.

Scott, K. 2009. *A Literature Review on Sustainable Lifestyles and Recommendations for Further Research.* United Nations Environment Programme Division of Technology, Industry, and Economics, Sustainable Consumption & Production Branch. Stockholm: UNEP.

Seguino, S. 2000. "Gender Inequality and Economic Growth: A Cross Country Analysis." *World Development* 28(7): 1211–30.

Seguino, S. 2006. "The threads that bind: race and gender stratification and the macroeconomics of inequality." *Working Paper.* Burlington: University of Vermont Department of Economics.

Seguino, S. 2013. "Toward Gender Justice: Confronting Stratification and Unequal Power." *Multidisciplinary Journal of Gender Studies* 2(1): 1–36.

Sen, A. K. 1981. *Poverty and Famines: An Essay on Entitlement and Deprivation.* Oxford: Oxford University Press.

Sen, A. K. 1984. *Resources, Values and Development.* Cambridge, MA: Harvard University Press.

Sen, A. K. 1985. "Well-Being, Agency and Freedom: The Dewey Lectures." *Journal of Philosophy* 82(4): 169–221.

Sen, A. K. 1990. "Justice: Means versus Freedoms." *Philosophy and Public Affairs* 19(2): 111–21.

Sen, A. K. 1992. *Inequality Reexamined.* Cambridge, MA: Harvard University Press.

Sen, A. K. 1995. "Gender inequality and theories of justice." Pp. 259–73 in *Women Culture and Development: A Study of Human Capabilities,* edited by M. Nussbaum and J. Glover. Oxford: Clarendon Press.

Sen, A. K. 1998. "The Possibility of Social Choice." *American Economic Review* 89(3): 349–78.

Sen, A. K. 2002. "Open and Close Impartiality." *Journal of Philosophy* 99(9): 445–69.

Sen, A. K. 2004. "Elements of a Theory of Human Rights." *Philosophy and Public Affairs* 32(4): 315–56.

Sen, A. K. 2005. "Human Rights and Capabilities." *Journal of Human Development* 6(2): 151–66.

Sen, A. K. 2009. *The Idea of Justice.* London, New York: Allen Lane.

Shah, K. and Rivera, J. 2007. "Export Processing Zones and Corporate Environmental Performance in Emerging Economies: The Case of Oil, Gas and Chemical Sectors of Trinidad and Tobago." *Policy Sciences* 40(4): 265–85.

Siddiqi, D. M. 2000. "Miracle Worker or Womanmachine? Tracking (Trans) national Realities in Bangladeshi Factories." *Economic and Political Weekly* 35(21–22): L11–L17.

Siddiqi, D. M. 2004. "The sexual harassment of industrial workers: strategies for intervention in the workplace and beyond." *Occasional Paper Series, Paper no. 26.* Dhaka: Centre for Policy Dialogue (CPD).

Siddiqi, D. M. 2009. "Do Bangladeshi Factory Worker Need Saving? Sisterhood in Post Sweatshop Era." *Feminist Review* 91: 154–74. doi:10.1057/fr.2008.55.

Simic, O. 2004. "Victims of trafficking for forced prostitution: Protection mechanisms and the right to remain in the destination countries." *Global Migration Perspectives No. 2.* Geneva: Global Comission on International Migration(GCIM). Retrieved November 16, 2013 (http://www.gcim.org/attachements/GMP%20No%202.pdf).

Slavery Convention. 1926. *Slavery Convention*. United Nations Human Rights. Geneva: United Nations Human Rights. Retrieved November 10, 2013 (http://ohchr.org/EN/ProfessionalInterest/Pages/SlaveryCOnvention.aspx).

Sloan, J. 2000. "Overview of Issues Affecting the Adult Commercial Sex Work Industry." Unpublished Paper presented at Conference on Adult Commercial Sex Work.

Smart, B. 2003. *Economy, Culture and Society*. Buckingham, Philadelphia: Open University Press.

Smith, A. 2013a. "30 million people still live in slavery, human rights group says." *NBC News*. 17 October. Retrieved November 20, 2013 (http://worldnews.nbcnews.com/_news/2013/10/17/21005059-30-million-people-still-live-in-slavery-human-rights-group-says?lite).

Smith, M. 2013b. "Potential Solutions to the Problem of Pregnancy Discrimination in Maquiladoras Operated by U.S. Employers in Mexico." *Berkeley Journal of Gender, Law and Justice* 13(1): 195–225.

Smithson, J. and Stokoe, E. H. 2005. "Discourses of Work-life Balance: Negotiating 'Genderblind' Terms in Organization." *Gender Work and Organization* 12(2): 147–68.

So, A. Y. 2010. "Post-Socialist State, Transnational Corporations and the Battle for Labour Rights in China at the Turn of the 21st Century." *Development and Society* 39(1): 97–117.

Solopova, A. 2013. "The Ongoing Tragedy: Women's Voices from Rana Plaza." *The Daily Star*, September 10. Retrieved March 23, 2015 (http://archive.thedailystar.net/beta2/news/the-ongoing-tragedy-womens-voices-from-rana-plaza/).

Sommer, M. 2014. "After Rana Plaza: Business as Usual?" *After Rana Plaza*: 5–8. November 7. London: Social Europe.

Spivak, G. 1988. "Can the subaltern speak?" Pp. 271–313 in *Marxism and the Interpretation of Culture*, edited by C. Nelson and L. Grossberg. Chicago: University of Illinois Press.

Spivak, G. C. 1996. "Woman as Theatre: United Nation's Conference on Women Beijing 1995." *Radical Philosophy* 75: 2–4.

Standing, G. 1989. "Global Feminization through Flexible Labour." *World Development* 17(7): 1077–95.

Standing, G. 1999. "Global Feminization through Flexible Labour: Theme Revisited." *World Development*, 27(3): 583–602.

Standing, G. 2008. "Economic Insecurity and Global Casualization: Threat or Promise?" *Social Indicators Research* 88(1): 15–30.

Standing, G. 2011. *The Precariat: The New Dangerous Class*. United Kingdom: Macmillan Publishing.

Stiglitz, J. E. 2002. "Employment Social Justice and Societal Well-being." *International Labour Review* 141(1–2): 9–29.

Taher, A. 1999. "Politicization of Trade Unions: Issues & Challenges in Bangladesh Perspective." *Indian Journal of Industrial Relations* 34(4): 403–20.

Tallontire, A., Dolan, C., Smith, S., and Barrientos, S. 2005. "Reaching the Marginalized? Gender Value Chains and Ethical Trade in African Horticulture." *Development in Practice* 15(3–4): 559–71.

Taylor, L. 1995. "Environmental and Gender Feedbacks in Macroeconomics." *World Development* 23(11): 1953–62.

Textile Today. 2013. "GIZ, CRP and BGMEA join hands six months after Rana Plaza" *Textile Today*: 6(11). Retrieved March 22, 2015 (http://www.textiletoday.com.bd/oldsite/magazine/766).

The Economist. 2003. "Special report: the promise of blue revolution: How aquaculture might meet most of the world's demand for fish without ruining the environment." *The Economist*, August 7. Retrieved January 16, 2012 (http://www.economist.com/node/1974103).

Theuws, M., Huijstee, M., van Overeem, P., Seters, J. v., and Paull, T. 2013. "Fatal Fashion Analysis of Recent Factory Fires in Pakistan and Bangladesh: A Call to Protect and Respect Garment Workers' Lives." *SOMO*. Retrieved July 8, 2013 (http://somo.nl/publications-en/Publication_3943).

Thompson, L. L. 2005. "Sexual Trafficking, Prostitution, and the Global Sex Industry." *CBE Bookstore*. Retrieved November 15, 2013 (http://www.equalitydepot.com/sexualtraffickingprostitutionandtheglobalsexindustry.aspx).

Tilly, C. 2007. "Trust Networks in Transnational Migration." *Sociological Forum* 22(1): 3–24.

Transient Workers Count Too (TWC2). 2013. "Proposals – Second Phase View of the Employment Act and the Employment of Foreign Manpower Act." *Transient Workers Count Too*. Retrieved November 7, 2013 (http://twc2.org.sg/wp-content/uploads/2013/10/2013oct_submission_final_v2.pdf).

Transparency International Bangladesh (TIB). 2014. "One year after Rana Plaza tragedy: progress in governance must be sustained." *TIB*, April 21. Retrieved March 22, 2015 (http://www.transparency.org/news/pressrelease/one_year_after_rana_plaza_tragedy_progress_in_governance_must_be_sustained).

U.S. Department of State. 2011. *Trafficking in Persons Report 2011*. U.S. Department of State. Retrieved November 15, 2013 (http://www.state.gov/g/tip/rls/tiprpt/2011/index.htm).

U.S. Department of State. 2013. *Trafficking in Persons Report 2013*. U.S. Department of State. Retrieved November 16, 2013 (http://www.state.gov/documents/organization/210737.pdf).

Uddin, J. 2014. "Bangladeshi rich people prefer Malaysia My Second Home (MM2H) Program." BDOpinion. Retrieved September 29, 2014 (http://www.bdopinion.com/2014/09/28/bangladeshi-rich-people-prefer-malaysia-my-second-home-mm2h-program/).

Ueno, K. 2008. "Foreign Domestic Workers in Singapore." Pp. 140–56 in *Asia's New Mothers: Crafting Gender Roles and Childcare Networks in East and Southeast Asian Societies*, edited by E. Ochiai and B. Molony. Kent: Global Oriental.

United Nations (UN). 1948. *Universal Declaration of Human Rights*. UN General Assembly. Retrieved March 22, 2015 (http://www.un.org/en/documents/udhr/).

United Nations (UN). 1993. *Vienna Declaration and Programme of Action*. UN General Assembly. Retrieved March 22, 2015 (http://www.unhchr.ch/huridocda/huridoca.nsf/%28symbol%29/a.conf.157.23.en).

United Nations (UN). 2009. *Agenda 21*. UN Department of Economic and Social Affairs, Division for Sustainable Development. Retrieved January 22, 2012 (http://www.un.org/esa/dsd/agenda21/).

Unni, J. 2002. "Globalization and securing worker rights for women in developing countries." *Working Paper No. 132*. Ahmedabad, India: Gujrat Institute for Development Research.

UN Women: Singapore Committee (UNW:SC). 2011. "Made to work: attitudes towards granting regular days off to migrant domestic workers in Singapore." UN Women: Singapore Committee. Retrieved, November 13, 2014 (http://unwomen-nc.org.sg/uploads/Day%20Off%202011%20June%2022.pdf).

Urbina, I. 2013. "Unions press to end special trade status for Bangladesh." *New York Times*, May 30. Retrieved March 22, 2015 (http://www.nytimes.com/2013/05/31/business/us-pressure-rises-to-end-bangladesh-trade-status.html?_r=0).

Vanaspong, C. 2002. "A portrait of the lady: The portrayal of Thailand and its prostitutes in the international media." Pp. 139–55 in *Transnational Prostitution: Changing Patterns in a Global Context*, edited by S. Thorbek and B. Pattanaik. London: Zed Books.

Velde, D. W. 2008. *The Global Financial Crisis and Developing Countries*. ODI. London: ODI.

Wadud, Z. F., Huda, Y., and Ahmed, N. U. 2014. "Assessment of Fire Risk in the Readymade Garment Industry in Dhaka, Bangladesh." *Fire Technology* 50(5): 1127–45. doi: 10.1007/s10694–013–0349–2.

Wagstaff, K. 2013. "China's Massive Pollution Problem." *The Week*, November 9. United Kingdom: The Week Publications. Retrieved November 11, 2013 (http://theweek.com/article/index/252440/chinas-massive-pollution-problem).

Walby, S. 2002. *Gender and the New Economy: Regulation or Deregulation?* Lancaster: Department of Sociology, Lancaster University.

Wallerstein, I. 1986. *Africa and the Modern World*. Trenton, NJ: Africa World Press.

Wang, V. W. 2005. "The US Japanese Alliance Redefined: Implications for Security in the Taiwan Strait." *Tamkang Journal of International Affairs* 9(2): 1–50.

Ward, H. and Ara, S. O. 2006. "Globalization, the Sex Industry, and Health." *Sex Transm Infect* 82(5): 345–47. doi: 10.1136/sti.2006.023044.

Ward, K., Rahman, F., Islam, A. K. M. S., Akter, R. and Kamal, N. 2004. "The Effects of Global Restructuring on Urban Women's Work and Income-Generating Strategies in Dhaka, Bangladesh." *Critical Sociology* 30(1): 63–102.

Wassener, B. 2012. "In an unlikely corner of Asia, strong promise of growth." *New York Times*, April 23. Retrieved March 26, 2015 (http://www.nytimes.com/2012/04/24/business/global/in-bangladesh-strong-promise-of-economic-growth.html).

Waters, J. J. 2013. "Achieving World Trade Organization Compliance for Export Processing Zones While Maintaining Economic Competitiveness For Developing Countries." *Duke Law Journal* 63(2): 481–524.

Wegner, L. and Zwart, G. 2011. "Who will feed the world? The production challenge." Oxfam International. Retrieved March 22, 2015 (http://www.oxfamnovib.nl/Redactie/Downloads/Rapporten/who-will-feed-the-world-rr-260411-en.pdf).

Weigley, S. 2013. "10 companies profiting the most from war." *USA Today*, March 10. Retrieved March 22, 2015 (http://www.usatoday.com/story/money/business/2013/03/10/10-companies-profiting-most-from-war/1970997/).

Weiss, L. 2003. *States in the Global Economy: Bringing Domestic Institutions Back In*. Cambridge: Cambridge University Press.

Westergaard, Kirsten. 1983. *Pauperization and Rural Women in Bangladesh: A Case Study*. Comilla, Bangladesh: Bangladesh Academy for Rural Development (BARD).

White, B. and Dasgupta, A. 2010. "Agrofuel Capitalism: A View from Political Economy." *Journal of Peasant Studies* 37(4): 593–607.

Whitehead, A. 2001. "Gender impacts of liberalization policies on African agricultural economies and rural livelihoods." Gender Inequality: Striving for Justice in an Unequal World. Geneva: UNRISD.

Williams, E. J. 1995. "Maquiladora Industry and Environmental Degradation in the United States-Mexico Borderlands." *St. Mary's L. J.* 27(4): 777–79.

Wood, E.M. 2002. *The Origin of Capitalism: A Longer View*. New York: Verso.

World Bank. 2013. "Bangladesh development update." Retrieved March 26, 2015 (http://www.worldbank.org/en/news/feature/2013/04/13/bangladesh-development-update-slower-yet-healthy-growth-with-remarkable-development-progress).

World Health Organization. 2012. *Nutrition: Global and Regional Food Consumption Patterns and Trends*. WHO. Retrieved January 22, 2015 (http://www.who.int/nutrition/topics/3_foodconsumption/en/index4.html).

World Wildlife Fund. 2011. "Aquaculture – Shrimp" . Retrieved January 30, 2012 (http://www.worldwildlife.org/what/globalmarkets/aquaculture/WWFBinaryitem18703.pdf).

Yan, H. and Weiqing, G. 2006. "The Transnational Network and Labour Rights in China." *China Rights Forum* 3: 57–62.

Yanklowitz, R. S. 2013. "Bangladesh: We Must Prevent Future Industrial Disasters." *Jewish Week*, May 24. Retrieved March 22, 2015 (http://www.thejewishweek.com/features/street-torah/bangladesh-we-must-prevent-future-industrial-disasters).

Yardley, J. 2013. "The Most Hated Bangladeshi, Toppled from a Shady Empire". April 30, *New York Times*. Retrieved November 4, 2013 (http://www.nytimes.com/2013/05/01/world/asia/bangladesh-garment-industry-reliant-on-flimsy-oversight.html).

Yeats, N. 2001. *Globalization and Social Policy.* Thousands Oaks, London, New Delhi: Sage Publications Ltd.

Yeoh, B. S. A. 2004. "Cosmopolitanism and Its Exclusions in Singapore." *Urban Studies* 41(12): 2431–45.

Yeoh, B. S. A. and Huang, S. 2010. "Transnational Domestic Workers and the Negotiation of Mobility and Work Practices in Singapore's Home-Spaces." *Mobilities* 5(2): 219–36.

Yeoh, B. S. A., Huang, S. and Gonzalez III, J. 1999. "Female Domestic Workers: Debating the Economic, Social and Political Impacts in Singapore." *International Migration Weekly* 33(1): 114–36.

Yip, G. 1992. *Total Global Strategy: Managing for Worldwide Competitive Advantage*. New Jersey: Prentice-Hall.

Yosef, S. 2009. "Rich Food for Poor People: Genetically Improved Tilapia in the Philippines." *IFPRI Discussion Paper 00925*. International Food Policy Research Institute (IFPRI). Retrieved March 21, 2015 (http://www.ifpri.org/sites/default/files/publications/ifpridp00925.pdf).

Young, I. M. 2006. "Responsibility and Global Justice: A Social Connection Model." *Social Philosophy and Policy* 23(1): 102–30.

Yu, S. 2004. Indonesia's Weekend Wives and Sex Tourists. Star TV Focus Asia.
Yu, X. 2008. "Impacts of Corporate Code of Conduct on Labour Standards: A Case Study of Reebok's Athletic Footwear Supplier Factory in China." *Journal of Business Ethics* 81: 513–29. doi: 10.1007/s10551-007-9521-2.
Yunus, M. 2013. "After the Savar Tragedy, Time for an International Minimum Wage." *The Guardian*, May 12. Retrieved November 7, 2013 (http://www.theguardian.com/commentisfree/2013/may/12/savar-bangladesh-international-minimum-wage).
Zhang, K. H. 2006. "Is China the world factory?" Pp. 257–74 in *China as the World Factory*, edited by K. H. Zhang. UK: Taylor & Francis Ltd.

Index

Lightning Source UK Ltd.
Milton Keynes UK
UKOW06n1257190216

268731UK00005B/38/P